CW01512384

MUST INCLUSION BE S. _ _.. ._.

Must Inclusion be Special? examines the discord between special and inclusive education and why this discord can only be resolved when wider inequalities within mainstream education are confronted. It calls for a shift in our approach to provision, from seeing it as a conglomeration of individualised needs to identifying it as a conglomeration of collective needs.

The author examines the political, medical and cultural tendency of current times to focus upon the individual and contrasts this with the necessity to focus on context. This book distinguishes the theoretical perspectives that are often associated with special or inclusive education and the broad range of interests which depend upon their ongoing development. This examination leads to a problematisation of mainstream education provision, our understanding of why social inequities emerge and how additional support can overcome these inequities.

Further chapters explore the underlying challenges which emerge from our use and understanding of the notions of special and inclusive, outlining an alternative approach based upon a community of provision. This approach recognises the interconnectedness of services and the significance of context, and it can encapsulate the aspiration of much international legislation for participation and inclusion for all. But it also assumes that we tend towards diffuse practices, services, policies, settings and roles, spread across provision which is variously inclusive and exclusionary. In seeking to create equitable participation for all, support needs to shift its focus from the individual to this diffuse network of contexts.

Must Inclusion be Special? emerges from the research base which problematises inclusion and special education, drawing upon examples from many countries. It also refers to the author's research into pedagogy, language and policy, and his experiences as a teacher and a parent of a child identified with special educational needs.

Jonathan Rix is Professor of Participation and Learning Support at the Open University, UK.

Current Debates in Educational Psychology
Series Editor: Kieron Sheehy

MUST INCLUSION BE SPECIAL?

Rethinking educational support within a community of provision

Jonathan Rix

Routledge
Taylor & Francis Group

LONDON AND NEW YORK

First published 2015
by Routledge
2 Park Square, Milton Park, Abingdon, Oxon OX14 4RN

and by Routledge
711 Third Avenue, New York, NY 10017

Routledge is an imprint of the Taylor & Francis Group, an informa business

British Library Cataloguing in Publication Data
A catalogue record for this book is available from the British Library

Library of Congress Cataloging in Publication Data
A catalog record for this book has been requested

ISBN: 978-0-415-71098-5 (hbk)
ISBN: 978-0-415-71099-2 (pbk)
ISBN: 978-1-315-71374-8 (ebk)

Typeset in Bembo
by Book Now Ltd, London

To Elspet and Velia

One would have tutted, the other would have sighed . . . probably

CONTENTS

ILLUSTRATIONS

Figures

Tables

Boxes

ACKNOWLEDGEMENTS

Particular thanks to Caroline and Dad for reading with such enthusiasm, honesty and speed. You have been fantastically helpful. Thanks also to Kieron. Your nit-picking has been invaluable.

Thanks to Colin Smythe Ltd and Random House for permission to publish an extract from Terry Pratchett's *Nightwatch*, Copyright © 2002 Terry and Lyn Pratchett; to Bloodaxe Books for permission to publish an extract from Linton Kwesi Johnson's *Tings and Times*; and to Random House for permission to publish an extract from Rachel Joyce's *The Unlikely Pilgrimage of Harold Fry*.

PART I
Inclusive and special

1

WHY DO WE NEED *SPECIAL* AND *INCLUSIVE* EDUCATION?

I begin with an idea from Tom Robbins (2002). In his novel, *Fierce Invalids Home From Hot Climates,* Robbins talks about trying to escape the Killer B's. These are behaviour, belief and belonging. If you do not belong you are either the enemy or inferior or both. To belong you must share others' beliefs and behave as they do (though even then you may not be accepted). Religions, political parties, towns, schools, countries, racial groups – you must believe, belong, behave or face damnation. Sadly, I cannot use an exact quote from Tom Robbins' novel though. I am still awaiting permission beyond the UK, Europe and Commonwealth. I may not believe, but I behave … so that I may belong.

Starting with some local issues

In carrying out a review of special educational provision across 50 countries (Rix, Sheehy, Fletcher-Campbell, Crisp & Harper, 2013a) the only unifying factors which we could say applied across all administrations and countries were that:

- Children are marginalised within all education systems.[1] (Who they are and why they are marginalised varies between systems.)
- Provision referred to as special involves time and space additional to that provided typically.

Subsequently, we wrote a paper discussing this lack of unity and submitted it to various esteemed journals. The reviewers kept rejecting it. They recognised the value of the research and the data we had collected but felt that the lack of patterns and groupings undermined its usefulness. The research, they suggested, would be more powerful if it was able to say 'these countries are Type A' and 'these countries are Type B' … and so forth.

Our problem was twofold. First, we could put countries into groups for an aspect of their provision but two countries within one group would not be together in many of the other groupings. So for example, Italy and Norway could be put in one group because they claimed to have closed their special schools, but they would be in different groups in relation to assessment and use of labels, since Italy still required a psycho-medical assessment to achieve additional funding, whilst Norway did not. Second, what was claimed in national documents and aspired to in policy was not what actually happened on the ground. So when we visited Italy and Norway we found that there were special schools and special classes in existence with varying degrees of official support at different levels within the system. In addition, some administrations in Italy were trying to provide additional funding without psycho-medical assessment, whilst in Norway psycho-medical labels were in everyday use as part of local funding distribution processes. This is not to suggest that this kind of discordance was only evident in Italy and Norway. As a research team we came to recognise that it was a factor across and between all education systems. Identifying patterns and putting countries into groupings gives a false sense of unity, implying a commonality which is actually undermined by all the other variables at play.

So let us go back to what everyone we spoke to did agree about. Education systems marginalise children; and special provision is time and space additional to that provided typically. This is not to say that:

- All additional time and space is referred to as special.
- Additional time and space is always provided with the intention of counter-balancing marginalisation.
- *Special* cannot mean more than this to some people.
- All people agree that some pupils should be provided with additional time and space.

But it does provide a point of agreement about what we have now. It provides us with a starting point. If we wish to understand marginalisation and additionality within any school or education system we must have a firm understanding of the aims and practices associated with the majority of children, young people and practitioners. To understand what is special we must understand the local processes of marginalisation and the nature of the provision which other provision is additional to.

But just as special is a localised phenomenon, so is inclusion. As much as inclusion is a matter of *being* rather than *doing* (Corbett, 1999) and about "community values" (p. 59), the nature of education systems means it is a process of a person or group of people *being included* within *something*. They are to be included within its processes, structures and everyday typical experiences. The nature of that inclusion will depend upon how people interpret, understand and enact the nature of the *something* and *being* within it. In Norway, for example, a key aspect of the *something* was an adaptive curriculum. The curriculum was meant to be adapted to meet the needs of each individual. As a consequence of this generic commitment to the individual, children with support could study a completely different curriculum to their peers in the same class or within a different part of the school. For example, in a primary lesson, we observed a boy learning English while his peers studied Norwegian; in a secondary school, a boy with profound and multiple emotional and physical needs was taken skiing, climbing, swimming and cycling on a daily basis but never spent any time with his peers; and in a strengthened school (they did not call them special), each child was taught in separate rooms despite management asking staff to open up their classes. Evidently, a commitment to inclusion within a system which is committed to individualisation can rapidly lead to marginalisation. But of course such a consequence cannot be generalised to any other school or education system … it can only serve as a warning, a possibility to be discussed locally.

Our starting point, then, for understanding both special and inclusive education is the system which is intended for all learners. If we wish to explore the underlying challenges which frame our understanding of the notions of special and inclusive, we have to begin with our understanding of what it is that this overall system is trying to achieve.

Understanding why we are here

Education has emerged for different reasons in different forms across different societies. This is an inevitable reflection of the cultural divergence within those societies. Despite this, many people speak of education as if it has some universally understood and agreed values. It is situated as part of international conventions, and the full range of legislation associated with gender, disability, race, equality, rights and "the exasperated etc" (Butler, 1990, p. 143).

> The reasons for providing all the world's children with high-quality primary and secondary education are numerous and compelling. Education provides economic benefits and improves health. Education is a widely accepted humanitarian obligation and an internationally mandated human right. These claims are neither controversial nor new.
>
> (Cohen, Bloom & Malin, 2006 p. v)

Yet, the egalitarian function of education is neither universal nor historically significant. It is also frequently contradicted by a range of other functions.

In their analysis of global educational expansion Benavot, Resnik and Corrales (2006) draw upon a broad literature to reveal the diverse motivations underpinning the development of education systems. Educational expansion has been an uneven process. Vested political interests had to create educational wholes out of "diverse, semi-related, and often non-existent parts" (p. 4). These social, political and economic processes created administrations which brought together competing interests and loyalties. These frequently involved religious authorities and leading figures from local communities and businesses. The impact of respected educational thinkers was far less influential in initiating education than broader social, political and economic pressures. The result was new social pacts and relationships. But the diversity of priorities and interests meant that the focus of these processes was often not primarily upon educational targets. Emerging policies,[2] structures and types of schooling[3] subsequently established and reinforced inequalities of participation and access.

Developing compulsion

Before compulsory education, frequently the role of schooling was to develop an elite class who could govern the state, run the administration and organise the faith. It provided a select number with the key skills, knowledge and social manners required for leadership within the fields of warfare, religion, politics and diplomacy. For the vast majority of other people, education was primarily an apprenticeship into a set of skills relevant to rural living or to a craft. Education therefore played an essential role in reinforcing clear social structures. It was committed to the status quo. Schooling of this kind was evident within ancient civilisations such as China, Egypt, Rome and Greece, as well as in pre-reformation Europe and countries associated with the European and Ottoman empires. It was not simply a matter of teaching the sons of the rich and powerful, though. For instance, in England some of the earliest schools (which were to become the elite's fee-paying 'Public' schools) were charitable institutions established with a clear duty to provide education for children from 'humble' backgrounds.

Within other regional contexts (North American, Scandinavian and Germanic states for example) social norms also emerged which required parents to educate their children, with a particular emphasis upon religion, morals and text-based literacy. In Islamic cultures, large networks of Qur'anic schools played (as they still do) a key role in socialisation, establishing regional and community identities. Their role was particularly evident in the early stages of learning, providing a focus upon literacy and religious texts. In many places education was not just a matter of individual development either. In Mexico literate adults were a communal resource supporting religious and bureaucratic functions; for example, to be a self-governing township required having a certain number of literate members (Rockwell, 2002).

In North America and North Europe, from the seventeenth century onwards, compulsory forms of education emerged out of the protestant reformation, leading to the development of localised education for many. However, the shift to a model of mass schooling within a nation state did not begin to emerge until the nineteenth century. There are seemingly practical reasons for this emergence. As a 'modern' society develops, so too does production and service. There is a concurrent development of specialised skills. The value of particular skills rises, whilst the capacity of the family or small local community to sustain and develop the required skills decreases (MacInnes & Diaz, 2009).

The reasons for the development of compulsory education are not just a practical and linear response to a changing economy, though. A narrative which emerged in seventeenth- and eighteenth-century Europe can be seen to be replicated across nations. As an industrialised society emerged, there was an enforced shift in land ownership and agricultural patterns. This created new pressures and population changes which drove people from the land and into urban environments (Hart, 2011). Education became a key tool in moving people from the thinking and lifestyles of their traditional and indigenous cultures. New kinds of work benefited from a literate society. Workers could have technical processes explained to them using a common industrial language, involving more explicit and precise communication than previously. This fuelled advances in technology and drove educational development as well as single, national, languages. In turn this became the means to create and transmit a communal culture. The coming together of universal education and a common culture and language was by necessity controlled, co-ordinated and driven by the state. Through them the 'nation' emerged (Rieffer, 2003; Gellner, 1983).

Competing interests

As people struggled to create unifying national systems and educational identities, the nature of the relationships and social pacts which developed varied between countries. It was not merely an emergent process. It had multiple and fundamentally political motivations which varied between contexts and across the years. For example, in many countries, the development of secular education was itself part of a wider battle to weaken the influence of the dominant religious culture. Compulsion to attend provided a means of directing the children towards non-religious learning goals. The focus on literacy, numeracy and appropriate behaviour could be linked to a developing economy and nation rather than an understanding of religious text. In broad terms, the economically dominant minority-world nations saw education as a way to consolidate the state. They could establish a sense of nationhood and drive economic change. In contrast, within the postcolonial majority-world,[4] education systems were seen as a way to break away from colonial legacies. They could rebalance economies and create a unifying national identity which might overcome ethnic divisions that had emerged from or been encouraged by colonial structures.

The existence of competing interests underpinning the introduction of compulsory education is evident when we look across nations. Benavot et al. (2006) cite a range of studies which suggest many different driving forces (see Table 1.1).

This is not to say that these were the only motivations in these countries. Different interests are also evident between writers and researchers. So for example, Benavot et al. pointed to studies suggesting that the focus of some US states was the future development of territory; in contrast, Richardson and Johanningmeier (1997) identified personal growth and individualism as priorities pre-1780. After this they saw an increasing focus on literacy and the use of education to create rational decision-making citizens, preserving order, productivity and social compliance. For them the common school and universal education emerged from this aspiration.

The legislative moves towards compulsory education also need to be measured against potentially contradictory impulses, such as issues of funding and

TABLE 1.1 Examples of some driving forces of compulsory education

Country/region	Some of the driving forces
France	Trying to control a powerful Catholic church
Prussia	Supporting the development of the Protestant faith
Scandinavia	Supporting the development of the Protestant faith
Japan	Developing industrial and military competitiveness; reorganising national institutions; creating national solidarity, a central bureaucracy, a skilled labour force and a future elite
Soviet Russia	Developing a literate nation; establishing meritocracy and the basis for industrial development
Ecuador	Overcoming parental disinterest and colonial gender bias
Arab states	Aiming to redress gender disparities
Spain	Aiming to unify geographically and culturally distinct regions
Sri Lanka	Aiming to reduce child labour
India	Aiming to build the nation

national income (Weiner, 1991 in Benavot et al.). In India, early attempts at compulsory education were possibly undermined by a middle-class concern with the disruption of the social order. Similarly, in England there was a concern that public education would encourage revolution, whilst in Spain the very regional disparities which compulsion sort to overcome were reinforced by the official language of education. In many countries there emerged not only a tension between secular and religious provision but also between public and private providers, and centralised and decentralised systems of control. These tensions produced varying responses within countries across the years, for example:

- Religious schools became part of national systems with a secularised curriculum.
- Private providers were publically funded.
- Decentralised systems were funded and directed through centralised curricula or centralised training or centralised standards.

Additionally, people frequently turned to pre-existing organisations as ways of thinking about schools and the problems associated with them. There was a particular link to the military, business and industry (Dorn & Johanningmeier, 1999). For example, in parts of nineteenth-century Europe, drill (based upon military training) was a basic physical activity included in the school day (McCrone, 1984). This made use of limited time, space and money. Importantly for militarised nations, it instilled discipline into the ranks of working-class boys (Winterton & Parker, 2009). It was a means of dealing with an increasing child population and a politically dangerous proletariat. It also responded to expanding international competition; for example, Britain's fear in the 1890s of a growing German militarism (Mangan & Galligan, 2011). Such was its significance, when the UK government nationalised all schools at the end of the century, they abolished fees in those schools which taught military drill but not in those which did not teach it (Mangan & Ndee, 2003).

The legacy?

Over the centuries, different people have been setting up and leading educational initiatives for very different reasons. In so doing they have set in motion a series of legacies which have worked their way into the education system as it expanded. For example:

- The imposition of a dominant educational language led to the loss of local or national languages and the marginalisation of individuals who did not speak the dominant language. It has created an education system in many countries which is primarily monolingual. This requires many children to learn in a language at which they do not excel. It creates systems which do not have the flexibility to take advantage of the bilingual skills that children and their families bring to the learning situation.
- The militaristic aspirations underpinning the notion of drill left a long legacy within the teaching of physical education. They are still directly evident within school cadet forces. They also had a profound impact upon the perceptions of generations of teachers about effective discipline. They still play a role in defining those pupils who need to be disciplined and the kinds of behaviours which require disciplining.
- The focus upon print literacy has led to a belief that it is a fundamental social need; that it is inherently more valuable to the individual and society than other communication tools. As McDermott and Varenne (1995) point out, there is little evidence to suggest this assumption is correct; but by agreeing with it we create it as true. The insistence that it should be taught in schools means it has come to be prioritised over numerous other communication tools which many people might prefer to use (e.g. imagery, practical or collaborative activities, artistic endeavours.)

These three examples can all be seen to play an underpinning role in some key components of our dominant notion of education: how children communicate; how they behave; how they engage with information. All the aims and interests raised above weave themselves into people's cultural assumptions in highly complex ways. Inevitably, these kinds of social divides have accrued at each of the points at which education has expanded its remit or has its established practices . . . and by now, the established practices and processes have very deep and complex root systems.

When we speak of universally understood and agreed values in relation to education, we need to recognise that even if our current aspiration is humanitarian and driven by a notion of rights, the system itself is driven by the legacies of drill, faith, nation building and so forth. Current schools systems may increasingly appear to resemble each other, speaking a similar language about aims and processes; however, they have taken very different emergent paths. At their heart is also an uncomfortable truth. Over the centuries, for many people, in all parts of the world, education has been imposed and has been seen as an imposition.

A coming together?

Given current political discourses and the complex development of education it is worth remembering that at the beginning of the twenty-first-century key egalitarian notions associated with schooling were still relatively recent arrivals in Europe. Initially, compulsory education was limited to primary and some lower-secondary children. Secondary education was generally reserved for those who could pay or could pass entrance assessments based upon academic or purported intelligence tests. This was supposed to encourage a meritocracy, but favoured a particular type of thinking and therefore a particular type of upbringing. It consequently condemned the majority to an education which conferred inferior social status. The nature of vocational training, which many were directed to at secondary level, may have changed with the development of science and technology; however, it was frequently seen as being of a lower status. It was the domain of non-academic children.

After the Second World War, stratified secondary-school provision still continued in many countries, maintaining this vocational–academic divide. This began to change as democratic principles emerging from the United States (which opposed talent being 'wasted' and opportunities being constrained by social background) met with the socialist principles which emerged from European states (which emphasised national responsibility and collective endeavour). Social scientists, intergovernmental organisations and politicians across the spectrum increasingly saw education as the means of delivering these goals. The models of education emerging from the United States (particularly comprehensive provision and student selection of routes of study) came to challenge the vocational and selective models. In many countries secondary education expanded, comprehensive school numbers increased, subjects became more diverse.

For a short while within the minority-world, economic and social disparity narrowed. This was not the case for most of the majority-world, however. Across the globe, governments took up the call, many aiming to come out from under the cloak of colonial rule, many in response to socio-economic pressure from international agencies. However, for many, the promised expansion never fully materialised. The new structures rarely improved social mobility or reduced economic disparity; old patterns of social disadvantage were reinforced. For example, in Indonesia there is evidence of improved living standards for some, but increased inequalities and job fragmentation which channels disproportionate resources to those at the top end of the socio-economic hierarchy (Martinez, Western, Haynes, Tomaszewski & Macarayan, 2014).

The dominant model of education which emerged from the minority-nations has also come to be seen by many as an import. The transfer of educational practices between nations largely ignored the historical configuration of countries and regions within countries. They did not shift their foci to reflect the local priorities and imperatives. In some countries, particularly in Asia, the mix of traditional and imported values and educational practices was relatively successful. In others, particularly in the Middle East and Africa, universal programmes of national enrolment have been blamed by elites for a range of ills. They have, for example, been perceived to encourage social unrest and cause fractures between the generations and their value systems. Benavot et al. (2006) discuss decentralisation conceived in "Anglo-Saxon cultures" (p. 67) being introduced into Latin America. This ignored the pre-established elitist nature of provision, and deepened social inequalities. Similarly, many reforms imported into Africa had little regard for local histories, in particular languages of instruction, indigenous philosophies and the role of the community in education. The reforms introduced concepts through learning which marginalised individuals, undermined the values and morale of the majority. They resulted in individuals who felt at home in neither the international community nor their domestic culture.

In competition with a discourse for everyone

It was only towards the end of the twentieth century that some kind of international agreement emerged that all children could and should be educated and that they might be educated together. Ironically, in many countries, this agreement began to emerge at the same time as vision of a comprehensive education system began to fade. In the 1950s, 60s and 70s, when the notion of the comprehensive school was in vogue in many countries, education was frequently seen as an international driver of growth and modernisation. The rhetoric around education did not shift its focus to incorporating marginalised groupings until the 1980s when comprehensive education was sliding down the agenda.

By the 1990s the rhetoric had become framed within the language of rights (Chabbott, 2003). The notion of equality of opportunity virtually disappeared from international discourse:

> The education of minority groups, the cultural rights of aborigines, gender equality and parity, and the emergence of the all-encompassing knowledge society became new themes in international policy papers. Earlier educational recommendations morphed into newer ones – almost all became integrated into world educational culture. Unchanged, however, was the power to initiate, diffuse, and adapt educational discourses, which remained unequal.
>
> (Benavot et al., 2006, pp. 64–65)

During this period, education also became increasingly positioned as ongoing, lifelong and work-related. It focused upon individual employability and the economic competitiveness of the individual and the nation (Gewirtz, 2008). This also coincided with a policy discourse of choice, efficiency and standards. In many countries, there was increasing independent provision within a decentralised marketplace, with the state securing the institutional frameworks which enabled this (Harvey, 2006).

Increasingly, the transformational notion of education had been co-opted to support calls for a flexible workforce and the increasing use of Information and Communication Technology. Global software and hardware corporations could be seen to have taken a lead in defining the nature of change (Rix, 2010). At the same time, an increasing emphasis upon issues of equity (as opposed to equality) became part of the process. This shifted the focus of participation away from its political goals and towards methods. An emphasis upon notions of diversity and equitable outcomes led to a rhetorical and policy focus upon diversity groupings. The focus became which ones had been included, as opposed to the nature of their participation and its transformational outcomes (White, 1996).

These policy and rhetorical models were supported both within minority-world national governments and also pan-national agencies (such as the World Bank and International Monetary Fund). At a time of increasing social disadvantage and inequality, there was an increasing use of targets and a positioning of education as a commodity delivering a product with measurable outputs. This was situated within a managerialist discourse of quality and effectiveness. These dominant belief systems worked against other values of social justice (such as inclusivity) and against creating politically engaged, critically aware, communal citizens (Beckmann & Cooper, 2005). In many countries, the development of marginalised groupings came to be framed as a personal issue. The individual and their skills and capacities seemed to provide an answer to overcoming their marginalisation. The contradictions and conflicts between the nature of opportunities available to them and their capacity to develop economically valuable skills could be put to one side. The opportunity to focus upon the processes of marginalisation within education was constrained by a model of personalised response and individual responsibility.

Who to leave out?

So far this chapter has outlined the wide variety of reasons underpinning the emergence of education, the range of interests it served and the diverse social, personal and political aims associated with it. This next section will consider who it is that is marginalised by the systems which have emerged from these competing interests and aims. I will attempt to explicate how the construction of the mainstream reinforces the historically rooted notions of difference and the in-groups and out-groups which emerge from wider society.

However equitable, diverse and personalised education may strive to be (within the discourse of our times), formal learning is still as much about exclusion as it is about inclusion. Over the centuries there have been many debates about which parts of the masses should be educated, with the suggestion that certain types of children or social groups were not educable. Educability has been defined in many different ways in many different cultures. Selection and access has been based upon very local notions and values in relation to physical, intellectual, social and cultural norms and what constitutes a successful education.

Within European settings, for example, assessments were being undertaken by local clergymen from the 1700s onwards. These aimed to identify who could be brought to God's grace through learning. As a result of developments in theological doctrine, a notion arose of "a specifically human intelligence as a natural phenomenon controlled by the necessary laws which operate on a person-by-person basis" (Goodey, 2011, p. 172). Alongside this a curriculum emerged with subjects largely identified by radical Protestants and their dissenter descendants. Their notions of righteousness allied to developing ideas of the rational provided the bedrock from which emerged the field of psychology:

> The first professionally administered psychological assessments and prototype intelligence tests in schools were not imported from some separate, already existing clinical setting or from beyond the educational sphere at all, but devised on the basis of the early psychologists' observation of existing methods of classroom assessment, themselves derived from catechical routines.
>
> (Goodey, 2011, p. 177)

White (2010) suggested that these early psychologists provided key arguments to support the development of a curriculum of discrete subjects (e.g. history supports memory and mathematics supports logic), and that this subsequently gave priority to the type of child they believed to be suited to academic learning. The boundaries of the curriculum defined those who studied it. At the same time in many countries purported tests of intelligence came to control entry to that curriculum (Richardson & Johnanningmeier, 1997).

Access to education is recognised as being dependent upon many factors. The United Nations Education, Scientific and Cultural Organisation for example points to the "powerful influence of circumstances, such as wealth, gender, ethnicity and location, over which people have little control but which play an important role in shaping their opportunities for education and wider life chances" (UNESCO, 2013).

At the head of that list of internationally recognised barriers should perhaps be disability. Certainly statistics cited by UNESCO elsewhere (UNESCO, 2007) state that 98 per cent of disabled children in the majority-world do not attend school (though they do not give a source for this statistic). Even in a country where disabled children do attend school they are still highly likely to experience extreme discrimination. For example, 321 families of disabled children took part in a UK charity survey in 2012–13. This looked at the children's experiences in English and Welsh mainstream and special schools. Twenty-two per cent of the children were illegally excluded once a week and 15 per cent every day for at least part of the day (Contact a Family, 2013).

Marginalisation of pupils may emerge in particular ways in different places, but it often reflects the kinds of strong social biases which are evident within many countries. In England, in the second decade of the twenty-first century, for example, even though the differences between ethnic groupings has been reducing in recent years, boys identified as Black Caribbean were still twice as likely to be legally excluded from school as boys identified as White. Boys identified as being Gypsy/ Traveller children were three times as likely to be excluded. The number of girls was lower, but even here a girl identified as being Black Caribbean was nearly twice as likely to be excluded as a girl recognised as being White British (DfE, 2013a). Within the United States there has also been a consistent over-representation of certain groupings within special education and under different categories of impairment, based upon notions of race, ethnicity, wealth, class and gender. As a consequence these individuals are frequently invisible within the formal assessment system and drop out without graduation (Connor & Ferri, 2007).

Even though statistics reveal patterns of inequity, the process of marginalisation cannot be regarded as purely linear or a result of absolute causational characteristics. For example, across the twentieth century, inequalities based upon social class reduced within many European countries (Breen, Luijkx, Müller & Pollak, 2010); however, class (with its associated networks and levels of wealth) remained a powerful predictor for educational outcomes. But it did not operate in isolation to other factors. So whilst in the English education system, white working-class students or those living in poverty did worse in terms of exam outcomes than most other ethnic groups, the percentage of white students who were working class was also much smaller than the percentage of most other minority groups (Gillborn, Rollock, Vincent & Ball, 2012). Meanwhile, whilst gender was frequently associated with difference in educational achievement, the most significant influences on exam performance was not gender but social class and ethnicity (Connolly, 2006).

However, even if there are not certainties, marginalisation can be frequently seen to operate as a complex self-perpetuating process. In Scotland, for example, as in many countries there is a gender bias in relation to entrance to special education; over many years boys have been more than twice as likely as girls to be sent to special schools (Scottish Government, 2009). However, entry into special education increases their statistical likelihood of being formally excluded from school. In the first decade of the twenty-first century (Scottish Government, 2010), children identified as having additional support needs in special schools in Scotland were fourteen times more likely to be formally excluded than the national average; in primary schools children identified as having additional support needs were seven times more likely to be excluded; and in secondary schools twenty-six times more likely. Yet again, other factors are interwoven with these processes. For example, children living in areas identified as most deprived on the Scottish Index of Multiple Deprivation were seven times more likely to be excluded than the average, whilst disabled children were six times more likely, and looked-after children were more than twenty-nine times more likely to be excluded.

It would be naïve to suggest on the basis of statistical evidence that a singular category experiences a greater degree of exclusion or marginalisation. Partly this is because of the great many variables which can influence school experience. You could, for example, also add:

- being summer-born (Sammons et al., 2012);
- having a parent deployed on military duty (White, de Burgh, Fear & Iversen, 2011);
- societal responses to sexuality (Taylor, 2007; Archer, Halsall & Hollingworth, 2007);
- the influence of parental involvement, family structure, home language, parental education, parental income, number of books at home and the national economic policy environment (Hampden-Thompson, 2013);
- experiencing difficulties with mental health (Tempelaar et al., 2014).

And this is just some of what research has identified so far. However, even if you could identify every category which is disadvantaged within a system, people cannot be summarised within a collection of such categories. Marginalisation and our responses to it are always experienced personally.

Reflecting upon marginalisation

Marginalisation within school is frequently a consequence of hidden processes or those which are rarely reflected upon. Osler (2006) suggests that marginalisation can be analysed at interpersonal, institutional and structural levels. In the context of considering the marginalisation of girls, she describes how everyday incivility and violence are parts of the cultures of schools which create problems for pupils. The social significance of fitting in with the majority can marginalise any group who is within a minority in some way, even those who might be considered most likely to benefit from current systems. Many schools' communities, for example, can marginalise those who are academically successful (Mendick & Francis, 2012) or create concerns for the welfare of the middle-class child (Williams, Jamieson & Hollingworth, 2008), even though typically they would be positioned as the most likely to fit within school systems.

Frequently, issues which one might assume to be at the heart of education (i.e. difficulties associated with learning, caring and relationships) are not obvious to those working within schools. This might be because it is not a priority to them or the system may not require them to be alert to particular (frequently less extreme) signals. For example, in the context of considering race in relation to the English education system, Parsons (2008) felt he had identified institutional racism in operation, and that: "There is poor awareness of the issues, relatively poor assessment and monitoring of policies and a limited range of targeted, positive action in response to monitoring information" (p. 417).

The lack of reflection and limited self-awareness within the system can result in powerful unchallenged biases. For example, within the United States some teachers would appear to identify individuals for special education to avoid having to teach them in general education classes (Connor & Ferri, 2007), whilst in Scotland, the official statistics (Scottish Government, 2010) showed that 32 per cent of children were formally excluded from school due to "general or persistent disobedience", 27 per cent because of verbal abuse of staff, and 17 per cent because of physical assault with no weapon. It is not too big a step to recognise that these were merely children who did not do as they were told and resisted when they were required to do something they did not wish to do. However, for those teachers who excluded the children these will have been very real acts of subversion; it is very difficult for them to see it otherwise, as the system in which they work requires conformity to function.

The inherent drive to marginalise is a consequence of a classroom in need of control. Difference which challenges the teacher's capacity for control (and their notion and experience of controlling) can seem to present them with a stark choice. As Bourne (2001) suggests in relation to linguistic diversity, the choice for teachers when faced with a child who does not speak their language is to change the way in which their class operates or to find a way to remove the child from the situation. The apparent starkness of this choice is at the heart of the problems which emerge from our socially and historically constructed education system. As McDermott and Varenne (1995) put it, culture results from "hammering each other into shape with the well-structured tools already available" (p. 326). Their analysis is that when people do not respond well to this hammering we can either focus upon what is wrong with them and their immediate surroundings or we can focus on what is wrong more widely with the world we have given them.

School is, of course, part of what we have given people, constructed by the myriad forces discussed above. It is by its nature a means of separating a 'child' world from an 'adult' world. Through its internal structures it further separates and sub-divides. The manner of this separation and sub-division is central to debates about special and inclusive.

Together or apart?

As with behaviour in schools, our understanding of impairment has always been socially and historically situated and constructed. Debates about whether to isolate groups on the basis of some category of impairment have long been part of that construction. For instance, in the UK in 1889, in presenting evidence about provision for the blind, deaf and dumb, representatives of residential institutions argued that parental choice and the need to have special approaches warranted separate residential schooling. Others presented evidence that generally the children made better social and academic progress in ordinary classes (Cole, 1989). At the same time in London there were active debates about types of education, risks to children and the desirability of segregation (Read & Walmsley, 2006). A quarter of a century later in England, at a time when the 1913 Mental Deficiency Act introduced a tripartite care system which included the locking away of so-called moral and mental defectives (Rolph et al., 2005), some school inspectors recognised that separation was not the solution and that "slum clearance, good nutrition and school health services would be better cures" (Cole, 1989, p. 45).

There is a tendency both to see our current times as an improvement on the past and to generalise our notions of the past to support our own ends and reflect our current priorities. Our tendency to separate particular groups of people leads us to infer that it would have ever been so. In a broad historical description of special education within the highly respected *SAGE Handbook of Special Education* (2006), Winzer notes how little evidence there is in relation to disability prior to the 1700s and that what there is has been paid little attention by historians. However, she echoes the standard view that:

> Prior to the mid-eighteenth century, individual deviations were rarely toler- ated and little was done for those who in some way disrupted the norms of a society. Disability was not an innocuous boundary; rather, it was a liability in social and economic participation. People perceived as disabled – whatever the type or degree – were lumped together under the broad categorization of *idiot*, scorned as inferior beings and deprived of rights and privileges.
>
> (p. 23)

However, there are a number of assumptions and generalisations within this accepted history which can be demonstrated to be questionable. First, as Winzer's careful use of the word 'perceived' highlights, disability is a matter of perception. Lord Admiral Nelson was not disabled in the 1790s even though he would now be recognised as having visual and physical impairments and unsuitable for active service; a young person we would label with Down syndrome would (if they survived the health problems they would have been more at risk from) have been able to carry out a range of useful activities within an agrarian community in the 1400s, whilst the obsessive tendencies associated with autism and quick-fire focus associated with attention deficit hyperactivity disorder would have benefited various jobs within the same community or within early industrial process. Similarly, the aggression and determination associated with emotional and behavioural difficulties would have been considerably valued in a physical feudal society which had, for example, to provide the King with young men for war. The evidence we have about attitudes towards the disabled therefore tends to be only those who were recognised as lacking one of the key senses, notably the profoundly deaf and blind. Yet there are plenty of examples of people who became deaf and blind, whose lives were profoundly affected, but continued to do well for themselves, such as the poet John Milton and the composer Ludwig van Beethoven. There are records of socially successful people blind from birth, such as Blind Harry, a poet and minstrel at the Scottish court for 20 years in the 1400s; and there are examples (from the start of reliable records in the 1500s) of individuals who relied upon sign language and lip reading. For instance, Edward Bone, manservant to a Cornish Member of Parliament, and Thomas Tillsye who confirmed his marriage through sign to Ursula Russel in 1575 (Woll & Adam, 2012). It does not seem unreasonable to suggest therefore, in the case of the deaf and blind, that there were some communities who at the very least sought to make adjustments for people if they could carry out tasks in a reliable manner.

The diversity and difference we associate with disability may have been less marked in a society which was not looking out for it, where it was far more the norm; in a society where priorities were around fulfilling your duties within a more tightly defined local community and within a wider social hierarchy governed by notions of honour and grace. The increasing visibility of individual isolation and loss of rights which is part of the accepted version of impairment in history may have been more of a consequence of the changes to the social structures which occurred with the shift from an agrarian to an industrial, urbanised economy.

It may well be true that many people we now describe as disabled would have been part of the category of idiots, but it seems very possible that historians have looked backwards, identified the word 'fool' and 'idiot' and read into them our current notion; or researchers have identified behaviours of particular people in the past and then mapped them onto the present syndromes or disorders. There is no certainty that at the time these differences would have been noted. Goodey (2011) demonstrates how in writings before the 1600s, idiot (and fool) was used for anyone who was not part of their elite group; agricultural workers, women, non-gentlefolk, melancholics.[5] It was even used to refer to the disciples before they met Jesus. Idiocy was a matter of class and background. Similarly, Goodey demonstrates how in the centuries prior to the mid-1800s, the gradual shift in arguments about religious texts and the nature of humanity's relationship with their God led to the emergence of the very categories and processes of categorising which made it possible and desirable to start to identify all these different groups and then associate them with disruption of the norm; the groups which subsequently became formally labelled as idiots, imbeciles, morons and so forth. The enlightenment of the mid-eighteenth century is frequently seen as a starting point for a modern focus upon improving people's well-being, but in many ways it can be seen as part of the ongoing process of identifying, justifying and maintaining the status of the elite; it simply marked the point at which our current processes of marginalisation emerged.

This is not to say that prior to the mid-eighteenth century, within the collective lives of the agrarian peasants, there was some golden era in which there was a universal welcome for those with a physical or cognitive difference. But it is definitely the case that what we value has changed. Our understanding and categorisation of difference has shifted with the social and moral codes of the times and our economic, medical and general living conditions. This should give us significant pause for thought when we reflect upon how we choose to treat those marginalised within our formal systems: "People are only incidentally born or early enculturated into being different. It is more important to understand how they are put into positions for being treated differently" (McDermott & Varenne, 1995, p. 336).

Where to go?

The last few sections have considered in relatively general terms who is marginalised within education systems and have touched upon how and why that marginalisation occurs in the manner that it does. This final section will focus upon the two concepts, *special* and *inclusion*, often associated with two extremes: removing the child or changing the operation of the class. This focus takes a very definite step towards the realm of a particular type of marginalisation, which might be broadly associated with special educational needs. It is not the intention of this book to constrain the notion of inclusion in this way; however, for the purposes of what remains of this chapter I will stick with its roots within the disability movement. I will attempt to outline how in relation to a particular population, special and inclusive provision have emerged as the means by which the in-school experience of the wider social inequities can be challenged. Both are explained and justified by the limitations of one another. Both create, reinforce and challenge in-school experiences and wider social experiences of marginalisation.

Special education has two dominant historical strands. The first strand emerges before the arrival of compulsory education with the development of institutions for groups of people such as those experiencing profound visual or hearing impairment or mental health difficulties, or identified with Down syndrome. The second strand, sometimes drawing upon the first, emerged after compulsory education. This was in response to the failure of mainstream schools to provide for all. Both strands have led to separation and at the same time have seen calls for unified provision. Their stories have also been told in two very different ways. Richardson and Powell (2011) for example notice a "tendency to portray the origins of special education in positive terms, and to link its contemporary, explosive growth to this confident, optimistic vision" (p. 10). Versions of this story maintain that disabled children were to be drawn up, raised out of a lack of activity and a lack of culture (Stiker, 1999), increasingly "not to be regarded as a race apart" (Gulliford, 1971, p. 3) with special schools brought "into closer relationship with the rest of education" (ibid.). The other version of this story recognises the development of institutions as forms of social control. Their function, as Wolfensberger (1975) described it, was:

1   curing the defective;
2   sheltering the defective;
3   protecting society from the defective.

From this version of history come the tales of "survivors of the system" (Mason & Rieser, 1994, p. 25), describing their experiences of a therapeutic, segregated, cossetted and disempowering system, where people learned that the problem was within themselves. People were led to believe that "it was not a good thing to be disabled and that the more I could reduce or minimize my disability the better off I would be" (Kunc in Giangreco, 1996, p. 2).

Inclusive education can be seen as emerging from the writings of sociologists, researchers and activists, who shared a desire to move away from an in-person deficit model of thinking about disability; they drew upon the insider's voice in order to understand the experience of disability and its social construction. They enabled recognition of the capacity of systems and communities to create, maintain and police institutionalised notions of difference and responses to difference. They sought to have difference seen as legitimate and valued. Much of this involved and served as a direct challenge to the process, practices and structures of special education. It highlighted the need to recognise where power lay within relationships and whose voice was dominant. As such, inclusion called for reconstruction, whereas special education supported the established structures.

However, as inclusion became the focus of governments and international discourse,[6] so special education engaged with its language and ideas, weaving them into its own structures and finding ways to accommodate its voice within the call for reconstruction (Rix, 2011). At the same time the notion of inclusion became associated with difference more broadly. For some this was an obvious conceptual shift useful in challenging the inequities of the status quo; but for others, as Slee (2008) suggests, the message of inclusion was useful in the ongoing expansion of compulsory education. It helped in situating challenges in the context of diversity. It helped situate the aspiration to increase certain skills in the workforce within the framework of anti-discriminatory legislation.

Inclusion within schools has resisted the drive to situate it more broadly. Slee concludes that it has experienced three acts from which current policy around inclusion cannot recover:

1 Understanding inclusive education to refer to children identified with SEN diverts focus away from the wider impact and structures of schools and undermines its capacity to drive social reform.
2 Allowing the ongoing dominance of psychological and medical understandings of disability which focus upon an in-person deficit undermines the complex economic and social factors which construct the experience of disablement.
3 A lack of engagement with the manner in which the culture and ideas of schooling construct the experience of disablement subsequently limits our thinking about how we can intervene.

These exacerbate "an absence of policy alignment [in relation to inclusion] across complex education systems" (p. 109) which "establish the conditions for failure and exclusion" (p. 110).

In competition?

A central challenge for those trying to make the case for one form over another is the double-edged nature of so many arguments associated with *special* and *inclusion*. For example, the child identified with special educational needs is both more likely to be the bully (Connor & Ferri, 2007) and more likely to be bullied if in a special education class (Christensen, Fraynt, Neece & Baker, 2012); and whilst some may see separate special provision as a refuge from bullying (Shah, 2007) for others it is the site of bullying (Shunit & Lapidot-Lefler, 2007). Connor and Ferri (2007) highlighted a range of other competing issues between special and inclusive education as they arose within newspaper editorial sections.

Stories emerged of children, in either kind of situation, being degraded and put in danger or being made welcome and feeling secure. *Inclusion* seemed to work for some and separation within special education seemed to work for others. They identified claims that the least restrictive environment (as mandated in US law) is best served both within segregated and mainstream provision. Similarly, they noted contradictory claims over where academic needs are best met, which way best serves social justice and which has inclusion as its goal (either inclusion within a school community or within wider society). They noted how some parents talked of their battles to claim mainstream education for their child as a right, whilst others talked of losing services that they had fought hard to establish.

Many stories noted how far social practices had shifted. They saw that special provision ensured access to education and services which had for so long been denied; it assured funding and instruction which was suited to their children. For some parents inclusion was taking resource away from their children and giving it to the services which had for so long rejected them. For other parents, funding separate provision was damaging to the individual and denied the benefits of inclusion for all the children. Teachers in both settings were seen to lack training. In mainstream they were seen to be unwelcoming. In special settings they lacked high expectations.

Connor and Ferri identified paradoxes in the views of parents around where to place the child – special or mainstream? Where would be best prepared? Where would they have the greatest opportunity to participate? Parents saw paradoxes too about whose rights and which rights should be prioritised, whether economic costs were greater or lesser; and they questioned whether rules around assessment marginalised or supported their child or merely served the economic ends of vested interests.

After acknowledging that their research was based on views expressed by parents within newspapers which also had vested interests, Connor and Ferri concluded that special education is highly complex and contradictory and very resistant to change. But they also noted that inclusion is often not inclusive and questioned whether the mainstream system is really that interested in change. They wondered whether the not-yet-disabled are really that interested in putting the required substantial changes for disabled people ahead of their own well established interests.

Perhaps unsurprisingly some parents tried to position themselves between the two extremes, seeing themselves as in transition between service types or being able to use both. Mainstream became a goal and special a gateway towards it, or special education became the safety net. It could catch the disabled child or remove a problem from the not-yet-disabled. Such findings seems to support those who suggest that the solution is not a matter of *either/or*, rather it is a matter of parental choice. However, the notion of choice does not resolve the problem. First, choice is no guarantee that parental aspirations will be delivered. Second, parents are frequently as torn between the arguments as anyone else … and it is their child who they are putting at risk. As a consequence they are strongly influenced by peers' experiences and the views of professionals. Their choice is rarely informed by support which might be seen as approaching impartiality (if such a thing is attainable).

The nature and availability of choice is also curtailed by geographical and organisational realities. As discussed in later chapters, much as we may wish to believe we can create the bureaucratic means to correctly allocate people to particular categories or settings, the evidence is very convincing that we cannot. The understanding and use of categories and labels varies enormously between nations and within nations (Rix, Sheehy, Fletcher-Campbell, Crisp & Harper, 2013b) and there is little reliability and consistency in both the form and use of many diagnostic psychiatric tests associated with special educational needs (e.g. Bickman, Wighton, Lambert, Karver & Steding, 2012). As parents in the Connor and Ferri research recognised, special education with its disparities across and within social groupings inevitably limits access to general education for some. Our regimes of testing trap many. The very existence of 'special' will invariably result in some people having a negative experience; but so will the existence of 'inclusion' within an unreconstituted mainstream.

Push-me pull-you

Special and *inclusive* seem to be caught in a two-way battle from which neither can be the winner. Unless we can achieve a truly inclusive system which does not marginalise people on the basis of their physicality, intellect or behaviour then our mainstream systems will go on recreating the need for special education and perpetuate the failure of inclusion. But to achieve this requires a shift in the huge array of historical priorities which have been outlined earlier in this chapter:

> The value or weight we give to learning X or Y or Z determines what we shall count as a 'special need', just as it determines what we shall count as a 'learning difficulty', or a 'disability' or a 'talent' or a 'gift'. In that sense, whether someone has a special need is not a matter of empirical fact: it calls rather for a judgement of value.
>
> (Wilson, 2002, p. 64)

Norwich (2002) concludes that in making the mainstream suitable for all there will always be minority needs which are not a priority for the majority, and these by their very nature will be additional. He suggests that a feature of inclusion therefore will be specialised support systems providing necessary additional support. Inevitably, the nature of this support will be dependent upon 'judgement of value'. Inclusion, like *special* education, therefore will always be a "separatist term relative to mainstream education" (Norwich, 2002, p. 493). It will carry the negative associations that arise from being marked out as a sector or process and being linked with an undervalued minority grouping. Replacing a segregatory special system with a genuinely inclusive one is therefore not a matter of shifting ways of thinking and talking about education but of shifting the social reality out of which education arises. This could be seen as prioritising one function (perhaps a humanitarian function?) over all the other functions which education fulfils. However, achieving agreement for such a priority (and what it might mean) seems unlikely; instead we will have to find ways to fulfil more than one set of values without undermining others.

Currently, we have a messy compromise whereby special and inclusion mixes integration, marginalisation, segregation and participation. If we wish to resolve this we will have to do so whilst being pulled in different directions. We will need to embrace the "continuous struggle" (Allan, 2008, p. 101) but we will also need to recognise that many people who work in education are already experiencing intensive change and for them the struggle is to cope (Ballet & Kelchtermans, 2008). This current messy compromise means that *special* and *inclusive* emerge as competing concepts despite the commonality of the challenges they face. These challenges are also shared by more than just the disabled population associated with these concepts. If you consider the range of issues touched upon in this chapter, these are the challenges which emerge from a system which in different ways marginalises the majority. It may be too cynical for some to describe this as a process of divide and rule; however, it is certainly a system which divides itself and the people within into numerous groupings. It offers ongoing patterns of reward and punishment as part of the process, operating mechanisms of collective and individualised banishment and support. In so doing, it reveals the confused morality of the whole.

The following two chapters will consider the manner in which the structures and processes of special and inclusion serve to both divide and support a key part of the school population. This is intended to both highlight the challenges which we face and to provide a platform for discussing possible ways forward.

Notes

1 The series editor suggested "Some children are marginalised". This implies that the experience is in some way constant though. Our interviewees did not suggest a level of constancy. Some children may be marginalised throughout their schooling life, some may be marginalised some of the time in some situations; all children may find their voices marginalised within some systems. Marginalisation can also be regarded as a momentary experience which depends upon the situation.
2 For example: selection, funding, exams, eligibility and curriculum.
3 For example: comprehensive, private, faith, vocational and technical.
4 The majority of people in the world are frequently described as 'the Third World', or 'developing nations' or 'emerging economies' or the '(global) south'. These are terms created by the minority.
5 According to the 1952 edition of the Shorter Oxford English Dictionary the etymological roots for idiot were the Greek for "private person" and "layman".
6 The international agreements which followed are discussed in Chapter 3.

2

THE STRUCTURES AND
PROCESSES OF *SPECIAL*

We see men of the very same rank and riches and education differing as widely as
the pointer does from the pug. The name, man, is common to all the sorts, and hence
arises very great mischief. What confusion must there be in rural affairs, if there were
no names whereby to distinguish hounds, greyhounds, pointers, spaniels, terriers, and
sheep dogs, from each other! And what pretty work if, without regard to the sorts of
dogs, men were to attempt to employ them! Yet this is done in the case of men! A
man is always a man; and without the least regard as to the sort, they are promiscu-
ously placed in all kinds of situations.

(Cobbett, 1825)

What confusion there would be?

I begin with doubt. With certainty comes unquestioned assumptions. The roots and
experiences of marginalisation vanish. I feel more comfortable if a question leads
to better-informed reflection (and perhaps further questions) rather than a defini-
tive answer. This influences the manner in which I approach my own research and
the research of others. It also influences the manner in which I present my analysis
of special education. It emerges from my experiences within diverse educational
settings, within institutions and organisations, charities and services, within families
and communities, as a practitioner, professional and amateur, as a parent, child,
sibling and peer. If you are not interested in the detail skip the next four paragraphs.

I grew up in the 1960s and 1970s with actor parents, Brian and Elspet, who
were constant campaigners and fundraisers. My eldest sister, Shelley, lived in a long-
stay institution; my parents led its League of Friends and were patrons, committee
members and chairs of various other charities. I witnessed not only the nature of
the institutions but also the development of special educational provision for those
previously identified as ineducable, then the closure of those institutions and its
impact upon their lives. In the 1980s my father led a major UK charity, and was

subsequently appointed to the House of Lords for his work, where more than two decades later he is still advocating (in particular for disabled people), whilst my mother was almost as tireless in her efforts elsewhere. Since 1980 I have also worked for or been a trustee of various charities as well as being a relatively low-level advisor to government and national organisations on issues of Early Support and special education funding.

At university I trained to be a secondary teacher, and in my third year was the sole participant on the special education course. After leaving, in 1983, I undertook a variety of jobs which introduced me to many people often seen as marginalised by our social systems. I spent 13 years, from 1987, as a secondary-school support teacher in Hackney, London, mostly working with children who were still learning English. I also worked as a prison writer-in-residence, writing plays with community groups and for Theatre in Education as well as dozens of audio tours (for people who in a UK social care context were described as having learning disabilities). In the 1990s I helped my wife, Caroline, on projects in Albania, Sri Lanka and Southern India which took us to many schools and long-stay institutions and which introduced us to international aid projects.

In 1998 I became a parent for the first time, to Isabel, who acquainted us with some national health and support services, but not as many as Robbie, born in 2001. Robbie was rapidly labelled and subsequently had a full range of support services (attending a special nursery, a local nursery, and then primary and secondary schools with full-time support). Caroline and I have been through a wide range of activities to achieve services for our children; I have also learned much through her work supporting early years provision and collaboration between services. We have also gleaned a great deal from Isabel's and Robbie's experiences as siblings and at school.

In my academic life, since 2000, I have been a founder of a heritage research group run by people with a range of labels associated with intellectual capacity. I have also conducted funded research into pedagogy for children identified with special educational needs, parents and children's experiences of early intervention, the nature of policy documents and funding systems, the discourse of special schools and inclusion, and international special education provision. I have run many modules at the Open University, but one in particular (on Equality, Participation and Inclusion) introduced me to thousands of students who shared (in online forums and through assignments) their hugely diverse views and experiences of all kinds of education and services.

I present this long summary of who I am because much of my experience has been due to my being a son, a brother and a father; not because of me but because of my life's circumstance. Frequently, doors have opened and conversations have been had with me because of my associations and not because of my CV. As the long summary shows, my CV is not bad. It gives me some right to have those conversations and for those doors to be opened. However, even when my CV alone might be enough … I have never been and never can be quite sure. I have always wondered if others who have far richer personal insights than me would have been granted the access I have.

Here, then is my first lesson about special, the one for which I cannot provide you research evidence, but I feel absolutely certain about . . . the one which gives birth to doubt:

• *Special* is a small world; it is profoundly influenced by who you are and not necessarily by what you know.

This view does not emerge simply because I have a tendency to be self-deprecating. It is also evident in tales I could tell if I was willing to name names. I have evidence because I was there or I was very close to what went on. In particular, I have witnessed on more than one occasion that many special organisations and services are personal fiefdoms (frequently with an honorary title as validation). There are charities set up or run with a heavy emphasis upon providing a living for the person who is setting it up or running it. Other individuals and services collude in the process. Frequently, these organisations are the mouthpiece of people who are good at marketing themselves or their ideas even if those ideas do not really stand up to detailed scrutiny. As a result, many speak as experts and are reified by people who should know better.

In the following sections I will return to this theme. I will try on a couple of occasions to give you examples. But my broader aim is to represent the range of interests associated with special and its ongoing development, to explore processes, practices, policies and attitudes which both inform and are informed by this development. I am approaching the issues from a critical perspective, so much of what I say can be taken in a negative light; however, I ask you to bear in mind the negative light in which I have already painted much of the mainstream and my intention to critically engage with other aspects of our educational system. It is very important to arguments that I make later in the book that people who see themselves as being part of special provision do not simply think I am attacking a system with which I do not agree. I can completely understand how people end up working, studying and living in special provision. It is full of people who are convinced by what they do and by the need for what they do. People may disagree with the existence of separate provision but they need to recognise that both in the context of a mainstream that fails us and as a vehicle of choice, to varying degrees special has satisfied customers and satisfied suppliers; there is a genuine perception that it is needed. My conviction is not that we need to agitate for change in this one part of the system; it is that if we are to change anything we have to change our understanding of the interconnected whole.

Establishing a history

We cannot approach a history of the treatment of people with an impairment with any certainty. As discussed in Chapter 1, our understanding and notions of what it is to be *able* and the characteristics which define us as *disabled* are too slippery to tie down in the general narratives of history. However, whilst historians must infer the meaning of intellectual or behavioural difference and terminology associated with it, two types of impairment (as we understand the notion of a type) are more easily recognisable; namely, hearing and sight. Because of their physical nature, the types can be most easily fitted into our current models of categorisation. So we can say with some certainty that a sixteenth-century Benedictine Monk (Pedro Ponce de Lion) developed a form of communication and instruction for the deaf and mute, and that a young Frenchman (Valentin Huay) developed in the mid-eighteenth century a method of communication for blind people using raised letters. We can also identify the birth of institutions such as that which emerged in Paris in the mid-thirteenth century for the blind or in England in the fifteenth century for unspecified mental health issues. There is also the evidence of legislation such as that which enabled fourteenth-century English kings to take control of the lands of those who in some way lacked capacity (*idiotarum et stultorum*) or the appearance of words such as *idiotae* in the work of Erasmus or *stupide* in Descartes, even if their meaning is unclear and open to interpretation. Our sense of certainty only increases with the development of specific categorical institutions.

Every nation has its own history of institutional development but it is clear that within a European context ideas took hold at similar times. So for example in the early 1600s there was a shift in England from a community-based poor law to the introduction of workhouses, which also appeared just a few years later in France. Subsequently, there was the establishment of the first French institutions for deaf-mutes (1750). These emerged slightly ahead of England (1760) as did educational institutions for the blind (France 1785 and England 1791), and institutions for idiots and imbeciles (France 1837 and England 1847).[1] Richardson and Powell (2011), in their analysis of key writings examining this process (e.g. Stiker, Serres and Abbott), concluded that poverty and charity bounded and enforced the exclusion of disabled people up to the late eighteenth century, but at the end of the eighteenth century, disability took on a value within systems of economic and social exchange.

> We are able to discern and name the long and intertwined genealogy of institutions that have confined, mistreated, corrected, and educated people with disabilities. The concept of nested self-similarity demonstrates that the historical antecedents to contemporary special education and the language of "special educational needs" reach back to the seventeenth century. These antecedents comprise a linked series of forms that vary but that embody enduring and common functions: the social and economic placement of the young and the reproduction of hierarchies in society.
>
> (p. 87)

The development of separate provision was not just a practical response to the difficulties of managing people of seeming difference. It was also a reflection of the ongoing development of ideas and practices and the identities of people associated with those ideas and practices. This includes both those who were being placed within the institutions and those who did the placing or the work within them. Our evidence for who supported people in the early years is scant, and the inclination is to make links to religious duty. However, the history of the professions associated with 'social and economic placement of the young' does not simply emerge from these roots, though its other roots are just as long. For example, we may associate the emergence of psychology in Europe in the 1800s with the emergence of modern scientific thinking, but its lineage is far longer. As was briefly mentioned in Chapter 1, the processes of assessment and teaching associated with the catechism profoundly affected the development of education and the subsequent emergence of modern psychological practices. Yet these catechetical routines themselves emerged from practices within a historical and political framework. As Goodey (2011) splendidly demonstrates, the teaching of these routines was a direct result of centuries of attempts to deal with changing religious and cultural practices and beliefs. They were in a long line of practices which exerted control over the populace. In particular, they emerged from the developing conceptualisation of Honour and Grace and the expertise which governed formal processes used to define those who were the in-group (the minority) and those who were the out-group (the majority).

Psychology and education (certainly in Western Europe) emerged from the same roots and these roots were not primarily about creating educational services for all, but were to do with debates about faith and social position. Goodey suggests that a key figure in this transition was John Locke and his "Essay Concerning Human Understanding":

> Even if the history of modern psychology is highly complex, as a significant social practice it is recognizably Lockean. Whenever psychologists are paid to assess someone or to deny social participation – on the grounds, for example, that this or that person lacks the ability to think abstractly, reason logically, process information, maintain attention, etc. – they are using criteria which Locke, in his seminal refashioning of theological doctrine, also used and from which he created for such people a separate space in society and therefore in nature.
>
> (p. 12)

It is in Locke's work that moral man emerges. With this concept we shift from 'those who don't try' cannot achieve a state of grace to 'those who cannot think' cannot achieve a state of grace. To prove that moral man exists however requires we identify those who do not think, 'changelings'. Those who lack the ability are "below the rank of rational creatures" (Locke cited in Goodey, 2011, p. 341). Emerging from Locke are key ideas which early psychology sought to measure. Goodey coherently argues that notions such as reasoning, attention and self-awareness, linked now to ideas of ability and intelligence, were picked up by writers such as Isaac Watts, John Wesley and Jonathan Edwards. These in turn profoundly influenced the development of classroom practices within which psychological frames of understanding and assessment were both situated and constructed. So it is that the key practices which justified and established the role of psychology in relation to education (such as the development and administration of IQ assessment), though they emerged over a century later, can be seen as "dividing practices" (Foucault, 1994, p. 326) which emerged to fulfil a preordained role.

Of course it was not just psychologists who fulfilled this preordained role, nor did the processes emerge universally at the same time. For example, Bakker (2012) describes the framing of early childhood in developmental terms[2] in a Dutch context over a nine-year period from 1929 to 1938. The focus upon young children began with paediatricians' concern over high death rates. Preventative approaches were identified as the way forward and urbanisation and domestication was seen to be the problem. The solution was fresh air and space to play in. Because of economic constraints, old institutions were adapted to create "residential health colonies for weak toddlers" (p. 81). The children found themselves in institutions subject to detailed observation by medical staff. As a result, norms of development were agreed and new problems 'identified'. This shift in thinking was evident in three key conferences across these years. The focus shifted from physical health to mental health and development and then to child rearing and emotional development. By the late 1930s, psychiatrists and educationalists were the key speakers at institutional conferences, with developmentalism and psychoanalysis to the fore. The earlier belief that play was what children needed had rapidly become subsumed into a belief that this play must be leading to some psychologically, developmentally defined goal.[3]

The historical roots of special are not certain, but seem to be profoundly linked to centuries-old issues of faith and social control. This established a tradition of separate categorical establishments and associated practitioners. It created institutional approaches to identifying, housing, controlling and supporting that category of person. This in turn provided a platform for society's response to compulsory education and those who did not fit.

A follow-up examination

Within a UK context, Tomlinson (1982) showed how from the earliest days of compulsory education, in the 1870s, the pressure to raise standards and the use of payment-by-results encouraged teachers to remove children who were difficult to school. At the same time the emergence of new professionals, in particular special-school teachers and psychologists, meant that there was an eager market for these children and for those with the means to identify them. Winzer (2006), drawing on a range of US sources, describes a similar social process in which teachers and administrators in the 'common school' rejected and stigmatised those who did not meet their views of acceptable behaviour and achievement. As in the UK, the presence of these young people enabled an expansion of special classes, institutions and services. These institutional services were administered initially by clergy and private philanthropy, until ideas of a bureaucratic, public service emerged.

Their leaders were zealous, regarded as progressive, and increasingly laid claim to specific expertise and a scientific underpinning to their work. From the earliest days they also sought to prepare teachers for working within their institutions (Connor, 1976).

The first US organisations of these educators (initially from institutions for the deaf and dumb, then for the blind and then the mentally retarded) emerged in the 1840s. These representative organisations both validated and underlined the separate nature of these practitioners and their seeming uniqueness, at a time when they were struggling to receive the kind of recognition given to mainstream provision. It was often suggested that these people had to deal with highly complex learners, requiring superior skills and particular personal characteristics. As a consequence, beliefs emerged about the status and relative power of these practitioners in relation to the children and young people within their institutions. These beliefs also influenced relationships both with other educators, other professions, parents and families and with the wider public. By the 1930s, this separate identity was being formally constructed by legislation requiring staff to have specific qualifications, frequently involving training supplementary to that received by mainstream teachers (Winzer, 2006).

At the mid-point of the twentieth century, medical and psychological professionals were vying for control over assessment processes alongside central and local administrations who distributed resources, controlling access to assessment and provision. Kirp (1982) described how these processes operated in the development of the English system in the middle of the last century, with professional and bureaucratic mechanisms to the fore. The 1944 act for example did not set out to create an expanded special-school system; however, a political process of persuasion arose for pragmatic economic and social reasons to make local authorities establish programmes based upon departmental categories of handicap. Through bureaucratic processes they created "a job market for educational psychologists as professionals uniquely able to identify and distinguish certain kinds of special students" within generously funded separated settings (Kirp, 1982, p. 144). Over the next few decades, a broadening of the notion of special education saw not only a growth of these professions within mainstream schools, but also a gradual shift of control towards educationalists. It also saw an increasing focus upon issues of rights, often led by parent groups (Wedell, 2008). In the UK "ineducable" students became the responsibility of local education authorities in 1970.

> By the late 1970s 'special' teachers in both segregated and integrated provision had, to some extent, realised that their common interest lay in enhanced professional claims to special expertise. These claims are currently being strengthened and the expansion of special education has created the opportunity for more expert special teachers, support staff, advisers and inspectors to be employed.
>
> (Tomlinson, 1982, p. 161)

It was professionals from this expanding special education network who were taking the lead in advising government too. The Warnock report committee for example only involved one parent of a disabled child (who was also an important figure in a national disability charity), one non-specialist (the chair) and no lawyer. One-third of members came from special schools and the rest from the medical, social work or teaching professions. Their findings seemed to sidestep convincing evidence submitted from alternative perspectives (Thomas & Vaughan, 2004). Their guidance underpinned the 1981 Education Act in England and Wales, reinforcing a process of professionally led assessment and an expansion of special within the mainstream. This expansion and approach to support was evident across the UK too. For example, in a detailed analysis of Scottish legislation from 1980 to 2004, Kay, Tisdall and Riddell (2006) noted how the system maintained an approach based upon individual assessment and models of support, "privileging bureaucracy and professionalism underpinned by legislative bureaucratic rights" (p. 377).

Tomlinson (1982, 1985) convincingly showed how special education had expanded because of the application of social or educational criteria arising in the context of diverse economic and political priorities and not because of children's fundamental qualities or lack of qualities. She also suggested that the expansion of special education would continue because of professional vested interest, dilemmas in relation to comprehensive schooling and decreasing youth employment opportunities. The previous expansion had persistently and perennially connected school-based problems of learning and behaviour to children associated with a manual working class and would continue to do so. This continued expansion has been evident across the world. For example, evidence from a study with colleagues (Rix, Sheehy, Fletcher-Campbell, Crisp & Harper, 2013a), showed that in Japan there had been year-on-year growth in numbers since 1955. In the United States, between 1996 and 2005, 41 per cent of all increased expenditure was on special education, to a point where it was estimated at 21 per cent of all education spending for 13.8 per cent of the school population (Scull & Winkler, 2011).

Special provision has also been very resilient to any efforts to curtail it or to a rhetoric of curtailment. For example, despite the supposed closure of special schools in Italy a few do still exist. Similarly in Norway, growth in special education support has caused constant economic challenges at a national and local level, whilst special schools and classes still emerge without any centralised control (Rix et al., 2013a, 2013b). In other countries, seeming large drops in special-school attendance have not been quite what they appeared. For example, in the Netherlands new regulations regarding severe learning difficulties (SLD) and moderate learning difficulties (MLD) came into play in 1997. In the name of inclusion the SLD and MLD schools were moved into the mainstream sector. Prior to this legislation 5.2 per cent of children were deemed to be in special schools, but after the legislation official statistics proclaimed 2 per cent now attended. Of course the 3.2 per cent in SLD and MLD schools were still in the same settings, just with a new school designation (Pijl, 2013). In the UK, despite many claims about special-school closures and of a bias towards inclusion (e.g. DfE, 2011), the amount of separate provision has remained constant (Barron, Holmes, MacLure & Runswick-Cole, 2007; Rix & Parry, in press). As a leading advocate of special schools, Peter Farrell notes: "The fact that the statistics over the last 20 years indicate that the number of pupils in special schools has remained the same has, for some reason, been ignored" (2012a, p. 42).

Some would even suggest that given the emergence of pupil referral units during a period of falling school numbers in England, and the nature of the students sent to these institutions, there was an overall growth of 6 per cent by the start of the 2000s (Sheehy & Duffy, 2009).

Who's interest test?

The growth of special can be seen to have been driven by forces associated with market economics. From its outset, special education has to some degree been about money, operating as a business, having to create and protect its own niche markets or provide economic justification for its existence. This is evident in examples that Tomlinson gave in her work; for instance the Braidwood family's Asylums for the Deaf in the early 1800s and the emergence of Edinburgh's Asylum for the Industrious Blind a decade earlier. It was evident too, nearly a century later, in the processes of the UK's 1913 Mental Deficiency Act, when doctors would share their fees for certification with the relieving officers who brought the imbeciles, idiots and lunatics to them. As the national press recognised at the time, once identified, these people "proved a very lucrative source of revenue to everyone with whom their misfortune brought them in contact" (*News of the World*, 15 July 1900).[4]

The economic pressures are still very much in evidence. Consider, for example, the report published by NASS, the National Association of Independent Schools and Non- Maintained Special Schools (Clifford, Hamblin &Theobald, 2011). This concluded that independent special schools were between 6-14 per cent cheaper than local authority (LA) provision. Put aside the debatable costing methods used,[5] and we are still left with what is effectively a marketing document. The figures too show the economic value of each child, with estimates of £118k for a child in an LA and between £102k and £112k in a NASS institution. This worked out at the very least to be £280 a day. This was more than:

- three times the amount for the most influential private and (arguably the most elitist) boarding schools in the UK (such as Eton, Harrow or St Paul's);
- over twelve times more than the most expensive secondary comprehensives (e.g. Tower Hamlets and Hackney);
- nearly 27 times more than the least well-funded comprehensives (Knowsley).

In addition, special is a source of income for the mainstream. In discussions with staff in Ireland (Rix et al., 2013b) it was evident that staff did not see formal diagnosis as of pedagogic value but as a means of securing resources. Similarly, a study in Sweden which has looked at cohorts of 10,000 students since 1961 (Giota &

Emanuelsson, 2011) concluded that increasing demands for assessments and diagnoses used to identify special educational needs was a response to budget reductions since the 1990s. This was partly because of under resourcing for special education support for students without an assessment. Budget reductions could therefore be seen as a driver both of increasing number of students with special education needs in mainstream and their placement in special schools.

I am not suggesting that everyone who is in special education is in it for the money. For example, evidence from the United States suggests special education does not attract people who are thinking of moving from high-status professions (Sindelar, Dewey, Rosenberg, Denslow & Lotfinia, 2012). Schools are not necessarily receiving huge amounts of funding for their provision either. For instance, West Sussex County Council allocated far less for a special-school day placement in 2013[6] than the figure cited above by NASS. They provided about £15,000 (13 per cent) of the amount. However, special's position on the margins of the mainstream requires that it operates by different rules. For example, special rarely appears to have the benefit of economies of scale. The consequence is that something which should be very cheap, such as a 'switch' for a computer (something akin to a simplified mouse) will be far more expensive than it could be.[7] Products or services which could be used by a great many children (such as the sign-supported English communication systems Makaton® or Signalong or the numeracy learning programme Numicon) become a luxury, something which is not publically available for all but has to be bought into. It is part of a closed world. In many situations a person's expertise is in knowing of such programmes, in having access to them, rather than the programmes or products containing anything particularly challenging or different for mainstream practitioners. This place on the margins both initiates, facilitates and justifies behaviours which do not have education as their priority. It also puts you in a place of doubt. You look at the price of the product and you wonder, why does it have to be so expensive? As a parent, you sometimes wonder who is becoming rich on the back of your child's situation.

Strategies and interventions

Our professional identities and economic benefit are not the only manner in which our interests are served. Genuine conviction can also lead us in ways which bring benefits to ourselves or our peers. For example, the emergence of attention deficit hyperactivity disorder (ADHD) involved teachers and physicians working together to identify and control those who stepped outside the norms which they valued. Brown (2005) explains how in 1937 a doctor was working with children experiencing severe post-spinal-tap headaches. These children had subsequently been identified for the difficulties their behaviour was causing. The doctor used an amphetamine compound in seeking medication to alleviate their discomfort. It did not help with headaches, but teachers noted a reduction in the behaviours which had led to the identification of the children. The use of the compound spread to other children identified with disruptive behaviour and then in the 1970s to those who were identified as inattentive.

Brown suggests that this tale reveals how: "Sometimes an effective treatment for a disorder is discovered by accident, before there is a full understanding of what is being treated or why the treatment works" (p. xix).

It also reveals a genuine belief that enforcing attention is an appropriate and positive action. Perhaps the practitioners concerned would have seen the changed behaviour as a platform for learning, perhaps they were gratified by having more control in the class, but they would not have been encouraged to reflect upon what it was about the structures of the class and school system which influenced those behaviours and framed them as problematic. As an approach it side-lined all the variables which make education so complex. By removing one of the signs of difficulty, practitioners might be less likely to seek a cure of potentially wider value.

The importance of such systemic supporting attitudes is well recognised. As Kirmayer (2001) noted when talking about depression and anxiety, our understanding of a condition and how it presents is not only influenced by a patient's ethnocultural background, but also by the structures of the system the patient finds themselves in. This includes, "the diagnostic categories and concepts they encounter in the mass media and in dialogue with family, friends and clinicians" (p. 27). Special's diagnostic roots do not encourage transformation of these structures.

A central part of special is its capacity to operate in ways which are supposedly specifically adapted or significant for particular categories of user. Mentioned above were the methods of Pedro Ponce de Lion in the 1500s and Valentin Huay in 1700s. In the nineteenth century, we could identify John Langdon Down's 'medical model of management' (for people we now refer to as having Down syndrome) and Alexander Melville Bell's and his son Alexander Graham's 'Visible Speech System' (for people identified as deaf mutes). It is not uncommon to find claims that particular approaches offer a solution or perhaps a cure for a condition or the experience of living with a condition or working with a person with that condition. There are, for instance, claims that we now know a great deal about teaching reading to children with intellectual disabilities if teachers can implement researched programmes precisely and consistently (Allor, Mathes, Champlin & Cheatham, 2009) or calls to develop specific ways of teaching specific types of children (Blackburn, Carpenter & Egerton, 2010).

Unfortunately, despite its long history, the research evidence and the evidence about the application of that research do not support such claims or the merit of such calls. For example, despite providing some of the earliest impairment specific approaches, an extensive examination of the literature related to educating children who are deaf and hard-of-hearing concluded that the limited nature of the research around particular interventions meant there was little to recommend (Marschark, Spencer, Adams, & Sapere, 2011). I shall explore this conclusion about the reliability and validity of research and its application further in Chapter 4. But for now, I will pick up on two fundamental overarching issues.

First, there is a fundamental problem of research process. Many people believe for example that combinations of narrative qualitative research and meta-analytic quantitative research can allow us to judge the effectiveness of different practices

(Spaulding, 2009). However, such a belief is challenged by reasonable concerns. Narrative approaches are too subjective for comparisons of intervention or impairment types or levels of efficacy. Meta-analyses cannot reflect the nature of variables within the numerous studies, tend to lack detail about method and have been shown to be inconsistent when they are replicated on the same sources. Others suggest a solution exists within randomised control trials (Goldacre, 2013) despite these requiring large samples, consistent and precise delivery of the intervention, a limited number of strategies to compare (preferably two) and a restricted notion of outcome. It might be as Hirsch (2002) suggests, that educational research is generally inconclusive because generalising findings from one educational setting to another is "inherently unreliable" (p. 53). This unreliability is not just a consequence of the complex variables in play within any educational grouping. It also results from the variables associated with the researcher and the questions the research asks, including the underlying biases within any paradigm and theoretical perspective that frame the question and the method. Such complications are endemic to social science.

Second, there is a problem about what is seen as special. For example, there are some approaches which have been shown to be particularly effective for children identified with learning difficulties but these are based upon a belief that all children learn in the same way; for example, the handle technique[8] (Sheehy, 2009). It is debatable therefore whether such approaches can be considered to be special. In Marschark et al.'s review (2011) mentioned above, the evidence highlighted the need to focus upon everyday strategies and materials. Similarly the variations between approaches belies claims to a fundamental difference in approach. So for example a 2004 literature review for the Department for Education and Skills looked for the best ways of teaching children identified with special educational needs using the principal theoretical perspectives of teaching and learning. The review concluded: "The teaching approaches and strategies identified during this review were not sufficiently differentiated from those which are used to teach all children to justify a distinctive SEN pedagogy" (Davis & Florian, 2004, p. 6).

Well-trained parents?

Despite this uncertainty about what constitutes best practice, in recent years in many countries special has expanded into the home, importing its values and processes to the domestic realm. Nearly half of studies (49/100) on children identified with autism for example in a recent international review of best practice provision focussed on pre-schoolers and only 18 per cent looked at children post-primary (Parsons, Guldberg , Macleod, Jones, Prunty & Balfe, 2009). A discourse has emerged which describes parents as the expert on our child, as their first teacher. This has turned us into ad hoc professionals (Rix & Paige-Smith, 2008). There is an implication that we will struggle to access support opportunities unless we incorporate or acknowledge professional values within our identity as parents and use those professional values and knowledge when we engage with the systems around us. This echoes a long understood premise within disability studies: "The more readily one adopts the disabled identity the smoother the process of dealing with professionals and other agents of rehabilitation" (Liggett, 1988, p. 270).

A central component of this professional view is that some children are deficient in comparison to others. The implication is that they have less worth than others. Consider for example this comment by a leading researcher in the field of autism, Professor Simon Baron-Cohen:

> "If there was a prenatal test for autism, would this be desirable? What would we lose if children with autistic spectrum disorder were eliminated from the population?" he [Baron-Cohen] said. "We should start debating this. There is a test for Down's syndrome and that is legal and parents exercise their right to choose termination, but autism is often linked with talent. It is a different kind of condition".
>
> (Boseley, 2009)[9]

This perspective, based around some selected norms and the relative value of people who stray too far from those norms, underpins much of the legislation and guidance that policy-makers and health professionals provide parents so they may choose the kind of child they have. This may reflect the thinking of the wider population, of course, but it also profoundly influences that thinking. This process continues once the child is born. Having had these children (now because they have chosen too or because of a mistake in the process of choice) or having had a child with an impairment which cannot be tested for, the authorities encourage parents to treat their children in a way that is different to the majority of children. The argument is that this will benefit the child and their family.

As mentioned above, part of this process is to tell the parent they are the expert and first teacher of their child. I fully appreciate that in recent years some parents have taken a leading role in fundamentally changing provision, for example by changing local authorities (such as Newham, London) or taking the 'last-resort option' of opening special schools (Treehouse®, n.d.) or inspiring research centres (such as Down Syndrome Education International). But at a more mundane level, as both parent and professional, I have found the call to treat parents as experts to be of selective value, more rhetoric than reality.

As a professional I have heard other practitioners being scathing about parents; as a parent there have been some warm and welcoming receptions, but generally I have found practitioners to be resistant to our ideas in a way they would not be if we were fellow professionals in a meeting. At the most basic level, practitioners rarely voice disagreement with parents and frequently look on with a slight sense of detachment. I often have a sense that people don't really want to listen or that they have had heard it wrong. An example of mishearing parents was reported by the BBC in 2010. Parents had raised money for an enclosed play area at their local school in Scotland, so that their teenage son (identified with learning difficulties and as being on the autistic spectrum) could play safely alongside his peers. The play area that was built is shown in Figure 2.1. Not surprisingly, having got the school to build the play area, the parents had to get them to take it down. Everyone was very apologetic and the school blamed a breakdown in communication with their supplier.

A common experience is simply having one's suggestions side-lined without any explanation. An example of this arose when I was asked to join an advisory group which produced a developmental journal with central government funding as a part the national Early Support programme. The journal turned out to be 229 pages of checklists and notes explaining the steps by which a child could be expected to develop. Such checklists are also evident in other countries, such as the Netherlands[10] (Tadema, Vlaskamp & Ruijssenaars, 2005) but can be based upon questionable reading of the research and its claims (Rix & Parry, 2014). The production of the developmental journal of which I was part was mainly driven by psychologists and therapists, with others providing feedback about the outcomes. In the hope that I might encourage some reflection on the tensions inherent within the checklist I made a number of suggestions about different assessment approaches, and also produced an accompanying document *Assessing the Effectiveness of Our Support*. This would have allowed families to assess the development and quality of support they were receiving as early interventionists, in a manner similar to that being used to assess the development of their children. This document was never circulated and I cannot remember the alternative approaches ever being discussed. My only achievement was to have some horizontal lines removed from

FIGURE 2.1   Play area? (Image provided by Scottish National Party.)

one of the columns. I always assumed that my model did not quite match up with the dominant professional perspective. I concluded that if I wanted to have strategic clout I needed to position myself closer both to the strategy-makers and to align myself more strongly with the strategy aims.

In England, the Early Support programme helped to professionalise parents as part of the wider pre-school early intervention process. As well as a family-held child checklist, it involved working with a range of professionals at home or in early years settings (with their own checklists) and coming up with activities in order to progress more rapidly against developmental norms. I was not only an advisor to this project but I also delivered an early intervention programme with my son. Sadly, this had a negative impact upon our relationship with each other. I have not been the only parent to experience this either. Consider for example the following quote from an Australian family:

> The thing that I resent about the whole business of Nick's infancy/babyhood is that I never actually took the time to just play with him like a baby. I always thought OK, the most important thing to do was stimulating him, OK, have him sitting up … instead of just bloody enjoying it.
>
> (Bridle & Mann, 2000, p. 13)

In the review of literature associated with autism mentioned above it was also noted that though some early intervention programmes might seem promising, parents needed support as the process was stressful and disruptive to families (Parsons et al., 2009).

It was very evident to me that my son did not enjoy what I was being asked to do with him, however creative I was about it. I came to realise after a great deal of endeavour that the processes I was being asked to undertake were utterly inappropriate for my son. I know that some children seemed to love learning from flash cards and the other various activities which were involved. I am sure to them it seemed like play. But to my son it did not. Of course, it could be my fault but I really did follow instructions and enthusiastically engage as best I could.[11] Certainly, nine parents we interviewed as part of a small research project all saw early intervention as a site of conflict, guilt and frustration. However, they also felt that they had to give it a go regardless, one describing the checklist she used as her "bible". Most also went on to take up formal roles in health or education (Rix & Paige-Smith, 2008; Rix, Paige-Smith & Jones, 2008).

I will return to consider the oppositional nature of parental responses in Chapters 4 and 5, but in the context of this chapter it is important to recognise both the divergent expectations which are placed upon special by its users and the impact which special processes, practices and thinking have upon the users' expectations. For example, in a study looking at the processes mothers go through in gaining recognition for their children with ADHD, many had to engage in ongoing battles with school which put themselves on the margins. Their struggle was to encourage schools to situate their children's behaviours in the same kinds of tolerable categories as other children. They sought to show that their children could be manageable if every day special processes were adopted, such as behavioural programmes or diagnosis leading to drug treatment (Carpenter & Austin, 2008). However, this study, of itself can be seen to be part of a wider public narrative, frequently constructed in the media, of the mothers as spokespeople and caretakers, the ones who bear responsibility for the predominantly male young people who are on the margins because they are exceptional or dangerous, victims, heroes or villains (Horton-Salway, 2013). These social representations in turn affect parental responses. So parents who see their child within the prototypical ADHD image will more readily agree with the treatment associated with that image, whilst the parent who does not see their child within the prototypical image will less readily agree (Schmitz, Filippone & Edelman, 2003).

As much as people may wish to dismiss discussion of language and attitudes to disabled people as political correctness, the language of special does have a profound impact upon families (or is that service users, customers or clients?). Neary (2013) examines the jargon and its rhetorical nature around Steven, his son, as he has moved into adult social care. His experience was that claims of *transparency* actually described opaque processes, where positive language disguised negative thinking. For example, Steven made a wish list of six everyday activities as part of his *person-centred plan* and all were refused as being not in his best interests. For his father this was a *system-centred plan*. He also showed how this rhetoric transformed normal activity into something special, because everything "must have a value". Here are some of the transformations which Neary highlighted:

- going out = *accessing the community*;
- his home = *his placement*;
- learning to make a pizza = *increasing independence skills*;
- being angry = *challenging behaviour*;
- choosing a meal = *being empowered*;
- friends = *circle of support and influence*;
- making unwise choices = *lacking mental capacity*;
- alphabetically sorting CDs = *inappropriately obsessive*;
- being greedy = *challenging boundaries*.

Neary's description of his sons life is one in which the everyday takes on a new professionalised meaning which separates him from other people's normality. His suggests for example, that being sad is an everyday part of his life, for his son being sad means a record being made, which requires analysis and input from a team of professionals.

Assessment summary

The discussion of the professionalisation of the family experience did not touch upon many other issues which might be pertinent, such as parent training programmes and a wider context of lifelong learning. Similarly, much has been missed from this first part of the chapter in its description of the emergence and migration of special from institutions for a relative few into the mainstream (for many but not all). The tales of the emergence of impairments, institutions, professions, charities, policies and social discourses have been merged in this section to try and give a sense of their interwoven histories which both created and were created by each other. I have attempted to show how it is that we have arrived at a model of special which is a fundamental marker of difference in the same way as gender, ethnicity, faith, age and sexuality.

Special has strong links to the model of childhood which sees children and young people as needing to be protected and nurtured. This situates adulthood and adult knowledge as the ultimate goal and adults and their knowledge as the means to achieve that goal. It is evident for nearly all children in education, who are in a place of "protection" ("artificial training rooms") so they can "get acquainted with social participation" (Jans, 2004, p. 39). But this notion has particular resonance in the delivery of separate provision for the minority.[12] For example, across the years, in the long-term, large-scale Swedish study mentioned earlier, practically all head-teachers attributed problems and difficulties in school and children's need for additional support "to the student's own shortcomings and individual characteristics" (Giota & Emanuelsson, 2011, p. 104).

The model of the deficient, needy child who requires specific adult (professional?) support also influences children's relationships with their peers. For example, a small case study in Australia explored a teacher's struggle to overcome the negative attitude of her class to two young children and negative attitudes of the two children themselves. The teacher saw this attitude as resulting from people's response to a behaviour label that trapped children in self-fulfilling organisational processes and removed any chance of the children reforming their own identities and social relations (Exley, 2008). The model contends that these shortcomings cannot be dealt with by everyday responses. As Adams, Swain and Clark (2000) identified in their analysis of classes within two special schools: "What's so special, from the viewpoint of teachers, is special expertise within special practice for special children" (p. 243).

This thinking will be explored further in Chapter 4, but in order to exemplify this viewpoint, consider Table 2.1. This is based on a table in the Statement of Purpose for Sunfield School, whose strapline is "Children at the heart of everything we do" (Sunfield, 2012). This was designed to be used prior to formal assessment, as guidance about access to the school.

The table from which this list came highlights the role of expertise, categories and selection. It also reveals the underlying uncertainty and contradictions at the heart of the process. Here we have absolute categories, identified through formal assessment, enabling choices to be made by the setting about who can attend. There is an implicit continuum of severity in evidence too. For example, how limited do your medical conditions need to be to gain access, and what happens if they worsen? Issues of comorbidity also seem to be unproblematic. If you

TABLE 2.1 Guidance to who can access school

	Access
Attention deficit hyperactivity disorder (ADHD)	Yes
Autism spectrum disorder	Yes
Blind	No
Cerebral palsy	Limited
Challenging behaviour	Yes
Deaf	No
Developmental uncertainty	Yes
Down syndrome	Yes
Hearing impairment	Yes
Medical conditions	Limited
Mental health needs	Limited
Mobility difficulties	Limited
Moderate learning disability	Limited
Physical disability	Limited
Schizophrenia	No
Self-injurious behaviour	No
Severe learning disability	Yes
Sexual abuse of peers	No
Sexualised behaviour towards others	Limited
Significant danger to others	No
Visual impairment	Limited
Wheelchair user	No

Source: Based on table in Sunfield (2012).

accept the notion of categories as being robust, what happens if you have autistic spectrum disorder and are blind? In addition, this table has been changed slightly over the years. So, for example, arsonists were not allowed to attend in the 2004 and 2008 version but now do not appear on the list. Does this mean something has changed about arsonists, the nature of arson, our knowledge of arsonists or the values of the school? Most perplexing of all, perhaps, despite robust anti-discrimination legislation, the school's Statement of Purpose suggests that Sunfield has remained consistent in its unwillingness to accept people who use wheelchairs. If you examine other publications from the school (e.g. Whitehurst, 2007), they have clearly been involved in building work which could have created wheelchair accessible accommodation. Why would they take this position? When I look at a table like this, I cannot help but feel confounded by its assumptions and underpinning beliefs. But I am even more discombobulated by why anyone would want to represent themselves in this way, particularly an organisation which wishes to be recognised as caring.

The following section will consider how the practices and process which have emerged from the notion of special are further complicated by the additional challenges of competing within the dominant economic, social and political environment.

Coping strategies?

In the UK, during the early 2000s there was a specialist schools programme. This government-led programme encouraged school to set targets, focus on particular areas of the curriculum and raise external funds. As a consequence they accessed additional centralised funding and could rebrand themselves as specialist schools or colleges. It was initially aimed at mainstream schools, but many special schools quickly latched onto the possibility of rebranding themselves as specialist colleges (Rix, 2011). These changes were frequently trumpeted by via external marketing consultants, in press releases and high-profile launches. One head-teacher described the process as providing parity with the mainstream, something which was incredibly important to her staff and students. However, it also involved political and strategic manoeuvring by these school leaders. In a presentation at the National Association of Specialist Education Colleges, Gillian Wills (Chief Executive of the Royal School for Deaf Children Residential Special School), advised attendees to:

- get in at the start of projects;
- liaise at the top of organisations;
- be shrewd;
- consider issues of competition;
- think strategically;
- 'be a politician!'

As new practices emerge, those who are strategic and competitive find ways to make money or expand their services. As two of the contributors to the hugely influential US *Diagnostic and Statistical Manual of Mental Disorders* (*DSM IV*), recognised, the third edition had made psychiatric diagnosis "a best-selling, financial bonanza" (Frances & Widiger, 2012, p. 122). Similarly the development of testing regimes, nationally and internationally, which some might assume drive up standards, enable parental choice and hold providers to account has coincided with expanding markets. There have, for example, been reports in the media of a boom in private tutoring programmes across the world (Burns, 2013; Sharma, 2013). In the United States the requirement that students sit state achievement tests and other standardized assessments has led to a rapid growth in the provision of 'remedial services'. Turnover for after-school tutoring passed $4billion in 2005. Annual reported revenues of supplemental services rose by 300 per cent between 2001 and 2004. In addition, firms which once developed assessment tests or who were established to work with children identified with severe emotional and behavioural difficulties now develop or deliver the interventions for 'failing' students and schools (Burch, 2006). Similarly, in the UK, education businesses are springing up in response to changes in local authority governance (Ball, 2009).

Dissociative identities?

In many situations these organisations are charities or required to be not-for-profit. However, the availability and nature of charities varies according to the socio-economic conditions of a community (Clifford, Geyne-Rahme & Mohan, 2012). They also have to balance the economic and strategic interests of the organisation with the benefits they wish to deliver. As a result an emphasis upon service-user interests can turn out to be rhetorical and subsidiary to strategic management priorities (Hedges, 2007). A study looking at 20 such care organisations in the United States (Sowa, 2008) identified how their decisions were informed by institutional pressures (particularly organisational survival, legitimacy and standing in the field). They were also under pressure from the market, funders and resources, and influenced by whether their primary aim was to meet needs or change practices. In addition, the tendency for charities (and other commissioned support organisations) to be funded for their services either generally or specifically by third parties and not end-users means that the quality and relevance of their services does receive the kind of direct feedback which typically governs a competitive market (Connor, 1999). Service is also vulnerable when funding sources move on.

Many organisations associated with special are also associated in some way with notions of care. This creates what Oliver (1996) describes as an "irresolvable contradiction". To put it bluntly, people in need of care cannot be empowered because the reason that they need care is precisely because they are powerless; if they were not, why would they need care?

Worse still, for many there is not only a lack of empowerment but also a lack of care. For example, Rae (1996) uses the phrase "special school survivors" when sharing four former students' experiences of bullying, isolation, loneliness and hatred of school (Rae, 1996). Also, in a study to find out more about the experiences of children and young people identified with a learning disability, undertaken in 46 special schools and units across England, Wales and Northern Ireland, 80 per cent had experienced bullying at school, 60 per cent had been physically hurt by bullies and 70 per cent had been verbally abused. These young people frequently experienced theft, were excluded from activities and struggled to enter the social networks of their peers. Moreover, 40 per cent said that the bullying did not stop even after they had told someone in authority (Mencap, 2007).

Historically, this "irresolvable contradiction" between care and empowerment and implicit powerlessness of users has been evident in the language associated with care organisations. Consider for example text from a special-school website I came across when researching a module for the Open University in 2003:

> Barbara Priestman School is a special school dedicated to meeting the individual and special needs of some very special children. Life is never going to be very easy for them. For many of them inclusion in mainstream schools will be no answer and bullying will be a threat. They have a variety of physical disabilities or some learning difficulty. These make it a bit more difficult for them to access the national curriculum and lead straightforward lives.
>
> Some are delicate, others have sensory impairment. Many have quite complex needs that advocates of inclusion may not know about and certainly may not understand.
>
> (Barbara Priestman, 2003)

Upon visiting this site ten years later, however, I found that they had become part of a federation of special academies[13] and the language was far more upbeat, with a sense of empowerment. In 2014, for example, their head-teacher's welcome included the following statement:

> We are very proud of our academy's positive ethos, one that values diversity and provides equal opportunity. We have high expectations for each individual, and are committed to developing each student's strengths and growing areas of need.
>
> (Barbara Priestman, 2014)

A similar process was evident in an analysis I undertook of 78 special-school websites (Rix, 2011). In 2008 a search for the Glyne Gap School turned up the description: "for children who will always need others to help them meet their needs, we aim to give a means of making choices and friendships". However, on visiting the site, this strapline had been replaced. When I revisited in 2014, there was no strapline at all and the text was all about encouraging, challenging, supporting and preparing individuals.

On all school websites there is still a strong focus upon safety and care, but it would seem that schools are avoiding language which disempowers children and are replacing this with language which empowers them. They seem to be focusing less upon the deficit in the child and are identifying themselves more by their expertise and their desire to work with the community.

The challenge of living with earning difficulties?

Organisations associated with special are by their nature predominantly focused upon a central issue. They are about a particular impairment or a particular approach or a particular service. They bring together particular shared mind-sets. This can be seen as a positive opportunity for expertise in a field, but it also risks creating an isolated perspective and 'silo' thinking. This can influence not only the services it provides but the way in which it represents the people it purportedly serves. Waltz (2012), for example, examines the understanding within creative industries and amongst autism charity brand-management professionals about the debates associated with images and narratives of disability. He cites the work of David Hevey (1992), a disability theorist and photographer, who noted in the early 1990s how charity branding sold fear rather than the desire associated with other organisations; something to avoid rather than buy.

Hevey's three stages started with building awareness through an image of need and a text of hope, then moved to creating an attitude change through the provision of information or a challenging statement, and third, showing disabled people doing 'normal' things. All three stages are fundamentally negative of course, at their best positioning the disabled as emerging and the charity as enabling. Waltz's examination of three campaigns between 2007 and 2009 concluded that charities still put out material that was offensive to some of the people they purported to represent. This was partly because of a lack of understanding of the social model and the way in which disability is constructed by social attitudes and structures. But it was also a result of financial pressure, not having input from autistic people and from being isolated from other disability charities. Waltz noted too that awareness adverts were more about brand awareness than accurate information; and particularly worryingly, when complaints were made to 'independent' arbitrators, different rules of proof were applied in comparison to other businesses.

It is perhaps unsurprising that the pressures on organisations to function in a purported market can encourage low-level disingenuousness. For example, in the summer of 2013, I was looking at the work of the successful Cambrian group, who run "specialist behavioural health services for children and adults". I noted with interest a claim that all their residential schools were rated as outstanding by OFSTED. When I looked at the reports, though, one was rated Good and two (which were outstanding for education) were adequate for care (Cambian Group, 2013). Evidence from schools and services from different countries would also suggest that they can become protective of resources which they have struggled to build up (Rix et al., 2013a) or resist changing practices or sharing resources because of the threat to their 'ownership' (Heath, McLean-Heywood, Rousseau, Petrakos, Finn & Karagiannakis, 2006).

Maintaining a position within this environment frequently involves shifting one's identity. Consider Sunfield once more, which in 2013 called itself on its website "one of the leading Curative Educational Communities in the UK" and began in the 1930s as a Steiner school. Over the years it has taken on different guises. For example, in 2005, Sunfield Research Institute was launched. At this time it made extensive claims about its international advisory group and began to publish its own research under its own publishing arm.[14] However, seven years later, the institute no longer appears in the school's literature. Sunfield's inevitable need to balance complex priorities is also evident within its organisational structure. It is an educational community, but to survive it has five departments answerable to the Principal, two of which are focused upon finance.[15]

I appreciate that any example of a single school is very partial and might be deemed by those associated with the school as unfair. My aim is not to mark any of these settings as being particularly bad or to suggest that all special settings operate in the same way. My aim is to exemplify the kinds of problems which emerge because of the challenges inherent within the model of special and the constraints which are fundamental to it, both as a result of its relation to the mainstream and the legacies of policy. If you are a small organisation it is very difficult to make ends meet. In many ways they have done very well to survive.

Special comorbidity

The consequence of these multiple organisations and individuals, with their complex aims, struggles and beliefs is that in almost every branch of special there are competing versions of truth, presented equally convincingly by contradictory experts. The competition which is inherent to nearly all aspects of special provision has encouraged a market place of confusion.

Consider what might happen if you were to try to decide how best to support someone with difficulties associated with print literacy – if you ignore the issues raised in Chapter 1 about the self-defeating nature of our obsession with literacy and numeracy. You might start with a claim from one expert that on the back of burgeoning research, educators can identify dyslexia early and step in to avoid a "downward spiral of underachievement, lowered self-esteem and poor motivation (Snowling, 2013, p. 1). However, as you explored further you could come across another expert who can argue convincingly that this belief in identification acts to "reduce overall educational attainment" and that "there is no clear discontinuity that provides an absolute categorical boundary for a diagnostic category of 'dyslexics'" (Elliott & Gibbs, 2008, p. 476).

In trying to resolve this contradiction, you would come across other experts – perhaps misrepresenting and/or missing the point of what someone has said – but claiming with equally convincing certainty that one or other is wrong (e.g. Stein, 2009) or to defend a position (e.g. Godsland, 2013). However, when you looked closer you would realise that the impartiality of their expertise was compromised. For example:

- Stein was a professor of neuroscience who researched "auditory and visual perceptual impairments suffered by dyslexic children" and was contributing his ideas to a website (Dystalk) which offered private tutoring services (Keystone Tutors), with a particular focus upon supporting those identified with dyslexia, which was itself validated by including a key advisor, Jane Emerson, who has run a school business focused upon dyslexia since 1991.
- Godsland was recognised within the reading and dyslexia field, running a frequently cited site, Dyslexics.org. On this site she quoted a range of literature to support her view, but it transpired her work had been focused upon advocating synthetic phonics as the means to resolve the problems of reading and she linked to many resources for this approach, including those which had made a great deal of money for their advocates (e.g. Ruth Miskin).

Can you trust these individuals? They have spent many years focusing upon a specific field. Does this mean you can have greater faith in them or does it mean they are less likely to question the validity of that field?

In seeking some resolution you might broaden your search. You might, for example, explore this latter phonics approach. But this would lead you into another furious debate, known by some as the Reading Wars. You might for example find yourself reading the much-cited, government-supported, Rose report on the issue; you might go to one of its robust rebuttals, such as that penned by Wyse and Styles (2007). Or perhaps you might find yourself drawn to advocates of approaches targeted at other specific conditions, seemingly well supported by research, such as a mix of sight word, letter knowledge and shared reading for children identified with Down syndrome (Burgoyne, Duff, Clarke, Buckley, Snowling & Hulme, 2012) or mixed teaching approaches for broad categories of students with intellectual disabilities (Allor et al., 2009).

In this world of contradictory explanations, how can anyone know what is right? Any decision a person makes is bound to be a mix of personal experience, beliefs and opportunities. Any outcomes will be dependent to some degree upon unpredictable fate of circumstances.

I return once more to special as a place of doubt.

Notes

1 All the dates above come variously from Richardson and Powell (2011), B. Rix (2006), Stiker (1999) and my own recollections which I confirmed using webpages and the websites of current institutions.
2 The notion of development can also be seen to emerge from notions around our capacity to achieve a state of grace (see Goodey, 2011, pp. 169–174).
3 I was attending a seminar series discussing Goodey's (2011) work when a leading European psychologist stated that Goodey's book was an unfair representation of psychology, because intelligence was no longer seen as the defining feature of humanity within his field. He made it clear that for some years at conferences and in papers the defining feature of being human had been presented as the capacity to empathise. In light of this comment a number of us noted that those previously identified as ineducable because of intelligence were now routinely included in mainstream, whilst those with a limited capacity to empathise increasingly had separate provision.
4 This quote was supplied by Kieron Sheehy.
5 For example, the full LA cost seems to be based upon a fully resident student but also includes individual travel costs and loss of income to family.
6 This figure followed central government cuts and excluded travel costs. It is still probably slightly more than mainstream support. In this LA in 2013/14, the first 20 hours of mainstream support were to be covered by the budget from central government. This disadvantaged schools with high levels of special educational needs. This LA paid another £3,200 for 7.5 hours a week additional support. Any further support had to be negotiated.
7 On 7 November 2013, at http://www.*inclusive*.co.uk/product-list?Text=Dome%20 and%20Disc%20Switches, the switches cost £59, whilst a mouse on Amazon could be got for as little as £1.46.
8 The handle technique involves identifying a word from the student's spoken or signed vocabulary. This is written on a flashcard, discussed with the child and a visual handle is then selected and added to the written word.
9 Thanks to Kieron Sheehy for identifying this quote.
10 This was adapted from the International Classification of Functioning, Disabilities and Health (ICF: WHO, 2002) removing reference to context and the factors which situated the behaviours. For example the assessment looked at whether the person could go to the toilet but removed things which seemed to overlap, such as whether they wash their hands afterwards and whether they were given enough time to dress and undress. It then added in things that "appeared to be important" (p. 409), such as "eats solid food". Evaluation of the assessment tool involved professionals reflecting on its value to them. Changes were made on the basis of their comments.
11 Coincidentally, on a module forum, the day I wrote this, two of my students were discussing delivering a different kind of programme. Both delivered an applied behaviour analysis programme to their children prior to school age (one training as a therapist). One

claimed it enabled their child to speak and the other that it had an entirely negative impact – she stopped the programme after four years.

12 And for them it does not end with school.

13 Academies are schools removed from local authority control, national curriculum constraints and national agreements over teacher pay and qualifications. They have a relatively long history within England but expanded rapidly from 2010.

14 Publications included an evaluation of new living accommodation at Sunfield (Whitehurst, 2007) which, despite claims to be evidence-based, cited only one paper. This paper is not referenced, and turns out to have been published in another Sunfield publication and a magazine. Both papers were subsequently cited by others writing in the field. The version published in a practitioner magazine was one of many cited in a publication in a peer-reviewed journal (Carpenter, 2007) which described how research had driven the development of Sunfield, how other schools could learn from the Research Institute, and how they must "accept the challenge for the sake of our young people, change and go forward" (p. 74).

15 These are led by the Head of Education, Head of Residential Services, Consultant Psychologist, Business Manager and Appeals Director.

3

THE STRUCTURES AND PROCESSES OF INCLUSION

People on the side of The People always ended up disappointed, in any case. They found that The People tended not to be grateful or appreciative or forward-thinking or obedient. The People tended to be small-minded and conservative and not very clever and were even distrustful of cleverness. And so the children of the revolution were faced with the age-old problem: it wasn't that you had the wrong kind of government, which was obvious, but that you had the wrong kind of people … . As soon as you saw people as things to be measured, they didn't measure up. What would run through the streets soon enough wouldn't be a revolution or a riot. It'd be people who were frightened and panicking. It was what happened when the machinery of city life faltered, the wheels stopped turning and all the little rules broke down. And when that happened, humans were worse than sheep. Sheep just ran; they didn't try to bite the sheep next to them.

(Pratchett, 2002, pp. 225–226)

Me

When I was studying at school and then began working in education the issue of inclusion was not even on the map. But as a 53-year-old writing this book in 2014, I have quite a lot invested in inclusion. It is how I make my living. It is in my job title.[*] I run a module studied by up to 500 students a year which looks at the issues associated with it. I conduct research which is published in journals that focus upon these same kinds of issues. My son has attended a local primary and secondary school, though if he had been born 30 years earlier he would have been deemed ineducable. It would seem therefore that I live in a world that has come a long way.

But then again…

Numerous families, children and young people (perhaps my son?) are still having a very (or relatively) poor educational experience and no opportunity for a self-directed and fulfilling adult life. For them the difference is of little meaning. They are parties to the rhetorical journey of the great and the good. They experience the reality of a politics of contradictory gestures, where professionals, policy-makers and opinion-makers battle over vested interest and influence. They experience a reality where folk just get on with their lives as best they can. And so, despite me being quite loud and quite pushy; despite Caroline and I having achieved much for our son that others may have not … our son is still not really in the mainstream. Partly perhaps because he will always have different rules applied to him. But also because the mainstream is itself a mirage, a complex mess of (the wrong kind of ?) people, a mix of orientations, interests, beliefs, histories, fortunes and characteristics.

The mainstream arises from multiple moments of self-interest overlapping with multiple moments of co-operation. It creates and is created by myriad experiences encapsulated by the full gamut of expressive nouns.[1] It is always the same and always different. It is where we live, verging on the edges of chaos, affirming some order and sense of self. It is about the groups we form and the practices, processes and social structures we reify. It is about symbiosis, tyranny, parasitism, alliances and chance. It is where we pass the time of day. It is all odd to someone and all normal to someone else. The mainstream is the "little rules" which keep the machinery going and by which most of us are judged acceptable. It is only by changing the "little rules" that we can shift the rhetoric beyond the realm of the gesture, so that we, The People, can hope to reshape the everyday without needing to take a bite out of each other.

Our starting point

In 2006, a research report came out in the UK which had been commissioned by one of the main teacher unions, the National Union of Teachers[2] (Macbeath, Galton, Steward, Macbeath & Page, 2006). A number of my colleagues were less than happy with the report and somewhat disparaging about its negative tones. It seemed to say positive things but always with a negative slant upon them. It never seemed to shift us away from the status quo. I am quite fond of this report though. It reminds me of my teaching days. I can hear the voice of the teachers in it. It also reminds me of the challenge which we face in changing the rules.

The authors of this report, in their initial description of the research, describe three worlds of inclusion:

- Their *first world* belongs to the policy-maker. This is the hyperbole of politics, unproblematically seeking contradictory goals which invariably lead to (or exacerbate) the marginalisation of some. The report gives the example of *personalised learning*. At the time this was touted as the means to really focus upon the individual and their learning needs. However, within the overarching standards agenda it can turn out to "mean little more than increased diagnostic testing, tighter target setting and additional pre- and after- school booster classes" (p. 13).

- Their *second world* of inclusion emerges from the aspirational sharing of pedagogy, in which best practice enables the mainstream classroom to be an effective site of learning for all children. They talk about this vision being underpinned by the notion of rights. This world is undermined in particular, they suggest, by the culturally determined nature of teaching and the legacies of earlier times (enacted through curricular assessment and notions of differentiation). It is undermined too by the inherent conservatism of teachers faced with a class whom they primarily have to control, regardless of their awareness of alternative approaches; "In reality it is the heart that more often rules the head" (p. 14). This, they also suggest, is why teachers tend to blame external factors beyond their control for their current practice. They feel justified if they can focus the blame upon resources, space, time or training.
- Their *third world* is the current classroom as it is, rather than as it could be. They present four vignettes around student's behaviour, concentration, over exuberance and controlling characteristics. They maintain that these exemplify challenges for which teachers have little or no training or prior experience. This demonstrates how teacher's decisions come to be political. Their actions and reactions define people's relationships to the whole, their identity and their standing amongst their peers and wider community. In the context of an "incompatible and often unreasonable system", everyday experiences become impossible tasks. In such circumstances we already require "courageous teachers and courageous leaders who are able to expand the repertoire of thinking and practice" (p. 16).

These three worlds are evident in their subsequent narrative which emerges from their findings about provision in England (see Box 3.1), a narrative which echoes the experience in many other countries (Rix, Sheehy, Fletcher-Campbell, Crisp & Harper, 2013a, 2013b). This then provides us with a reasonable starting point for considering inclusion. It is understood and experienced by people in different ways. It is full to bursting with contradictions, tensions, constraints and possibilities.

Box 3.1 The experience of inclusion in English schools

Key issues identified in National Union of Teachers evaluation

- The increased numbers of children in England in independent special schools and pupil referral units (for behaviour) with an increasing numbers of children experiencing health and educational problems as a result of surviving through medical intervention.
- The increased chance of exclusion for those with an identified SEN and

(Continued)

(Continued)

from particular ethnic backgrounds.

- The lack of recognition of mental health issues.
- The need for increased resources. (Decisions were frequently made on the basis of funding.)
- Parents frequently struggling to get services for their children.
- The support provided is often not what is required or promised.
- Teachers passing responsibility on to teaching assistants for teaching and planning, seeing these unqualified support staff as experts. This leads to a nurturing and less academically challenging relationship, isolating the child further.
- Teachers acknowledging how school processes and pedagogical approaches create learning problems and how subsequent frustrated behaviour leads to disruption and sanctions as well as concerns for well-being. The focus upon behaviour thus overshadows learning issues.
- Staff feeling they have to rely on their common sense, that they do not have adequate specialist help and that, with high numbers of special needs, effective teaching becomes nearly impossible.
- Staff identifying the curriculum and testing as creating inappropriate demands, particularly when children and young people move into secondary school.
- When the teacher did work with children identified with special educational needs they often do so in isolation, asking the teaching assistant to teach the rest of the class.
- A feeling that inclusion takes a disproportionate amount of time in planning and preparing.
- As a consequence of all these factors, head-teachers had to find ways of 'working the system'. However, the collective structures which would better support them become increasingly difficult as the system further fragments and become framed as a competitive marketplace.
- Few mainstream schools felt they could take all children without fundamental change in systems, structures and conventions.
- The best provision, however, is already flexible, pragmatic and drawing on all available expertise, whilst being actively engaged in self-monitoring.

(Based on Macbeath et al., 2006)

As Winzer (2006) notes, there is a stated commitment to the philosophy but a clash with policies that serve diverse priorities; education is a 'pragmatic' response to the limited availability of resources. This is why the problematic realities of current classrooms have remained in place despite the calls and claims of school restructuring. This chapter will consider if the problems of inclusion are unresolvable.

A brief history of seeking togetherness

Chapter 1 touched upon the history and development of segregated settings in the context of developing compulsory education. In previous centuries, however, even if many disabled children were unserved by schools and were either at home or within residential institutions, the increasing compulsion to attend school did not always lead to calls for separate provision.

Cole (1989) reported a debate in Scotland in the late 1800s where staff from institutions for blind children argued for residential provision because of parental choice and special approaches to learning. Others at the meeting maintained that children did better within ordinary classes. The meeting passed a resolution supporting the view that children should be in school with their peers unless exceptional circumstances meant they could not be (Cole, 1989). Winzer (2006) reports a publication from a US school for the feeble-minded which recognised the need for disabled and disadvantaged children to take their place in the 'commonwealth' and that they should attend schools so they did not become institutionalised and lose touch with the wider community. In Leicester in the 1890s the inspector of schools sought to place all children in "the ordinary school if they are at all fit" (Copeland, 2001, p. 7). He would not place them within the newly formed special classes on the basis of impairments or medical examinations. He conducted an educational assessment and had to be convinced that there was no aspect of the regular classes which offered them the opportunity to thrive. Other individuals, such as Marjorie Chappell (2003), would find themselves attending their local schools because of the actions of their family or parents. It is possible too that there would have been a connection between rurality and inclusion, where the practicalities of providing transport and separate provision discouraged educating children away from their local schools; it has certainly been shown at a national level (in a study of 15 countries) that there is a strong connection between population density and levels of segregation (Meijer & De Jager, 2001). In the UK, for example, you are statistically more likely to attend a special school in an urban unitary local authority than a rural county authority (Black & Norwich, 2014).

Of course, despite these exceptions the growth of special education continued in many countries and a concerted challenge did not emerge until the 1950s and 60s. There seemed to be three drivers for this challenge. There was contested research which suggested that special schools were no better than mainstream (Hornby, Atkinson & Howard, 1997), a rejection of the long-established view that some people were ineducable (B. Rix, 2006), and the emergence of a range of social movements which argued that division on the basis of social, ethnic, gender, physical and intellectual differences could not be justified on moral, educational or socio-political grounds.

This last factor, in particular, was evident globally. In 1960, for example, there was the United Nations Convention Against Discrimination in Education, in 1971 there was the United Nations Declaration on the Rights of Mentally Retarded Persons, in 1975 the UN Declaration on the Rights of Disabled Persons, and then the 1981 International Year of Disabled Persons. This last is frequently represented as a historic moment when there was a paradigm shift in relation to participation, accessibility and civil rights (Richardson & Powell, 2011). It certainly helped prepare the ground for the 1990 conference in Jomtien, Thailand, where a World Declaration on Education for All was adopted by participants from 155 countries and representatives of 160 governmental and non-governmental agencies. This commitment to universal primary education reaffirmed that education was a fundamental, essential human right, central to personal and social well-being (Miles & Singal, 2010). However, it did not include a clear statement that all children should learn together within inclusive schools (Peters, 2007; Kiuppis, 2013) and so four years later in 1994 there was the World Congress on Special Needs Education, Salamanca. This set the global policy agenda for inclusive education and marked the global linguistic shift from integration to inclusion (Vislie, 2003).

Are we talking about the same thing?

The seeming unanimity which such international agreements imply is not always evident on the ground, of course. During the early wave of inclusive rhetoric, Evans & Lunt (2002) surveyed English Principal Educational Psychologists in relation to their local authority's policies on inclusion. The response represented 37.5 per cent of local authorities in England. Across the country inclusion was variously interpreted as: part-time placements in special and mainstream; outreach support from special schools; units attached to the mainstream; and modified facilities, additional resource or individual support in the mainstream.

At around the same time, Booth and Smith (2002) noted the shifting position of policy-makers in their use of the term 'inclusion'. It was used to refer to:

- special educational needs;
- access to and participation within mainstream schools for students categorised as having special educational needs and/or disabilities;
- social inclusion/exclusion relating to issues such as truancy, behaviour and looked-after children;
- issues of racial discrimination;
- community stresses brought about by poverty, lack of housing, etc.;
- inclusion as an underlying general principle for education;
- reducing exclusionary pressures on and supporting the participation of all children and young people in schools (summarised in Black-Hawkins, Florian & Rouse, 2007, p. 20).

Inclusion has been also widely represented as an ongoing process (UNESCO IBE, 2008), active and without end (Flem & Keller, 2000). There is a strong message that people work towards reaching out to all learners, they continually strive for this goal, but do not arrive (Ainscow, 2000). It can be seen as mixed with exclusion in "a messy series of compromises, adjustments and individual preferences" (Corbett, 1997, p. 55).

As suggested at the start of Chapter 1, what appears to be a commonality is actually undermined by all the other variables at play within the day to day practice and policy environment, as it operates at local and national levels. Things may have the same name or be associated with similar concepts or terms, but this does not mean that they describe equivalent processes, practices and people. Inclusion, because it is such a fluid concept, can be used to support very contradictory arguments and practices. In England, for example, there are many schools which have 'Inclusion Rooms' or 'Inclusion Units' which are filled with children who have been excluded on a short-term or long-term basis from the mainstream class. In Italy, where legislation to close special schools was introduced in 1977, data suggests that 5 per cent of children included in the mainstream school are out of class the whole time. Further, practitioners suggest the nature of the 5 per cent is variable, and depends upon the values of the school and the tenacity of the parents. In contrast, in Japan, children who are formally in a special class can spend some of the week included in the mainstream class (Rix et al., 2013a).

Contradictions are widely accepted as being interwoven with other policy agendas too. Parents, for instance, recognise inclusion as a site of competing rights situated alongside a choice agenda and a drive for higher standards (Connor & Ferri, 2007). This tension is exemplified in a project within the United States which adopted standardisation approaches in the name of learning-for-all and inclusion, but created marginalisation in new forms. Waitoller and Kozleski (2015) describe how this project, involving a university and three elementary urban schools, aimed to transform schools for inclusive education. At the heart of the project was a notion of quality for all students. This notion was used to drive change. It was evident in team curriculum design, classroom observation and the use of public displays of data. These 'data wall' displays were used to judge, compare and purportedly control quality. They presented the scores for all the students' standardised tests, serving as a discussion point at weekly meetings. They were seen as objective and neutral, serving as a rationale for remediating teaching practices.

The intention was for teachers to inspect, appraise and correct themselves. The university partners soon realised, however, that the dominant professional focus of the teachers in using these standardisation approaches was the identification of students who were falling behind their peers: "In the professional vision of the school, inclusion for all students meant auditing and inspection for all" (p. 28).

Students came to be represented as single scores, graded for their performance on a narrow skill. Waitoller and Kozleski concluded that as a result of these work practices: "Inclusive education has resulted in the continuation of labelling and segregation of those students considered different from the dominant culture of the school" (p. 43). These were not the old special education labels though: "We demonstrated that though teachers and administrators aimed to erase special education disability categories from their discourse and practice during Friday meetings, new labels and sorting mechanisms emerged according to the assessments dictated by the school district" (p. 43).

It is not just in the United States that the operationalisation of the inclusive impulse has expanded the categorical approach associated with special. Consider, for example, the introduction of the notion of Additional Support Needs in Scotland. Originally intended to move away from the constraining notions of special education (Allan, 2008), its introduction was accompanied by a marked growth within the mainstream of certain categories of difficulty, particularly social, emotional and behavioural difficulties, as well as an increase in types of categories (Figures 3.1 and 3.2) (Riddell & Weedon, 2013).

The contradictory pressure of polices was also evident in a longitudinal study of two secondary schools in the UK, undertaken with colleagues at the OU (Parry et al., 2013). These schools had professed aims to develop provision in a more inclusive and collaborative manner but on revisiting them a decade later it was evident that:

- New facilities that had been predicted as encouraging inclusive practice had encouraged separate spaces and did not bring about systemic structural change.
- A focus on standards was used as a rationale for increasing separate provision within the schools.
- Shifting policy priorities at either a local or national government level eroded capacity to deliver on planned school changes.
- The rapid introduction of top-down policy was demotivating.
- The legacy of past policies had a profound impact on attitudes and practices.

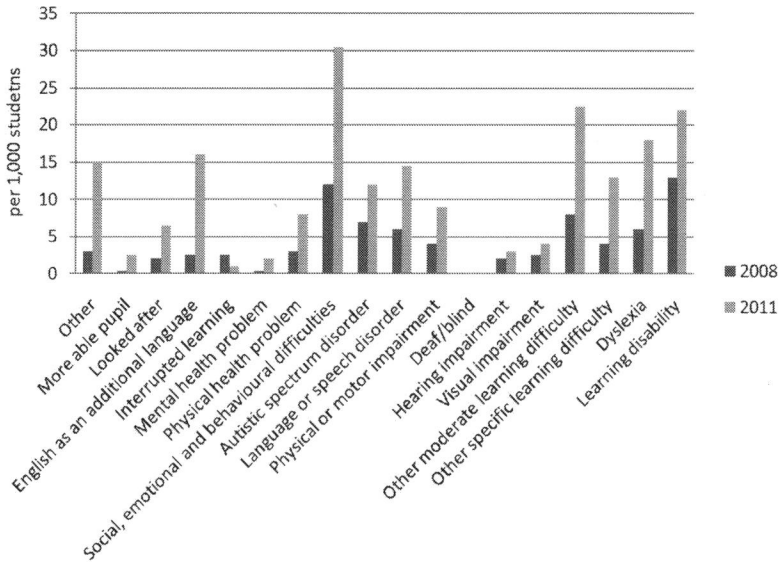

FIGURE 3.1 Changes in categories of difficulty in Scotland with introduction of Additional Support Needs (rate per 1,000 pupils).

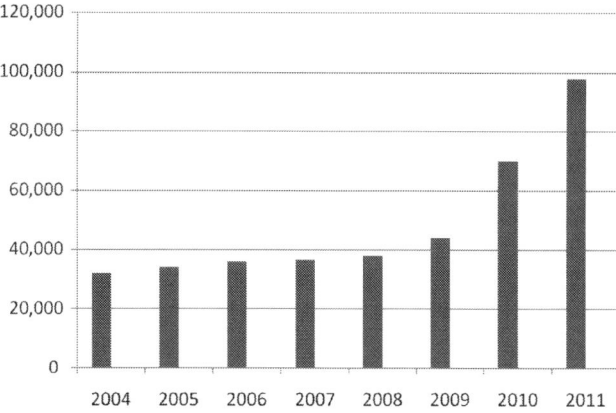

FIGURE 3.2 Number of pupils identified as having Additional Support Needs in Scotland (in 2012 it rose to 17.5 per cent of pupil population).

Ainscow, Booth and Dyson (2006) examined the findings from four national research networks working with 25 English schools from 1993 to 2003, to consider the impact of standards and inclusion policies. Although the schools in the project were invited to develop inclusive practices, there were many instances where the outcomes were not what one would associate with inclusion. For example, many schools chose to focus on questions of attainment as the primary means of enhancing student achievement rather than consider potentially more inclusive options. However, in examining how the schools had gone about this, the authors felt that there was evidence that some schools had engaged in a rethinking process which was fundamental. Some were talking in the language of standards but they had managed to shift some practices and ways of approaching problems in an inclusive direction.

Is it a matter of reaching enough people?

In trying to resolve why the schools responded in different ways, Ainscow, Booth, and Dyson suggested that some schools had an established, communal way of understanding and working, which pulled them in an inclusive direction, whilst others had not. This might seem to be a very nebulous explanation. Some might conclude (given the leading role the three researchers played within the academic construction of inclusion) that they were bound to seek out the inclusive needle in the standards haystack. But these authors are not alone in recognising that inclusive practice involves something intangible. In our research in Italy (Rix et al., 2013a), one principal of a secondary school suggested during a discussion (with a number of teaching and in-school staff present) that only 20–30 per cent of teachers in the school were planning and teaching as collaboratively as he would like. The rest of the staff concurred. At another secondary school in a discussion about inclusive practice, staff noted: "The other 50, 60 per cent [of teachers] they are struggling [with collaboration]. The 30, 40 per cent [who collaborate inclusively] doesn't count the working hours".

In developing inclusive practice within settings, it would seem that there is a tendency towards partial concurrence. A number of writers have talked about the need to achieve a 'critical mass of staff' (Visser, Cole & Daniels, 2002) who are committed to the values of inclusion, including 'key players'. But it seems quite possible to have large numbers of staff who are committed to the processes of inclusion (or to seem committed) and for this not to be enough. The critical mass may have to be 'just about everybody'. Engaging 'just about everybody' is enormously challenging, of course.

In the 1990s, in the UK, a developmental programme, the Index for Inclusion (Booth, Ainscow, Black-Hawkins, Vaughan & Shaw, 2002) was created. This was distributed to 26,000 primary, secondary and special schools and all local education authorities in England, as well as being translated and used in a number of other countries, including Norway (Vislie, 2003). A study began in 2009 to investigate if and how the Index was being used in the 10 partner countries of the European Association of Service Providers for Persons with Disabilities (EASPD, 2012). It transpired that all countries used some kind of tool to encourage reflection upon inclusion issues, some of which were only available in the national language. Whilst six countries used the Index, it was well known in four countries, being used by schools and external organisations. The six countries which used the Index, however, were the countries which had a higher percentage of children and young people in special schools (3 per cent for users vs 0.8 per cent for non-users). In these countries, schools used it for setting goals, but found these difficult to realise. The Index was seen to encourage reflection on inclusive ideas and ways of working and to have some benefit for planning, but again applying this was challenging.[3] In the context of this discussion of partial concurrence however, it seems particularly significant that people only used part of the Index, choosing what they perceived to be relevant. As Slee (2006) suggests, the Index may be a useful and adaptable tool which encourages reflection. But it may also excuse or encourage an administrative response which seeks simple solutions for complex issues. It may be a way of leading people without them fully understanding what it is they are following or why.

This is a real challenge for advocates of inclusion. It seems very likely that when people in schools put new ideas into practice their established ways of working and their lack of understanding of the theoretical roots means that they cannot recognise that their actions undermine the possibility of the new processes (Brown, 1994). They might feel inhibited by an expectation to experiment or unlearn trusted ways and challenge the accepted position and knowledge. It seems inevitable that schools will experience resistance when attempting fundamental changes to long-standing relationships, learning goals and ways of working across the institution and within the class (Mitchell, 1999). We might also doubt the capacity of professional communities, particularly if they are insular, to improve practice through collective and reflective processes. Their discussions have been seen to be selective, partial and highly contextualised (Warren Little, 2003).

The bottom line may be that there are many practitioners who do not wish to engage in 'ceaseless struggles' (Betteney, 2010, p. 96), which are so often at the heart of calls for inclusion. This underlying hesitation may mean that the critical mass can never be reached.

Some difficulties with the narrative of inclusion

There is a long history of people arguing that the drive for inclusion emerged not from pedagogic considerations but because of arguments about budgets and about rights (Hornby, Atkinson & Howard, 1997). Winzer (2006) maintains that inclusion emerged from specific notions of social justice, ethics, and rights which had themselves grown from "a liberal-democratic social philosophy focusing on individual civil rights, mobilizing the discourse of equity, and guided by axiomatic moral imperatives" (p. 31). Inclusion came to be seen by many as a transformative approach. In particular, its focus upon the individual's location within a school setting meant it was associated with transforming educational structures. Winzer suggests that subsequently, what began as an aspiration for sameness in relation to treatment came to be interpreted as seeking sameness in relation to experience, which in turn became associated with a shared space. This led in the early 1990s to calls for full inclusion.

Winzer's commentary seems to describe processes in some countries, such as the UK and USA. However, a couple of countries had moved much further and faster, such as Italy and Norway, and some, such as those in Eastern Europe, have followed a somewhat different pathway. Whatever international treaties they may have signed, many countries have never really considered inclusion-for-all within the mainstream, often because of economic constraints or because of cultural attitudes towards certain groups of disabled people. Regardless of the differences and similarities in hyperbole, though, the reality of full inclusion is not in evidence anywhere but at the most local of levels.

It is perhaps unsurprising, however, that calls emerging from a social justice agenda should meet with such a response. The suggestion that inclusion is primarily about rights means that its critics can position it as a matter of ideology. This has led to a number of debates (e.g. Wilson, 2000a, 2000b; Thomas, 2000) about the ideological nature of inclusion, carrying the implication that other approaches are backed by reason and evidence (Thomas & Glenny, 2002). Of course, somewhere in these arguments one or more of the participants explains how one's own ideology is not noticed by oneself but by others (rather like eating garlic). They also suggest that the range of definitions for 'ideology' mean that using it is itself an ideological position. Almost invariably someone then points out that in applying it to others there is a derogatory implication.

The combination of this association with social justice and rights along with the diversity of definitions connected with inclusion creates a double bind. It means that any number of organisations which position themselves as fighting for issues of social justice and rights can associate themselves with the notion of inclusion.

Just to confirm this statement, on the 12 February 2014, I visited the websites of large charities which have supported separate provision and utilised the tragedy model at different times in their history. This was not a scientifically constructed study, just an informal visit to the first charities that came to mind. The first six charities I thought of (all of them based in the UK: SCOPE, MENCAP, RNIB, Action on Hearing Loss, Barnardo's and Oxfam) had major projects linked to the notion of inclusion. This brief search identified books, pamphlets, articles, research projects, policy documents, campaigns and assessment tools framed around the notion. It was only the seventh charity name which sprung to mind that came up a blank.[4] When I visited the Camphill Communities site, my search found nothing. But when I burrowed down and did a manual search, there it was too. One of their schools, The Sheiling School (an independent residential school for children and adolescents aged 6–19 with special educational needs) was able to claim it had an inclusive ethos because it had pupils from all over the world.

This school connection did not surprise me though. In 2010, I conducted a study of the online presence of 100 special schools (78 had websites) which identified a common use of ideas associated with inclusion[5] (Rix, 2011). Over 50 per cent sites linked themselves directly with the term 'inclusion', 23 per cent made reference to either: integration; links to the mainstream and other settings; opportunities to attend classes and/or socialise; or the return of pupils to the mainstream. Some of the 25 per cent of school sites which made no mention of their links with the mainstream still used the language associated with inclusion.

This presents an additional problem for the supporters of inclusion. Provision associated with special and with charities associated with traditional categories of impairment and social disadvantage demonstrate an ease and alacrity to position themselves as a pragmatic response to mainstream problems. In the process they take ownership of the language of rights and social justice associated with inclusion. This is not to say that they are being disingenuous or self-seeking. SCOPE, for example, have taken some highly contentious decisions as a consequence of their commitment to inclusion within the mainstream. These kinds of organisations and the institutions which they run are also key players in this process. They must be key targets for supporters of inclusion. They must be part of the critical mass. However, the intermeshing of inclusion with the old institutional ideas and values of separate provision and thinking about disability adds to the complexity of challenging the status quo and reforming practice. To those outside of the small and somewhat insular world of charities, inclusion and special, these institutions seem to be largely what they always were. They represent the values which people grew up with. Their support for inclusion implies it is a continuation of what came before rather than a transformation. They are still about separate groupings, they are still about fund raising, they are still about able people campaigning on behalf of disabled people, they are still about providing services additional to the universal, local and national provision. They were and still are the key storytellers in the dominant and pre-existing narrative which inclusion is trying to rewrite.

Our investment in inclusion

As has been outlined above, by the early 1980s one of the strongest educational reform movements was around equity and opportunity for all, with special education claiming the territory of reform (Winzer, 2006). This increasingly led to calls for restructuring of the mainstream to enable full access. Inevitably, funding of additional support was a key part of this restructuring process. However, as Sigafoos and colleagues (2010) report (in their systematic review of the cost impact of special education funding models), despite every country developing their own funding processes there have been very few cost impact studies. The wide range of models and variable research methods means that the few studies that are available cannot be effectively compared. In addition, funding arrangements for special education and other support services are kept separate. This administrative separation makes it very hard to evaluate the costs of inclusive provision. Where studies have been attempted, the costs of inclusion seem to be lower, but they cannot compare like to like. Odom et al. (2001) for example suggested that the hidden costs to parents within the inclusive model are greater, and that issues beyond instructional costs needed far greater analysis. My personal experience, in discussion with parents whose children attend local special schools, is that funding costs are slightly lower for my son in the mainstream. However, focusing upon the cost per individual can serve as a distraction to the primary goals of inclusion. It can be seen as discouraging a transformational perspective and prioritising a bean-counting one. This can also turn the argument into one primarily about economics.

Arguments of economics cut both ways. Some parents, for example, perceive inclusion as a way of reducing costs, whilst others see inclusion as being constrained by the restraints of funding (Connor & Ferri, 2007). Hallahan (1998) asserts that additional cost is a key reason against "full-inclusion", but believes that some administrators see inclusion as a way to save money. Other studies suggest that administrators believe that inclusive practice adds to costs (Williams, Pazey, Shelby & Yates, 2013). These economic arguments perpetuate the idea that special and inclusion are equivalent, though. They put inclusion and special in the same economic place. Economically, they are both understood as being additional to the current system. The mainstream remains as it is. Inclusion becomes the economic equivalent of special. Regardless of where the additional resource is situated or delivered it is supplementary to mainstream finances. As a result, special and inclusion are set against each other, as if they are distinguishable and comparable.

It is not just that economic arguments of effectiveness support arguments which support a non-transformative (non-inclusive?) model of inclusion. It is also that inclusion (even if it has been one of the strongest educational reform movements) has not had the same level of priority as other policies (Barton & Armstrong, 2007). Issues associated with the economically correct, political, dictum of growth, competition and choice have meant that inclusion has been subsumed within a wider discourse. As Liasidou (2012) highlights (by drawing on a range of literature), successful inclusion has been linked to those whose behaviour puts the school and the economy at risk rather than the creation of communities. Social justice is framed as a promise of choice, and those who don't add value and interfere with efficiency cannot be allowed to interfere with the 'free' choices of others. Restructuring the system in order to save money therefore is not going to influence policy-makers unless it contributes to the wider economically correct narrative. Costing less does not help them if it compromises the promise of standards and choice.

The lack of investment in inclusion as a transformative process is also evident within the training and development of personnel. Internationally there is a belief that staff lack skills (e.g. TALIS, 2008). In our study of provision in 50 countries (Rix et al., 2013a, 2013b), we also noted that inclusion was an identified need for the development of practitioner roles and skills. However, few countries, if any, appeared to provide a coherent, connected pathway for significant numbers of practitioners throughout their career. The nature of training and available routes seemed to be largely constrained by two factors; first, other priorities within practitioner development and second, the capacity and character of further and higher education facilities.

Even when there is a small amount of initial training, the impact may not be that long lasting either. For example, Hodkinson (2005) reports on a small-scale research project looking at the shifting attitudes of first-year teachers. When they left training they viewed inclusion as an issue of teaching related to a range of students; however, after a year in school 90 per cent had changed their views on inclusive education in some way. There was a general trend towards seeing it as a whole school issue which particularly pertained to children with special educational needs. It was no longer a matter of classroom teaching. In reflecting on this shift, the paper suggested that it demonstrates the impact of the realities of classroom life. It suggested that on arriving in schools the new teachers come to recognise how constrained they are in what they can achieve if they are to succeed within the dominant educational context. The children who are most clearly marginalised by this reality are those with special educational needs.

However, it is also possible that the new teachers' views change because it is these children which the discourse of the schools position as being the primary focus of inclusion. Such a view enables schools not to deal with the reality of inclusion for all and the need for all staff to change their classroom practice. At the same time it enables them to retain inclusion as an overall policy goal. This is perhaps why the new teachers had not turned against the policy of inclusion, but still supported its maintenance. As a consequence the new teachers, like those who had been there a while, did not have to invest time and energy in seeking ways to ensure the engagement of all the pupils. They could focus their attention on those who engaged with the way they worked already. These teachers would have worked very hard, but they had invested their time and effort in the status quo and not its transformation.

Is it good for people?

This inability to maintain a focus upon inclusion as an issue beyond special creates another double bind for supporters of inclusion. Inclusion's dominant association with the mainstream experience of children identified with special educational needs forces us to ask whether it benefits individuals above and beyond any theoretical issues of rights and social justice.

It is tempting to begin with the evidence base. The research evidence leans towards inclusion but it is hardly overwhelming. Lindsay reported that findings from 1,300 studies published between 2000 and 2005 suggested a marginally positive effect overall (Lindsay, 2007). Most studies and reviews have found that mainstream does not disadvantage students either with or without special educational needs (Meijer, 2001; Kalambouka, Farrell, Dyson, & Kaplan, 2005; Farrell, Dyson, Polat, Hutcheson & Gallannaugh, 2007; Gruner Gandhi, 2007; Canadian Council on Learning, 2009) whilst some found positive correlations between mainstream placement and a variety of outcome measures (Curcic, 2009). There have also been mixed results for specific groups of pupils in specific curriculum areas. For example, significant gains in language and numeracy skills for children labelled as having Down syndrome (Buckley, Bird, Sacks & Archer, 2006; Appleton, Buckley & MacDonald, 2002; Laws, Byrne & Buckley, 2000) and in maths for children with a broad range of special educational needs characteristics (Vanlaar & Van Damme, 2012). But this can be juxtaposed with a review of 30 years of studies into the education of children facing speech and language difficulties, which concluded that in-class support was no more effective than 'pull out' models (Cirrin et al., 2010).

These broad studies can reassure us, but they do not help us when we are confronted with individual examples of social injustice in which competing rights are being prioritised. As is evident from the views of the 24 parents in Rogers' (2007) study, mainstream is not an easy option for many nor is it straightforward. This particular research used snowball sampling so it is possible that it attracted parents of a like mind rather than a representative sample, but it highlights how many children seem to be practically excluded from classrooms and/or intellectually excluded from the curriculum accessed by their peers and/or emotionally excluded from friendship and social networks. Parents also recognise the contradiction of placing people in a system without support when they need support to thrive within that system. The act of including can seem synonymous with isolation, as a chauvinistic top down, enforced assimilation, which works for some but marginalises others (Connor & Ferri, 2007).

If there are just a few children who are having a negative experience in mainstream, then it does not matter to them or others concerned with their lives what the research says. It does not matter if outcome reviews do not find advantages for specialist settings (President's Commission on Excellence in Special Education, 2002) or if rigorous reviews of the literature show that the academic achievement of children identified with and without special educational needs is comparable or better than outcomes in non-inclusive classes (Ruijs & Peetsma, 2009). We have to be concerned for the child who is currently experiencing marginalisation. We might agree with Thomas (1997) that educational inclusion has to be seen as part of a bigger social inclusion agenda, and cannot be judged on narrow and often inadequate educational research; we might concur with Mittler (2000) that the human rights agenda has moved us beyond a time for evidence about whether to work for inclusion. But we have to be able to respond when a charity such as Ambitious About Autism (2014) reports that in a survey of 500 parents, 40 per cent said their child with autism had been excluded illegally during their time at school. If we are serious about an agenda of rights and social justice, we cannot simply question the research methods or the self-interest which such a survey serves, nor can we switch the discussion to possible solutions in the future.

But this too creates a dual problem for supporters of inclusion. First, the purpose of inclusion is to overcome such social barriers. Simply acceding to demands to remove an individual from an exclusionary situation denies the opportunity to improve the situation for the individuals concerned and those who may follow. Second, it feeds the widely held perception that disabled people are invariably marginalised by their peers, social networks, social systems and structures. This is what the research evidence and subsequent campaigns seem to suggest. Regardless of where they go to school or what activities they engage in, children identified with special educational needs seem to have a less favourable social position than their peers (Ruijs & Peetsma, 2009).

But things are rarely quite what they seem. For example, a study of 983 children in Norway (Pijl, Frostad & Flem, 2008) showed that peers nominated fewer children having special needs[6] as friends. These children were also far more likely to have no nominations and no mutually agreed friendships (see Table 3.1). It was evident that some children needed extra support to participate in a group. However, Pijl and colleagues emphasise that this sociometric analysis gives an overly negative picture. The students identified as having special needs nominated more friends. They did not feel as isolated as the other data might suggest.

Drawing on the work of Skaalvik and Skaalvik (2005), they pointed out that when we evaluate the social experiences of children our most important criterion must be the pupils' subjective experiences of their situation. By focusing upon the negative too, we also risk overlooking the vast majority of people identified with special educational needs who feel that they do have friendships. We feed the widely held perception that disabled people are marginalised by their peers. Perhaps the most important point, however, is that the last row of Table 3.1 not

TABLE 3.1 Nomination of friendships in Norwegian school study

	Age 9–10 (n = 491)		Age 12–13 (n = 498)	
	Special needs (n = 42)	Peers (n = 449)	Special needs (n = 37)	Peers (n = 461)
Average nominations	2.6	4.2	2.3	3.9
No nominations	14.3%	2.4%	24.3%	3.9%
No mutual relationships	16.7%	4.9%	24.3%	7.4%
No friends according to self-report	4.8%	1.6%	10.8%	5.9%

TABLE 3.2 Approximate numbers of children who feel they have no friends in Norwegian school study

	Age 9–10 (n = 491)		Age 12–13 (n = 498)	
	Special needs	Peers	Special needs	Peers
Number of children who report having no friends	2	7	4	27

only shows that people identified with special needs perceive themselves to have fewer friends than their peers, but it also reveals that there are a lot of friendless people in the school more generally (see Table 3.2); and this, of course, brings us back round to the first point that supporters of inclusion would make about assuming that removing the child will solve the problem. One may well ask, if we are to consider removing the six children identified with special needs that feel friendless should we consider removing their 34 peers too? Would this be an act of social justice which supported their rights?

How might 'the wrong sort of people' do the right thing?

The everyday scenario described above does not just raise particular questions in the context of student placement but it also highlights the kinds of challenges teachers face in identifying who to support and how to support them. In this study, teachers tended to be more optimistic about friendships than in other studies, but whatever their perceptions, the approaches they should take and the support they should offer in order to facilitate the relationships was a "largely open question" (Pijl, Frostad & Flem, p. 403).

Chapter 2 discussed some of the complexities around educational research and its inability to provide definite answers. It is perhaps unsurprising therefore that there is a widely reported lack of research in relation to inclusive practice. Danforth and Kim (2008), for example, note the paltry nature of research literature on the inclusive education of students diagnosed with attention deficit hyperactivity disorder (ADHD) who qualify for special education services in the USA. This is not the same as saying there is no evidence however, and the practices which the evidence supports will not be unfamiliar to the vast majority of teachers. Marschark et al.'s study mentioned in Chapter 2 (2011), for example, extensively examined the literature related to educating deaf and hard-of-hearing children. They highlighted the lack of coherent research in relation to effective practice, but what there was suggested a focus upon familiar strategies and materials.[7] Evidence suggested that by engaging with flexible modes of representing activities, teachers provide a richer context for learning than they might typically provide for hearing students.

This everydayness was also evident in a three-year systematic literature review of effective special educational provision in mainstream classes undertaken with colleagues (Rix, Hall, Nind, Sheehy & Wearmouth, 2009). We found enough research rated as having medium or high reliability to say with some certainty that teachers had to:

- recognise their central responsibility for all pupils that they teach;
- engage with a 'teacher community' – either within the school or more often from outside the school – who have a shared model of how children learn;
- see the other adults within the school community as both teachers and learners;
- develop a shared philosophy around respecting everyone in the class and all their learning;
- recognise that social interaction is the means through which student knowledge is developed;
- understand the aims of the structured programme and subject, with a shared understanding of the characteristics, skills and knowledge associated with the subject to be taught;
- plan to scaffold both the subject's cognitive and social content;
- carefully plan group work, delineating the roles of group members;
- explore pupils' understandings, encouraging questioning and the making of links between new and prior knowledge;
- work on (basic) skills in a holistic way, embedded in classroom activity and subject knowledge;
- utilise pupils as resources for learning;
- use activities which the learner finds meaningful;
- use a range of different modalities, which are frequently 'hands-on' and offer diverse opportunities to engage with the concepts and with others' understandings of those concepts (Rix et al., 2009, p. 92).

McLeskey and Waldron (2011) examined research outside the mainstream and considered whether these practices could be delivered in mainstream settings. They noted that instruction should be provided to small groups of students (from one to three students for optimal results) and that students should have similar instructional needs. They identified the need to focus on a small group of clearly defined skills and/or concepts, using instructional sequences and materials that meet individual needs, which are well structured, providing explicit information with demonstrations, models and concrete examples. The instruction should be at a pace to allow sufficient time for mastery of targeted skills, providing cognitive support, carefully structured and sequenced, scaffolding to ensure high levels of success. They noted too the need for encouragement, feedback and emotional support, having opportunities to practice, respond and succeed, both as part of a group and independently. Independent practice therefore needs to be actively supervised, and continued until responses come automatically. To achieve this, teachers needed to monitor student progress at least weekly or biweekly, to assess the effectiveness of learning strategies being adopted and to ensure sufficient progress was being made, providing feedback to the student on that progress.

This everydayness and its relevance to inclusion are evident when the broad scope of educational research is considered too. Figure 3.3 is an adaptation of The Education Endowment Foundation Teaching and Learning Toolkit, cited in Coe (2013). It is a visual representation of the educational research summarised within the Sutton Trust–EEF Teaching and Learning Toolkit, which collates research in the field. The first thing worth noting is how evidence for socially based, collaborative and peer to peer approaches is strongly supported by the findings mentioned above. However, as Coe suggested, it is not just a matter of starting in the top-left corner with the cheapest approaches that seem to have the biggest impact. First, evidence may exist but it may be thin, it may not have been carried out in everyday class-room situations and it may also be dependent upon context and quality of support. Second, how do we know if we are doing it correctly, and how do we get large numbers of colleagues to duplicate the process appropriately, effectively and consistently? Lastly, many of these practices have been around a lot longer than the research findings and the problems have not gone away. It is also worth considering at least two other matters. Are 'effect' and 'cost' the two key parameters by which to judge the worth of a practice? And just because research says something does not work does that mean it needs to be ditched or does it mean it ought to be developed in a different way?

A range of practices and strategies will be considered in the next few chapters but suffice to say at this point, the weight of evidence within international reviews consistently rests with methods which relatively accessible to practitioners. These are deliverable as part of current everyday practices within well-structured contexts, as opposed to requiring highly specialised expertise requiring highly specialised environments. The problem for supporters of inclusion is that these approaches represent the minority of teacher activity. As Scruggs, Mastropieri and McDuffie (2007) noted in their meta-analysis of the literature, techniques which

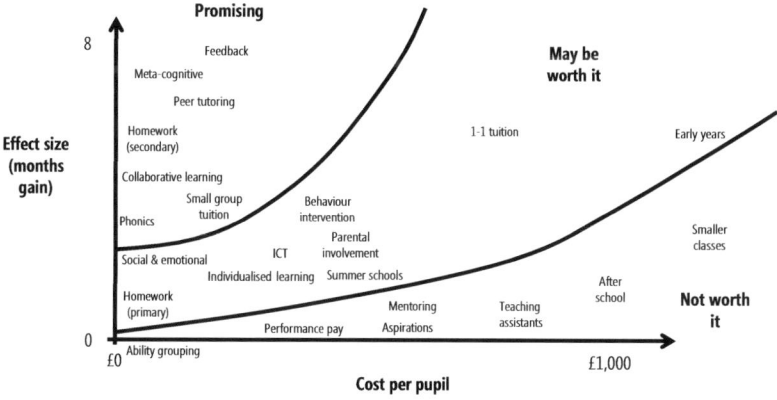

FIGURE 3.3   The research view of the effectiveness and value of teaching approaches. (Based on Coe, 2013.)

are supported within the literature are observed infrequently in practice. It is not how teachers work most of the time or are encouraged to work. It would seem that such practices are undermined by the traditional nature of the curriculum, subject areas and assessment as well as the school spaces, structures, relationships and roles within which inclusion is situated.

Biting the 'wrong sort of person' next to you?

The difficulty of delivering change is clearly exemplified by the role of the additional adult in the class. Support staff, under a great many titles, are a cornerstone of support in mainstream (and special) schools. Globally they are the means by which inclusion is frequently managed (Abbott, McConkey & Dobbins, 2011). However, according to Figure 3.1, the English version of non-teaching-qualified in-class support staff (teaching assistants) is just about the most expensive and least effective solution. This finding is supported by a large-scale, longitudinal study (Blatchford et al., 2009) which found a negative relationship between the academic progress of pupils and the amount of additional support provided by support staff. This finding was widely publicised and created a widely held perception that there is something fundamentally wrong about their use.

Blatchford and colleagues identified a great many other factors too, however. They suggested that reduced academic progress was due to a combination of issues, which included: the experience and knowledge of staff; the separation of pupils from the class teachers and curriculum; the nature of interactions with pupils; and the availability of time for planning and training with teachers. Their findings suggested any negative impact was primarily a consequence of how the system chooses to employ, train and organise the support staff.

It might be tempting to assume that this relationship would change if the teaching assistant had the same status as the teacher and was equally qualified. However, evidence from other systems suggests the challenge is deeper than this. Within our NCSE study, Italian practitioners talked about team teaching and wanting to engage in it, but it was suggested that generally they did not do so. Despite support staff being qualified teachers with at least one year's additional training, partnership teaching mostly involved one teacher leading the class and the other working with a small group, the 'other' generally being the support teacher

In comparing the deployment of teaching assistants in England and qualified support teachers in Italy, Devecchi and colleagues (Devecchi, Dettori, Doveston, Sedgwick & Jament, 2012) concluded that support in both countries is frequently provided in isolation and without collaboration with the class teacher. The line of professional demarcation can be slight in both countries but leads to unclear and inequitable status in the class and in the organisation of the school. The child is still seen as being the 'problem' of the support staff; effective collaboration is further constrained by the lack of resources and time. In both situations the role of this additional adult reinforced the class teacher's view that certain children require specialist knowledge which they did not have access to. It is not surprising therefore that in a review of 32 qualitative investigations of co-teaching, Scruggs et al. (2007) identified instruction that was traditional, a lack of planning time and training, and the dominance of the 'teacher' and 'assistant' model with the additional adult in the subordinate role.

Despite the lack of benefit for students' learning, though, teachers tend to like having support in their class. Blatchford et al.'s study noted that the support staff enhanced teacher job satisfaction and perceived effectiveness whilst reducing their stress and workload. They also seemed to benefit classroom control and teachers' perceptions of pupil learning and behaviour. Teachers felt support staff could give children individual attention, particularly those who the teacher perceived needed most support. This enabled the teacher to deal with others in the class, uninterrupted. Differentiation could take place easily and without disrupting the majority. Would it be unfair to suggest that teachers like support staff because they make it easier for them to carry on with things as they always have?

It would appear that the class teacher is the key to effective additional support. Teachers' belief structures about the nature of ability, disability and learning appear to affect who they see as their responsibility and how they subsequently teach those they take responsibility for. Jordan and colleagues (Jordan & Stanovich, 2001; Jordan, Glenn & McGhie-Richmond, 2010), as part of their extensive research into teachers and their classroom interactions, noted that effective teachers maximise instructional time through their preparation of lessons, clearly communicating expectations that all students will be engaged in learning to a high standard. These teachers had routines which allowed them to instruct individuals and small groups for large parts of the teaching time. They worked with *all* pupils. They engaged in interactions intended to foster student understanding and development of thinking skills. In particular, they engaged in prolonged interactions with pupils with special educational needs and used most of the available time to offer learners the opportunity to problem-solve, to discuss and describe their ideas and to make connections with their own experiences and prior understandings. This contrasts with teachers who did not have the same priorities. Their interactions primarily focused upon non-academic, organisational issues or offered space for closed, short responses.

Here, then is another double bind for supporters of inclusion. The people who can deliver inclusion are the people who can be the main barrier to inclusion.

Can all the little rules break down?

Considering the impact which it has had upon the public discourse, it is remarkable how limited the field of inclusion is. Inclusion is not like a subject area or an impairment-specific expertise or a separate space. Inclusion cannot claim a specific body of professionals. The individuals and agencies which are called upon to advise in the delivery of inclusion come from fields with very different vested interests: speech and language therapists, occupational therapists, educational psychologists, paediatricians, behaviour intervention agencies, special teachers, special educational needs coordinators, social-pedagogues, history teachers, maths teachers, physical education teachers, music therapists, psychotherapists, and so on . . . a myriad of names and different professions in every country. These are the people who may have reason to commandeer inclusion, who may use it to recoat old practices with which they feel comfortable and which they value.

Apart from those who have claimed it for their already established practices, there are just a few pressure groups, a few consultants, and some policy-makers, parents and practitioners spread around the system. All of these have also emerged from the old ways; many have emerged as a result of their frustrations and unhappy experiences within the established systems mentioned above, or because of moments of epiphany. They come with a huge range of priorities and degrees of commitment. There are no other career pathways (apart from a few of us academics and a few inclusion advisors in local authorities) and no specific expertise which can be claimed. The pedagogy of inclusion turns out to be the pedagogy of teaching. The training modules for inclusion have to be part of everybody's training or exist as an occasional add-on or afterthought. As Graham (2006) notes, inclusion by its nature implies an act of placement, of "bringing in" (p. 20). It can easily encourage the reification of otherness. It becomes the inclusion of those who have been identified as other. The only means of overcoming this is for the system to operate on the basis of a norm which is premised upon diversity and the multiplicity of difference. People within the system have to start from a place of uncertainty and variability rather than certainty and typicality. Whereas all the other groupings had a separate identity to carve out and fight for, could build alliances or establish institutions, inclusion by its very nature must strive to do exactly the opposite. It has to convince everyone (or nearly everyone) of the need to change.

The problems for inclusion are well established. Norwich (2008a) suggested that there are three key dilemmas, which involve two choices that both lead to negative consequences:

- should children be identified as having a disability (needing special education);
- should identified students study the common curriculum or a different curriculum;
- should identified students study in ordinary or separate locations.

Allan (2008) identified unresolvable tensions in the training of teachers, aporias that are unreasonably seen as resolvable to one choice:

- how to acquire and demonstrate specific competencies as a teacher and to understand you are part of an ongoing learning process;
- how to be autonomous and collaborative;
- how to maximise achievement and ensure inclusion;
- how to help others understand impairments and avoid disabling students;
- how to enable learning to deal with exclusionary pressures as student teachers and avoid becoming closed to the possibilities of inclusion.

These tensions mean that inclusion in practice does not resolve the problems it sets out to transform. As McMenamin (2011) concluded, when considering the tenacity of special schools in New Zealand, the debate about inclusion is misunderstood. It confuses people and lacks consensus, whilst mainstream experiences are often negative and parents have to/can make choices. Perhaps this means that there is something fundamentally wrong with inclusion as a notion. It exists in a world which is set against it, where mainstream rules are endlessly changing and yet where norms always push people to the margins. It exists as a way of evoking change and sharing best practice and yet is experienced as complex and challenging. It is a singular term which is understood and experienced by people in numerous different ways, and so supports contradictory arguments, policies and practices. Its problems are the problems of the mainstream but it is dominated by special answers which can only be on the margins; it has to live with purportedly new practices and processes branded inclusive which create new categories of marginalisation.

At the heart of inclusion are unresolvable quandaries. It is both a call to be transformative and a tool for maintaining the status quo; it needs to transform the vast majority but its means of transformation are the established structures, relationships and practices. It needs to transform those who are not aspiring to become inclusive, yet it requires them (many who may not wish to change) to have some of the skills associated with inclusion in order to become inclusive (or make the change to being inclusive). It aims to achieve this through the use of argument and example, yet many of the institutions which use the arguments of inclusion and participation have long been associated with separation and care. It cannot demonstrate economic benefits without being a rebrand of special and can only call upon evidence which by its nature must be partial.

In day-to-day situations, inclusive practices which are accessible to all practitioners are little used. They are not encouraged by institutional priorities and traditions; they call for time and resource which the status quo does not provide, they rely upon staff that are additional and essential but not integral. As a consequence, the practical experience of mainstream education remains profoundly exclusionary for some, and inclusion has become its name.

I believe in inclusion because we are The People whether we like it or not, and many of us experience exclusion. Yet, it would appear that our capacity to confront this issue is undermined by our ongoing, narrow assumption that we can support the few in order to resolve the problems of many.

So where do I go from here?

Notes

* At the time of writing the author was Senior Lecturer in Inclusion, Curriculum and Learning.
1 I started this list: oppression, control, division, entertainment, sharing, hope, boredom, violence, love, inspiration, emptiness, completion … but I gave up, as I could never complete it.
2 I was a member in my classroom days.
3 It was largely seen as a means of: encouraging positive behaviours; looking for possibilities in a situation and offering insights into their inclusive nature; framing discussions and

planning lessons; highlighting the importance of learning from each other; working and collaborating with external partners, particularly parents; and promoting teamwork (though teamwork was challenging).

4 And by now I was trying hard to find someone to buck the trend.

5 Namely, a focus on rights to access the mainstream; the overcoming of barriers; and the creation of a collective vision and ethos, which recognises, respects and supports the full diversity of individuals and engages with their perspectives.

6 Since Norway does not use formal categories, these individuals were identified as having special needs by the teachers in the study.

7 They identified the use of concept maps and other diagrammatic representations, games and targeted activities aiming to demonstrate conceptual similarities and differences associated with such matters as: language, perception, practical experiences and taxonomies. By explicitly linking information to what young people know, using authentic interactive activities and cognitive scaffolding strategies, teachers increase the possibility of students who are deaf or hard-of-hearing achieving at the level of their peers.

4

THINKING AND TALKING ABOUT *SPECIAL* AND *INCLUSIVE*

The balding, middle-aged author chewed a sunflower seed, a snack which did not raise his already high cholesterol levels. He had planned to use a poem from his wife's 1977 reprint edition of the writings and drawings of Bob Dylan. But when he read the publisher notes on references, he could feel his diagnosed high blood pressure rise: "Fair use exception does not apply". The publisher required him to clear copyright on the first six lines of *I shall Be Free No. 10* because they had been recorded on the 1964 album *Another Side of Bob Dylan*. He looked on-line and realised that this would be a long and potentially costly process.

The diabetic writer sighed. Why had he chosen this quote? It was because Dylan presented himself as an everyman, as being the same as everyone else; it was because he suggested that there was no use in talking to him because that would be the same as talking to yourself. How else could this bearded stereotype of an academic make the point that people are all riddled with assumptions and that in the words of Linton Kwesi Johnson (1991) "all a tun prime ministah in dem hed" (p. 55)? Then it dawned on him. He could tell his readers to enter the name of the song into a search engine. A different technology could bring them together!

Talking to me

In the spring of 2010, I was at a meeting, stood in a smart London professional establishment, talking to an illustrious, esteemed and very well-connected colleague. We were pouring coffee together in a third-floor room, with the sun filling the window behind him. He said to me: "Have you seen the latest Down's brain scan studies?". I overcame my desire to ask him not to refer to people in this way and smiled to encourage him to go on. "It's remarkable", he said, "these studies prove that they are visual learners. It is a real breakthrough. Now we really know how we should be teaching them!". He beamed enthusiastically, whilst I stared at him, at a complete loss for words.

In the autumn of 2010, I was at a meeting, sat at an oval table in a small London office talking to a highly respected, knowledgeable and well-connected colleague.

There was a pause in the discussion whilst we were waiting for someone to return to the room. To fill the silence I began to explain some research I had recently been involved in. We had examined nine years of paperwork related to a nine-year-old boy and identified only two mentions of the context in which he lived and studied. There was nothing in this paperwork about friendships or relationships or working practices or collective processes. It was all about him and what he had done, could do or couldn't do. Nearly everything written about him placed him in isolation. It ignored what was really important, our interdependence. I spoke for about three minutes and then my widely travelled colleague, nodded and muttered, "Oh, I see, the social model". She turned away from me, back to the table, and I stared after her, at a complete loss for words.

In the summer of 2004, I became involved in an email exchange with a very well-known UK comedian about a joke he told on his smash hit tour. This was all about him going to a gathering with people with learning difficulties and the punchline revolved around his reference to them as retards and mongs. I had expressed my disappointment at him choosing such an easy target for his comedy and he responded: "I can tell jokes about disability but I find it very difficult to deal with 'Race'". As a result of our email exchange he changed the nature of the joke to be slightly more self-deprecating, but kept in the term 'retards and mongs'. Our discussion continued. He told me he had made further changes. I went to see the show in Brighton. He had kept the joke but settled on the term 'window-lickers'. I sat in a hall full of laughter and I was at a complete loss for words.

It is remarkable how ignorant well-informed people can be. It is remarkable how we allow our world view to justify our actions and limit our questions and our possible answers. It is remarkable how we want to explain things to suit our purposes.

Or perhaps it is not remarkable at all.

Where does our thinking begin?

In three short articles, Wilson (2000a, 2000b, 2002) asked a series of questions about inclusion and special needs. Laying aside the discord around the articles themselves, it is worth revisiting a few of his thoughts. Wilson noted the ambiguity of meaning in the terms, as well as some underlying assumptions associated with them. In particular he questioned:

- whether a *need* is inherently beneficial or desirable or can be identified;
- whether it is evident what it is people will be *included* into, who will be *included* and who will do the *including*.

He noted that both concepts require an *other*, either to be special *to* or included *within* or *included by*. Any discussion or examination of these two phenomena therefore requires reference to criteria associated with what is more generally seen to be desirable, important and necessary. Without this reference empirical observation and research will produce results which are incoherent and make comparison between systems impossible. However, any such reference varies within and between systems and cultures. Meaningful comparison, he therefore suggested, is not widely attainable.

This theoretical conclusion seems to be borne out by the evidence. In the previous chapter we gave a flavour of the diverse understandings of inclusion. Following our study of provision in 55 administrations in 50 countries (Rix, Sheehy, Fletcher-Campbell, Crisp & Harper, 2013a, 2013b) we recognised the incoherence associated with the notion of special:

> It seemed evident that no two countries dealt with the issue of support for pupils with special educational needs in the same way. No two countries shared a view about who needs support, the nature of the support they provided or the nature of an appropriate curriculum. No two countries had the same mechanisms for assessment, resource distribution, in-class support or support service provision. There was no identification of a special pedagogy in international documentation, and people's descriptions of a special pedagogy were the same as their descriptions of good teaching for all. We are not merely reiterating that international practices are unified by international language or that official statistics cannot usefully compare much of the special educational provision. We are suggesting that the differences are such that they undermine any sense of a coherent whole.
>
> (Rix et al., 2013a, pp. 388–389)

This should not, perhaps, surprise us. The way we think is culturally situated. Edwards (2005), for example, maintains that psychology in Russia has historically emphasised how the collective is incorporated into the self, whilst North American psychology has been concerned with how the self adapts to different social situations. This is exemplified by the emergence of the social-constructivist views of Lev Vygotsky in Soviet Union in the 1920s and 1930s at the same time as the ideas of eugenics and behaviourism and the constructivist views of Piaget were developing in the West.

Our cultural roots lead most of us to starting points in our thinking without us realising their significance. For instance, Borthwick (1996) discusses how we understand intellectual impairment, particularly in relation to Down syndrome. He concludes that when Langdon Down detected "mongolism" these identified individuals were perceived not as damaged versions of "us" but as an order of lesser beings. One hundred years later, when Borthwick was writing, he felt that achievements for anyone with a "mental retardation" were seen as exceptional peaks arising from a low base, rather than as troughs from a common starting point. This attitude, he maintains, encourages a low level of expectation. Subsequently, each new generation has had to surmount parental and professional presumptions of relative limited capacity.

Whilst Borthwick encourages us to consider our starting point for what is normal, Graham (2006, 2008b) explores the role played by the media and within an Australian school system in constructing normality. Her interest is in how this has created the space for and the identity of attention deficit hyperactivity disorder (ADHD). Drawing on a wide range of literature, she outlines discussions of ADHD and the predominant focus upon:

- causes broadly associated with modern entertainment media, diet, parenting or individual temperament;
- claims that parents seek the label to avoid blame or to access scarce resources, with the label implying exoneration or forgiveness.

Graham identifies the dominant role of professional "experts" in these discussions. She highlights how notions associated with developmental psychology have been so taken for granted that people cannot see how they can be or why they should be questioned.

> As educationalists have become so used to thinking in terms of the 'norm' and categorizing educational endeavour according to bell curves and developmental age/stage theory, it can be unsettling to acknowledge that the 'norm' is a fiction. It is, however, a man-made grid of intelligibility that attributes value to culturally specific performances and in doing so, privileges particular ways of being.
>
> (2006, p. 7)

Developmentally established educational 'norms' do not just describe what it is to be a *normal* child within school, but also what it is to be *not normal*. It becomes a reality, delineating how we come to understand a child's nature, aptitude and character. As part of this process, the practices and spaces that broadly suit the majority become *normal* and those which are prescribed for the minority become *not normal*. The process itself constructs and applies tools of measurement, creating (or reaffirming) winners and losers both amongst the *normal* and the *not normal*.

The processes of research can also demonstrate this reality and support its perpetuation. Bell, Long, Garvan and Bussing (2011) for example, analysed responses to the ADHD Stigma Questionnaire from 268 teachers who had also carried out behaviour rating scales on their pupils. They concluded that special teachers were far more sensitive to the stigma experienced by students with ADHD. They recommend therefore that other teachers needed to have more training and experience with children with ADHD. This might seem like quite a reasonable conclusion. However, it is also an acceptance of the norms of the status quo. It is premised on 26 questions asking you to rate how badly people with ADHD are treated and perceived. In a manner similar to the Borthwick study mentioned above, it attributes value to culturally specific performances; its starting point would seem to be that ADHD characteristics are negative.

Snowling (2013) provides a further example, but this time in relation to dyslexia. Her robust research showed how teacher assessment[1] in England provided a statistically valid measure of 5-year-olds' development and predictor of their literacy attainment at age 7. She went on to argue for using teacher's developmental assessment of 5-year-olds to identify those "at high risk of educational difficulties" and to accept that the "best predictors of educational success are measures of language, communication and literacy" (p. 11). There is a contradiction within these conclusions however, which rests with the papers own recognition of the complexity of the classroom situation. The paper explained that neurodevelopmental disorders that affect learning are a "behavioural outcome of a multiple risk factors" (p. 8). The conclusion that teachers are the best predictors (though possibly true) seems to play down this multiplicity of risks. The research shows that it was statistically likely for teachers to undertake the assessment and get it right; but this is not the same as saying all will get it right or even that some will get it right all of the time. If we approach the data from this perspective we will recognise the capacity for teacher's to err as one of the multiple-risk-factors, we will assume that some teachers will get the assessment wrong and that many might find their own behaviours affected by the judgements they have made. We will return to consider some other alternatives to this conclusion in Chapter 5.

Evidence would suggest that there are potentially significant consequences from expecting teachers to carry out assessments which associate the child with a life-long label. In Queensland, for example, school-based identification practice, based upon developmental models, was used to identify those with difficulties in learning and to apply labels to them (Graham, 2006). The category criteria were very specific and qualified the child for specific kinds of support. They not only identified but also disqualified children based upon measurements of such things as "attention, memory, processing speed, impulsivity, disruption, organization, compliance and self-direction" (p. 17). Through these mechanisms schools could justify variation in treatment. Importantly to Graham, however, they also constructed and reinforced a deficit, negative view of the individual child. The problem was within the child. For those who fell outside the recognised categories, however, such a view meant their differences were ignored or drew punitive responses from the system.

Some may argue that this should not matter to us. As Gewirtz, Ball and Bowe (1995) noted: "Not only are schools and school services but also children themselves are coming to be viewed as commodities, some of whom are more valuable than others" (pp. 175–176).

People may feel that all cultures have values, that without norms and coherence around norms there would be chaos and anarchy, and that the values of our system are by and large reasonable or to the betterment of the majority. They may feel that separation and some unfairness of the kind that Graham identified in the Queensland system are an essential corollary of all human systems. After all, inequality can be seen to encourage hard work, innovation and risk-taking (Birdsall, 2001). So, if teachers can get it right for the majority then that should be good enough. However, even if this is the case, it underlines the importance of recognising what our view is.

Our collective view of what is normal and where the problem lies has significant implications for how we think about inclusive and special and how we develop practices associated with them.

A clear divide?

The theoretical divide frequently associated with inclusive and special education is that problems are either *within the setting* or *within the child*. These ways of viewing problems are frequently referred to as the social model and the medical model (deficit model or in-person deficit model). Drawing on a wide range of literature, Connor and Ferri (2007) explore the tensions around how special and inclusion have dealt with these models. They suggest that despite seeing itself as being at the service of disabled people, special education has been associated by many with the medical model and the ongoing oppression of disabled people. By linking itself to clinically developed approaches it has been seen to be in opposition to the social model and the initial drive for inclusion. To many supporters of special education, however, inclusion has threatened an undoing of the services and practices they value. They do not accept inclusion's challenge to ableism. They dismiss its aims as possibly desirable but practically unachievable. However, in side-lining their ideas within teaching and training, by colonising the language of inclusion and in the continued use of old practices and structures they suggest to disability activists that they do not recognise disabled people's political struggle.

These two very different ways of seeing the child and the situation can appear to be profoundly at odds with one another. For example, during our research across 55 administrations, Norwegian academics told us of the divide between departments within the same university as well as between universities and colleges. Teaching staff pointed to each other and explained how their views differed because they had been trained at this place or that place, either in the social method or the medical method. They openly recognised that this dissonance made it far harder to collectively agree about how best to approach day-to-day challenges.

The understanding of staff influences both their relations with 'outside' professions and with colleagues within their schools as well as their ways of working and approaching a situation. Lindqvist, Nilholm, Almqvist and Wetso (2011) surveyed 938 preschool teachers, teacher assistants, SENCOs, special teachers, class teachers and subject teachers in Swedish settings to explore how they described children and how the school should support them. The research team noted that the deficit perspective strongly influenced explanations of school difficulties, and that a medical diagnosis was seen to be an important precursor to receiving special support. There was a general assumption too that special educators rather than teachers should take the lead in creating the pedagogical content. In contrast, special educators were more much more likely to identify school and teacher factors as reasons for children's difficulties, and were less likely to emphasise medical diagnosis, separate support and the use of support staff.

The existence of this theoretical dissonance is not always quite as clear in practice. For example, Jones (2003) explored this tension in relation to emotional and behavioural difficulties in British education. She described a historical shift from a religious view of the child as sinful, to one informed by a psychoanalytical view in which lack of childhood security creates a deficit in development. This *maladjusted child* became one of the UK categories for identifying and referring pupils. It led to placement being decided by clinicians, with a focus on therapy rather than education. Subsequent critiques from educational sociologists highlighted the range of vested interests in this process, using semantic, ethical and social science arguments. This led to a shift towards seeing behaviour as a matter of school discipline. Jones could find no evidence of people defending the medical model, however. She believed this was because psychology had always associated emotional disturbance to some degree with the environment. The ideas also chimed with the reformation of special education in the 1970s. The locus of perceived expertise, suggested Jones, shifted away from medical psychology and towards sociology and social-psychology. The issue of labelling and the context-dependent nature of problematic behaviour came to the fore. How teachers understood and defined a situation and their idea of the ideal student came to be seen as a major causal component. Yet this (perhaps unwitting) appropriation by education of ideas from social-science served a rhetorical purpose, shifting the power balance away from health agencies.

However, Jones maintained that the polarised "either or" position (which suggests that some believe behaviour problems originate in the school environment and that some believe they originate in the child) is false, particularly since she believed the critiques of psychiatry upon which the polar positions were based did not necessarily equate to the psychiatry practised 30 years later. She suggested that the benefit of this debate has been that it has drawn attention to relationships and communications in class, but the negative consequence has been that teachers are derided for claiming that a pupil 'has' a problem. This goes against the reality that some children are troubled by challenges which do not appear to be resolvable by changes to their schooling. At the same time, she suggested that education feels it has "successfully negotiated the medical model" and has to find educational solutions to the challenges it faces. This, however, is not a theoretical position which frames teachers' understanding of young people and ways of working; it is closer to a working model which leads to recommended practices. It also ignores a reality that educational psychologists still serve as the gatekeeper to provision for many pupils (Sheehy, 2013).

Norwich (2002) suggested that there is a false theoretical opposition between what he calls the individual and social models. He contended that in reality the individual model always exists in context of the social whilst at the same time the social must also always make reference to the individual. His view was that the tensions and divergence between these two perspectives become increasingly evident as one seeks to argue from just one position.

What's your theory?

These frequently cited theoretical positions are just two of many which can be associated with inclusion and special. Different theoretical perspectives are associated with many different professions or different groupings within professions who work within this field. For example, the authors of *The Psychology of Education* (Long, Wood, Littleton, Passenger & Sheehy, 2011) identify five perspectives which are key to educational psychologists: psychodynamic, behavioural, humanistic, psychobiological and cognitive; whilst Cooper (2011) suggests a slightly different five in relation to social, emotional and behavioural difficulties: psychodynamic approach, behaviourist, humanistic, cognitive behavioural and systemic. Other authors attempt to situate philosophical positions as the theoretical underpinnings for diverse approaches. Farrell (2012b), looking across the broad spectrum of research which he associated with special education, identified theoretical positions associated with positivism, empiricism, phenomenology, hermeneutics, historical materialism, critical theory, holism, constructivism, structuralism, post-structuralism, pragmatism, symbolic interactionism, post-modernism, historical epistemology, as well as the ideas of two people in particular via Freudian and Lacanian psychoanalysis.

As much as some approaches to analysis or practice are underpinned by singular theoretical perspectives, attempts have been made to create a coherent practicable application, situating these different perspectives within a unifying whole. The International Classification of Functioning, Disability and Health (ICF) in particular aims to pull together some of the diverse models, using the biopsychosocial model, which integrates biological, individual and social perspectives of health. This, its originators suggest, is the only way to overcome the shortcomings and build on the strengths of the two dominant models, the medical and the social:

> On their own, neither model is adequate, although both are partially valid. Disability is a complex phenomena that is both a problem at the level of a person's body, and a complex and primarily social phenomena. Disability is always an interaction between features of the person and features of the overall context in which the person lives, but some aspects of disability are almost entirely internal to the person, while another aspect is almost entirely external. In other words, both medical and social responses are appropriate to the problems associated with disability; we cannot wholly reject either kind of intervention.
>
> (WHO, 2002, p. 9)

There is a fundamental risk, though, in any attempt to encapsulate the diverse theoretical positions which might be associated with special and inclusion. The theory becomes reified. Over the years, repeated discussions and descriptions of these ideas results in them seeming to be real; a genuine truth encapsulating what happens in the world. For example, a common problem for students analysing data on Masters modules on which I have worked is their use of a wide range of contradictory theories to explain phenomena. They fail to take an identifiable singular or complimentary theoretical position against which their work can be judged. The student is adopting a layperson's approach to an academic problem. They are drawing upon the wide range of conflicting ideas available to them, rather than narrowing their focus to enable precise debate. They treat a theoretical position as if it as object which can be laid alongside any other, rather than as a way of seeing, thinking, talking and behaving.

Such a tale of non-specialist generalisation and over-simplification is evident across professions. It is not just people in training who fall into this trap. Consider for example the English Early Years Foundation Stage Framework. This framework was underpinned by reviews about children's learning and development which identified a great deal of evidence from a sociocultural perspective and some from an interactionist perspective. There was virtually no evidence presented from an individualist perspective. However, the framework which was produced under the auspices of civil servants in a government department, gives equal weighting to these three different perspectives. It sets the three ways of thinking alongside each other, suggesting we can operate these three views at the same time even if in everyday situations they produce very different practices (Rix & Parry, 2014).

All professions have a need for specified thinking and communication. The inherent constraints upon language and thought are evident in all walks of life. They are also encapsulated in terms associated with boundaried communities or fields, terms such as discourse, genre, frame and jargon. The consequences of this separation were pointed out by many of the interviewees in the four country visits undertaken as part of our 55-administration review. The different professions speak different languages, often meaning different things even when they sound similar. As a result we overlook important issues or opportunities. It was suggested by a number of interviewees that we need someone to translate between them. Even this may not be enough, however. Jones (2003), coming from an educational psychology perspective, goes as far as to suggest that education is insular. She noted the diverse consequences of adopting approaches informed by different psychological perspectives within an educational context. But she felt that this was largely regarded by educationalists as immaterial in relation to their area of specialisation: pedagogy. Education pragmatically accepted imported perspectives from outside professions. However, there was a fundamental problem when educators sought evidence-based[2] solutions from purported experts from outside education and did not engage with the current and historic arguments going on within the outsiders' field: "Turning to the social and/or behavioural sciences raises the question of who is the expert, and sets in motion professional rivalries that unfold in a dialectical relationship with changes in policy and practice and the wider political landscape" (Jones, 2003, p.149).

This dialectical rivalry will not go away either. The problem for theory is that just because your theory results in you coming up with a hypothesis which leads to a solution that solution does not categorically prove a hypothesis nor make your theory 'right'. For example, my theory that great trade routes can be opened up by sailing west from Europe may lead me to a hypothesis that if I set sail I will reach the rich market of India. This will bring me to land and it will open up trade routes, but it will involve the Americas. Similarly, my behaviourist theory may lead to the development of programmes which produce empirically proven changes in behaviour. This may support my hypothesis, but it does not mean that these changes could not be explained through other theoretical perspectives, or that they are not supported by proven hypotheses. Consequently, because of the complex multi-factorial nature of evidence, the diversity of research methods and the partialness of any research question, contradictory theoretical perspectives can build up a range of supporting evidence which will further convince the believer and can always be used to counter another's certainty.

Given the significant emphasis placed by many policy-makers, researchers, parents and practitioners on the need to work with empirically proven techniques, this needs to be considered further.

Are there reasons to doubt?

Nearly 20 years ago, Gallagher (1998) noted that any claims of a scientific basis to special were undermined by the lack of cumulative development. Two decades later, things have not changed much. We are still dealing with the same questions or ones that are very similar. Gallagher maintained that if scientific research could answer the central questions about who, what, where and how we should educate, then debates about inclusion and special could be closed down. In contrast, many still assert that conclusive findings are achievable and regard scientific study as being the defining feature of special provision. Farrell (2012b), for example, has described special education as "essentially a positivist endeavour". He suggests:

> Many aspects of special education can be associated with a positivist stance. Special education assumes that disorders and disabilities are describable as individual phenomena. It also recognised that social and other factors can be influential. Furthermore, it is maintained that disabilities and disorders can be meaningfully identified and classified. Special education concerns approaches it is said can be linked to particular disabilities and disorders in evidence-based practice. It seeks and uses what it considers evidence of approaches that lead to academic progress and better personal and social development.
>
> (p. 40)

The questions we need to ask therefore are first whether disorders and disabilities are describable, identifiable and classifiable and second whether patterns they identify and categories they create are either all encompassing, consistently applied or particularly illuminating.

Type 1 – Doubting the category

The first question mark against categories is that there is much disagreement about what they are. It would seem, for example, that countries' definitions of special educational needs cannot be categorised for comparison without creating a deceptive sense of commonality (Riddell, Tisdall, Kane & Mulderrig, 2006) and consequently can only be listed as a tool for reflection (see OECD, 2012). In our study of 55 administrations the number of categories of impairment or special educational needs varied considerably between countries, ranging from 3 to 22 categories. Once all the obvious similarities were grouped together there were 60 different categories which emerged across the 55 administrations (see Table 4.1).

The assumption that each country felt that they were using a robust category is evident in that nearly all countries used them for formal allocation of resources. Only one administration claimed not to have categories within the system and three suggested that the categories were just for administrative purposes.

Florian and colleagues (2006) suggested that these numerous categories fall into three main types, based upon:

- clinical classification (type of impairment);
- educational classification (type of special educational need);
- administrative categories (types of setting, support or funding).

They noted the limited educational relevance of these classifications however, since children with different difficulties in learning can be assigned to similar categories.

TABLE 4.1 Clustered categories across 55 administrations using unifying headings

Visual impairment	Physical impairment	Assessed Syndrome
Deaf blind	Physical and health	Orphaned
Hearing impairment	impaired	Experienced a
Speech-language	Health impairment	bereavement
impairment	Metabolic or nutritional	Looked after by a local
Communication and	disorders	authority
interaction	Students with fits	Internally displaced
Social-interaction	Disabled children	Interrupted learners
disabilities	Multiple disabilities	Of nomadic/pastoral
Autism spectrum disorder	Global development	communities
ADHD	disorders	Heading households
Intellectual impairment	Tactile impairments	Abused
General learning	Traumatic Brain Injury	Living in the streets
disabilities	An incapacity which	Drug addicts or with
Dyslexia	prevents using	parents abusing
Learning, adaptation	educational facilities	substances
or functioning skills	generally available	Children in schools
Students with an	Giftedness	attached to paedological
educational sub-	Learning problems in	institutes
normality	specific fields of	Learning environment
Dyspraxia	education	Family circumstances
Dysphasia	Pupils subject to judidical	Living with parents with
Severe behaviour	measures	issues of mental
disorder	Teenagers failing at school	health
Psychological impairments	Not attending regularly	Have English as an
Chronic somatic and	Epilepsy	additional language
neurological disorders	Cerebral palsy, students	Being bullied
Psychomotor disturbances	who have cerebral palsy	On child protection
Sensory and multi-sensory	Down Syndrome	register
disorders	Albinism	Young carers others

In order to overcome this kind of inconsistency, in the late 1990s the Organisation for Economic Co-operation and Development (OECD) established three unifying data collection categories:

A   *Disabilities*: having a clear organic basis for their difficulties.
B   *Difficulties*: not seeming to have a clear organic basis or clear basis in social disadvantage.
C   *Disadvantages*: resulting from aspects of the social and/or language background.

Subsequent research (Robson, 2005) indicated that individual countries were even using these very broad catch-all categories differently. Evans (2003) also found that whilst category C children were educated in similar locations, children in categories A and B were educated in very different locations in different countries. It was suggested that the inconsistency of their use emerged from their one-dimensional nature. Florian et al. (2006) noted that the model presumed that a child would be classified in only one category and ignored the broader demographic and socio-economic data.

Type 2 – Doubting the diagnosis

Obviously these kinds of international findings highlight why we cannot use the formal collation of statistics in relation to special needs education to develop an accurate picture of trends and developments (Vislie, 2003). However, it also seems very likely that there is a fundamental problem with the notion that disorders and disabilities are describable and can be identified and classified. Consider research led in the 1990s by Leonard Bickman, subsequently the highly decorated Professor of Psychology, Psychiatry and Public Policy and Associate Dean for Research at Peabody College, Vanderbilt University, in the United States. They reviewed a study of 984 dependent children of military personnel (ages 5-17) who received mental health treatment. Bickman and colleagues (Bickman, Wighton, Lambert, Karver & Steding, 2012) evaluated the scale characteristics, internal consistency, reliability and application of the measures. The kinds of conditions looked at were attention deficit hyperactivity disorder, oppositional defiant disorder, overanxious disorder, dysthymia and conduct disorder.

The study concluded:

1) Few of the diagnoses for children are only slightly more internally consistent than symptoms selected at random.

2) Comorbidity [having more than one condition] can often render the determination of a "primary diagnosis" similar to tossing a coin.

3) While scales of functioning impairment have a fair predictive validity for hospitalisation and cost, the addition of diagnostic information from parents and children results in only a negligible improvement.

4) Agreement between parent, youth, and clinician-based diagnosis is low.

5)   Children may receive diagnoses that favor their chances of obtaining treatment in their service/insurance system and not truly reflect their mental health problem.

This study provides little support for diagnosis as a useful tool for services or evaluation research and policy.

(p. 19)

These findings cannot be extrapolated to other settings, other countries and other professions but it does clearly raise doubt about the methods, purposes and consistency of diagnostic processes; doubt which is supported by evidence from elsewhere. For example, consider the American Psychiatric Association's (APA) *Diagnostic and Statistical Manual of Mental Disorders*. Two of the contributors to the fourth edition wrote a paper examining the process of compiling the fifth manual, *DSM-5*. They observed that previously unrecognised disorders would now be "among the most common of the psychiatric disorders, potentially creating false epidemics of misidentified pseudopatients" (Frances & Widiger, 2012, p. 122). They also pointed out that the deletion of half the diagnostic sets for personality disorders had led to many complaints that the decisions "were sorely lacking in objectivity or comprehensiveness, emphasizing instead the research by work group members and failing to give due consideration to alternative perspectives" (p. 124). They concluded that DSM-5 is evidence of "high-risk proposals and sorry methodological performance" (p. 125).

Similar uncertainty around issues of diagnosis has been raised in the UK by the British Psychological Society's Division of Clinical Psychology, which called for "a paradigm shift in relation to functional psychiatric diagnoses" (BPS-DCP, 2013). This shift needs to acknowledge how behaviour is contextualised and dependent upon multiple factors, reflecting "the complexity of the interactions involved in all human experience". Their position statement included the following:

> It should be noted that functional psychiatric diagnoses such as schizophrenia, bipolar disorder, personality disorder, attention deficit hyperactivity disorder, conduct disorders and so on, due to their limited reliability and questionable validity, provide a flawed basis for evidence-based practice, research, intervention guidelines and the various administrative and non-clinical uses of diagnosis.

Even the most established categories come with some doubt. For example, early on in a book on the genetics and aetiology of Down syndrome, involving numerous international contributors, the editor can challenge the ubiquitous statement that Down syndrome results from an additional chromosome 21: "Although several hypotheses have been put forward, it is still unclear as to whether particular gene loci on chromosome 21 are sufficient to cause Down syndrome and its associated features" (Dey, 2011, p. ix).

Yet whilst the causes of the identified condition are still open to question, other researchers can go as far as to suggest that the personality of people identified with Down syndrome can be regarded as a secondary phenotype arising from a primary behavioural phenotype (Fidler, 2006). Other researchers in the field warn against this approach, suggesting that behaviours and personalities can be changed but that such a model leads to a perception of inevitability (Buckley, 2008).

Attempts to define or attribute causes in widely recognised conditions such as Autism are even more problematic. The general evidence is that causes of autism are still largely unknown (Ecker, Spooren & Murphy, 2013); that autism spectrum disorders are the extremity of normally distributed autistic-like traits (Lundstro, Larsson & Anckarsa, 2012) and that some people can meet the diagnosis for autism at one point in their life and later in their lives no longer meet that diagnosis (Fein et al., 2013). Seemingly robust research methods which underpin many claims of knowledge have questions raised over them. For example, announcements that neuroimaging approaches can reveal differences related to autism at six months (Wolff et al., 2012) are undermined by a recognition that magnetic resonance imaging (MRI) studies have the statistical power of 8 per cent[3] (Button et al., 2013). Similarly, claims that genetics are providing the answers alongside neuroimaging and multi-factorial studies (Ecker et al., 2013) must be set against statements that a common genetic variant is still inferred and that rare genetic variations may have the greatest effect (Anney et al., 2012). This is alongside a recognition by leading figures in the field such as Professor Simon Baron-Cohen, that a key challenge will be understanding how the genes that are discovered may interact with environmental factors (Geddes, 2009). Set against such evidence, some authors have asked if we can have any faith in claims that genetic tests can predict autism in very young children (e.g. Hughes, 2012).

Given the levels of disagreement about what it is that is being diagnosed and how to diagnose it, it is perhaps unsurprising that in 2013, in England, Department for Education figures showed huge variation in diagnosis between local authorities across all categories. On average, across all 12 categories used in England, there was four times more chance of being identified in the highest 10 diagnosing local authorities than in the lowest 10 local authorities (see Table 4.2). The only category which was noticeably lower than 1:4 was 'Behaviour, emotional and social difficulties', which of course is largely based upon a child causing problems in the classroom. Even those categories which would seem to be fundamentally self-evident, such as visual, physical or hearing difficulties still showed this wide kind of variation in diagnosis between local authorities.

Similarly, a study in 2009 in one large UK education authority identified significant variations in placement recommendations between educational psychologists. This showed that "half the EPs were responsible for referring 91 per cent of the children who attended special schools for children with EBD [emotional and behavioural difficulties] and MLD [moderate learning difficulty]" (Farrell & Venables, 2009, p. 118). It was evident that those trained more recently were less likely to recommend separate provision. This would suggest that a factor

TABLE 4.2 Percentage of types of diagnoses of children identified with special educational needs in English local authorities (LAs) in 2013

	Number of LA returns[a] (n = 152)	Mean %	Median %	Lowest LA %	Highest LA %	Average % of lowest 10 LAs	Average % of highest 10 LAs	Ratio lowest to highest	Ratio lowest 10 to highest 10
Specific learning difficulty	118	10.71	10.30	2.50	24.34	4.84	18.96	1:10	1:4
Moderate learning difficulty	147	19.94	18.44	6.93	38.12	8.97	35.75	1:6	1:4
Severe learning difficulty	130	4.66	4.33	1.50	11.16	2.08	8.60	1:7	1:4
Profound and multiple learning difficulty	89	1.65	1.39	0.63	4.17	0.76	3.21	1:7	1:4
Behaviour, emotional and social difficulties	141	21.23	20.70	13.47	34.94	15.07	29.53	1:3	1:2
Speech, language and communications needs	141	19.72	19.43	9.67	40.88	10.65	31.56	1:4	1:3
Hearing impairment	104	2.63	2.42	0.84	13.11	1.09	5.75	1:15	1:5
Visual impairment	102	1.34	1.24	0.41	3.84	0.54	2.56	1:9	1:5
Multisensory impairment	54	0.15	0.13	0.0	0.50	0.0	0.35	0:1	0:0
Physical disability	128	3.96	3.90	1.41	7.70	1.94	6.06	1:5	1:3
Autistic spectrum disorder	147	10.37	9.95	3.48	22.37	5.01	18.98	1:6	1:4
Other difficulty/disability	111	4.27	3.95	0.71	12.04	1.24	8.06	1:17	1:7

Source: Data extracted by Rix from DfE (2013b).

Note: a Lower returns are because an LA did not submit figures for at least one of the primary, secondary or special school categories.

in the variation was training or length of service. It seems likely, though, that these were just a couple of reasons amongst many.

Type 3 – Doubting the research

The reasons for doubt are not just related to the categories themselves and our capacity to allocate people to them, but also to the quality of the underlying research, the assessments we create and the manner in which this is used by others. Consider the highly influential notion of Intelligence Quotient (IQ) which underpins many assessments of intellectual impairment. The origins of these tests emerge from corrupt research practices (Mackintosh, 1998). They have a long history of racial and gender biases (Mirza, 1998) and have been culturally influenced in an equivalent manner in relation to people with Down syndrome (Borthwick , 1996). The outcomes they do produce can be better predicted by measures of social and family background (Howe, 1997) and the scores have been subject to an ongoing upward creep since they first began. James Flynn, for instance, identified that in 1942, adults in the sample for one such test, the Ravens Progressive Matrices, scored 27 IQ points lower than equivalent adults in the 1992 sample. Such recorded annual changes meant that we can reasonably conclude that at least 84 per cent of people in Victorian England had an IQ below 75. Flynn (2000) concluded that in 1949, 1 in 23 could qualify as mentally retarded, whilst in 1989 it was 1 in 213. As a result of such changes, intelligence test manufacturers have to periodically renorm their tests. This has a profound impact for many people. For example, in 1993 in the United States, classification rates for mental retardation ended a period of decline and began to climb once more. This coincided with the introduction of a renormed, harder version of the major IQ test (Ceci, Scullin & Kanaya, 2003): "Behind the facade of constancy, the hidden history of IQ testing shows huge fluctuations in the IQ criterion of mental retardation and paucity of evidence for any particular criterion" (Flynn, 2000, p. 197).

In addition to these tales of inconsistent processes, the aims of research can also be questioned. It is important to recognise, for example, that many disabled people and disability activists feel research upon them is alienating and disempowering. There is a sense that it is often unrepresentative and not in the best interests of participants (Kitchin, 2000). There is also a strong current of thinking that the research is not relevant to those for whom it is or might be intended, particularly practitioners. For example, McLesky and Waldron (2011) examined a range of different study types in segregated settings to identify components of high-quality, intensive instruction for elementary students with learning disabilities. They concluded that these approaches were used rarely if at all in either separate provision or the mainstream. Similarly, in considering the role educational psychology could play in teacher education, four US educational psychology lecturers (Patrick, Anderman, Bruening & Duffin, 2011) point out that its relevance is not apparent, that there is a "disconnect between much educational psychology research and practitioners' needs and concerns" (p. 75) and that the field need to prove its relevance and effectiveness. Similarly,

Professor of Educational Psychology Dennis McInerney (2005) suggests that "recent theory and research seems to have had a disappointing impact on educational policy and practice" (p. 596) and that outdated ideas from earlier eras dominate.

The lack of practical engagement with research also undermines the conclusions of that research. Wang and Spillane (2009) in their meta-analysis of social skills interventions for children with autism note the lack of evidence for their effectiveness, apart from video modelling and to a lesser extent social stories and peer-mediated strategies. They note that these last two practices (and the 20 other practices lacking evidence) need to be implemented with great care and continuous monitoring, given the uncertainty of the supporting evidence. The risks of adopting these approaches are further highlighted by the observation that most of the interventions across all 23 practices were conducted by researchers and not practitioners or families: "If the interventions implemented by professional researchers yield mixed results, it would be a real challenge for classroom teachers and parents with limited resources and time to achieve the same or better outcomes" (p. 339).

It is also worth noting that if the practitioner is following the programme and believes that the programme is sound, they will be trying to make sure they deliver it as it is designed. The lack of success could all too easily be put down to their own lack of skill or the inadequacy of the child. Much time could be wasted and opportunities for learning missed because the programme is the focus.

This tale should not surprise us. It is commonplace for systematic reviews of the available evidence related to some aspect of special educational needs or a particular impairment group to begin by recognising the lack of evidence they have to work with. This was the case in our systematic reviews of effective pedagogic approaches (Rix, Hall, Nind, Sheehy & Wearmouth, 2009), just as it was with a review of the evidence around effective best practice provision for children placed on the autistic spectrum (Parsons, Guldberg, Macleod, Jones, Prunty & Balfe, 2009). These researchers noted that independent evaluation of all interventions is evidently lacking and that well-known interventions (such as Lovaas, ABA [Applied Behavioural Analysis] and PECS [Picture Exchange Communication System]) might not be as effective as earlier findings suggested, when more robust research methodologies have been applied. They concluded that previous evaluations tended to be too short term, with too small a population and conducted by researchers involved directly with implementing programmes or with centres providing services. They noted too, a frequent lack of objectivity and rigour in classroom-based studies and a lack of research in post-primary and post-compulsory educational contexts. Perhaps, given the structured approach of these models, it is unsurprising that there was also a heavy reliance upon quantitative research, but the reviewers noted a lack of qualitative insights. This meant that little was understood about such things as contextual factors which could influence outcomes and the usefulness and relevance of skills learned during interventions.

The limited, reliable evidence base is not restricted to one impairment group either. A review of research into learning disability, examined the capacity of 15 meta-analyses to provide robust evidence for teachers (Therrien, Zaman & Banda, 2010). It concluded that the lack of reporting about student characteristics and teaching strategies in primary studies meant researchers could not identify the potential impact of specific interventions. All they could provide was more general statements about what is effective.

Reviews looking at specific interventions are similarly constrained. For example, PECS shows promise in promoting communication in children with autism, but this is not yet proven and needs to be set alongside the lack of evidence for gains in speech and the generalisation of skills (Flippin, Reszka & Watson, 2010). This finding is partly down to the very small number and size of studies alongside the lack of clear structured methods.

When studies clearly present their methods it often reveals underlying problems too. For example, in a consideration of bias in behavioural research (Podsakoff, MacKenzie, Lee & Podsakoff, 2003), the reviewers suggested that there was a general agreement that variance attributable to the methods used in measurement was a problem in this field. They pointed to the difficulty in recognising the most significant bias within a situation (such as implicit theories, consistent practices, and scales) and the lack of measures for such biases. This was particularly important given the small scale of many of these studies and the small differences which generate statistical significance. However, most studies only took account of random measurement error and not systematic measurement error or other possible sources of bias.

Type 4 – Doubting the underpinning beliefs

An excellent example of the complexity of underlying beliefs arises from the literature around foetal alcohol syndrome (FAS) and its variations foetal alcohol syndrome disorders (FASD), alcohol-related neurodevelopmental disorder (ARND), alcohol-related birth defects (ARBD) and partial foetal alcohol syndrome (PFAS). The first challenge arises because many of the markers of FAS and its variations are the same as those associated with ADHD and there is frequent comorbidity between the two categories (Coles, Platzman, Raskind-Hood, Brown, Falek & Smith, 1997). This challenge is exacerbated by the inaccuracy of behavioural diagnoses as discussed earlier. There also seems to be a lack of robust literature. For example, a cornerstone paper in the field (Sampson et al., 1997) is premised upon the only two studies the authors felt they could rely on in the United States.

One of the two studies Sampson et al. trusted included their own. This is based on 581 children of mothers who self-identified as heavy drinkers (out of 1,439 families who had given birth in a Seattle hospital in 1974–75). The authors retrospectively analysed this sample to estimate total FAS and ARND percentages. Their subsequent reanalysis of the data enabled them to estimate that in the Seattle study 0.91 per cent had FAS and ARND. However, this 0.91 per cent involved using assessment based upon many variables:

These include tests of copying designs, memory for designs, memory for stories, and differentiating rhythmical patterns. Salient outcomes from other blocks defining the pattern of alcohol related deficits at 4 and 7 years include IQ and achievement measures of arithmetic, teacher ratings of attention and cooperation/impulsivity, overall ratings of academic adjustment, and false alarms on laboratory vigilance tests.

(p. 324)

Such assessments would all be influenced by contextual factors, many associated with cultural background and socio-economic status. In reaching 0.91 per cent the authors also assumed that the figures they actually found (12 children out of 1,439 families or 8.3/1,000) were underestimates. They felt a need to statistically alter their findings to account for these assumptions.

By October 2013, according to Google Scholar, this paper had been cited 666 times. But it is not just its questionable figures which have spread. The paper also includes a picture (cited elsewhere as being from teaching materials produced by one of the authors) purporting to represent "The face in fetal alcohol syndrome". As the authors made clear, biological differences mean that it was not possible to provide a specific list; however, the image can be found in many places as if they were being very specific indeed. They also felt confident enough to say: "When this characteristic clinical expression is complete, many diagnosticians believe that the FAS diagnosis can be made without knowledge of maternal alcohol exposure" (pp. 318–319). This is despite saying a few lines later that diagnosis is "particularly prone to unreliability and bias" because of the lack of training, checklists and laboratory tests (p. 319).

A third interesting issue arising from this paper is that it dismisses claims in two other important papers in the field (Abel & Sokol, 1987; Abel, 1995). These papers suggest a worldwide figure for FAS. Abel and Sokol (1987) claimed that worldwide FAS represented 1.9 births in 1,000 (0.19 per cent). This figure was based on an average of 19 studies from eight countries. This suggested that out of 88,236 children, 164 developed FAS. However, if you excluded the United States and looked at the 35,634 children in the seven other countries, this dropped to 1.26 births per 1,000. Across the whole sample, in nine of the studies (involving 18,240 children) no children developed FAS. As the authors note, over half the cases of FAS came from one study in the United States in 1980, involving people from the Navajo, Pueblo, Apache and Ute tribes.

This pattern of higher US figures led Abel (1998) to coin the term "American Paradox" in relation to FAS, as it seemed to be 20 times higher in the Unites States than in Europe. Looking across all studies up to 1993 he noted that the "most critical determinant for the presence of FAS continues to be the country in which the study is conducted" (Abel, 1995, p. 439). He suggested that this may be because countries followed very different clinical procedures and that practitioners in the United States may be more prone to associate child behaviours and features with FAS. However, when Sampson and colleagues critique Abel's conclusions, they choose to put differences down to research method issues.

Some of the subsequent international research does seem to identify FAS and its variations in other countries. However, it is still not straightforward. For example, a recent significant study from Italy reports that "FASD in this Western European population may be 3.5 per cent" (May et al., 2006, p. 1573). This study involved 22 children identified with FASD and 63 control children all in first grade (presumably aged 6–7). The researchers went into schools and identified children with and without FASD and then interviewed the parents. The findings were based on interviews about current and past drinking habits. They could not get information from up to 50 per cent of mothers about their drinking. It was also noted that the researchers did not believe 19 per cent of the mothers (four interviewees – all with children identified with FASD) and were informed by professionals who knew them that they did drink. They perceived therefore that they could only rely on the interviews of 12 parents of children identified with FASD and 48 not so identified. There was also virtually no difference in the reported drinking levels during pregnancy of the parents of children identified at one of the three levels of FASD and parents of children not identified, though the 12 parents reported drinking more at the time of the interviews. The researchers also acknowledge that they had problems with translation and their research instrument.

Finally, given the dramatic impact of the American Paradox identified eight years before it is worth noting that:

- The majority of researchers came from the United States.
- The US researchers trained the Italian researchers.
- A US government agency (the National Institute on Alcohol Abuse and Alcoholism) was instrumental in the training and the research's funding and organisation.

Is it unreasonable to wonder if this is an example of the exporting of the American Paradox? Is there is a motive for extrapolating a small study to a whole region and to use phrases which imply that the findings may apply to a large part of a continent ?

It seems reasonable to raise doubts, particularly as some might claim quantitative research of this type can attain objectivity. If this was ethnographic or qualitative research one would expect the researchers to explore their own biases and assumptions. We would expect considerable self-reflection in research seeking to identify a condition notoriously hard to diagnose, particularly if it was making strong claims on the basis of 12 participants, using a flawed research instrument, in a field which recognises the limitations of its own studies. The authors of this paper, however, do not feel any need to discuss the American Paradox, even though the author is associated with the Center on Alcoholism, Substance Abuse and Addictions in the United States.

It is important that readers understand that I am not saying that these are individually bad papers or bad studies. I do not know enough to make this claim. The issues identified above mean that we can ask about their validity and reliability. It seems clear that we need to maintain doubt about this literature because a range of cultural issues and underpinning beliefs may be at play.

Building on unstable foundations

It seems unquestionable to me that the categories, diagnosis, underlying research and beliefs which are seen to be fundamental to special education are questionable. As a positivist endeavour it merely leads to the asking of more questions. This is not a bad thing unless it is not recognised by those who work within this particular paradigm; if, for example, there is a belief that evidence-based practice provides answers and clear guidelines. Unfortunately, this belief is widely held. Fox (2003), for example, discusses the political view that we could eradicate the variations in the quality of service (between areas, service types, individual practitioners, groupings of patients and across time) if only we could get practitioners to use the same evidence-based practice.

Such attitudes can take us in some very unnecessary directions.

A case study without doubt

Consider a paper on FASD written by a leader in the field; a researcher who has a great many academic and honorary titles, and who lectures and advises in many parts of the world. This paper (Carpenter, 2011) had 12 citations on Google scholar as of 4 April 2014 and was also extensively cited in the two books its author published on the subject. The paper stated with certainty that FASD was learning disabilities' most common non-genetic cause; it gave a figure for number of births in Europe, gave estimated costs nationally and across a person's life, as well as listing the top challenges faced by teachers. It also included a specific pedagogic profile for children with FAS which was cited as coming from a Training and Development Agency research project run by the author. This work therefore appears to represent rock-solid, government-backed evidence upon which practitioners can base effective practice. Except it all falls apart when it is looked at in any detail.

The lack of solid evidence in relation to numbers has already been discussed. In this paper they are cited with confidence. In addition, figures are cited for European countries without a source, whilst figures for South Africa come from an abstract for a conference (Molteno, 2008). There is similar room for doubt over the costs cited without question in the paper: "FASD costs the US $36 billion dollars per year, and the total lifetime cost of an individual with FAS to society is estimated at $2.9 million (Peadon et al., 2008)" (Carpenter, 2011, p. 41). If you go to Peadon, the $36 billion did not come from their research but was a citation for someone else (Lupton, Burd & Harwood, 2004). Peadon does not cite this figure either. The figure Peadon took from Lupton was $3.6 billion. Accepting that we can all fail to notice typos, it is still worth going to see just how Lupton et al. reached their figure. They drew on many US studies, but all of them demonstrate questionable assumptions and cultural biases. For example, many of their costings assumed full-time residential care either up to the age of 21 or from 21 to 65; others attempted to include an estimated loss of earnings as a result of being identified with FAS. Many of the figures did not anticipate these individuals being supported to be economically productive members of society or that they might live quite happily within a supportive local community. The \$3.6 billion figure was also a median figure (the one in the middle) in estimates which ranged from £200 million to £9.3 billion. These figures had also been adjusted for inflation on the basis of estimated costs in earlier studies (with a range from \$75 million per annum in 1984 to \$4 billion in 1998). It is this very obvious variability and inconsistency which led Popova and colleagues (Popova, Stade, Bekmuradov, Lange & Rehm, 2011) to conclude (after a systematic review of the literature) that there were no comprehensive, sound and generalisable assessments of economic impact.[4]

Of course, I have chosen this paper not just because it doesn't check its stats, but because it demonstrates how a paucity of evidence and lack of reflection can underpin fundamental notions associated with special (and by default with inclusion), whilst being in a position to inform the approaches and attitudes of educational practitioners. The title of the paper is "Pedagogically Bereft", invoking the tragedy/charity model which has for so long been associated with disability and special provision. At the same time, its framing of its recommendations fit within the medical model. However, it turns out that the "top challenges faced by teachers" resulted from personal research by the author, whilst the "specific pedagogic profile", which seems to be cited as coming from Blackburn, Carpenter & Egerton (2010), was not in that paper. The "specific pedagogic profile" had therefore not been published before, and was being presented with no description of method and no substantiating evidence.

This paper exemplifies a belief that there are types of children who can and need to be identified through assessment in order for an appropriate pedagogy to be made available to them. It highlights how the process creates experts. The consequence of this process is that the rest of the population are encouraged to believe they lack the capacity to help. A market for expertise is developed and deepened. Ironically too, after all this, the practices which the paper recommends for this category of child are practices which you might expect any teacher to undertake with any class.[5]

Talking to you

The 1960s–70s was a period of rapid growth in training for special education, largely premised upon a continuum of severity and types of impairment (Brownell & Kiely, 2010). As a result, despite the subsequent emergence of non-categorical and integrational approaches (which is discussed further in Chapter 5), the categorical continuum mind-set underpins the training of many still working today, many of whom will now be in senior or advisory positions. This reality also applies to those who are working within the mainstream sector.

The past does not go away. Its ideas and beliefs inform the new paradigms and practices which emerge, even though they can seem so fresh, exciting and original. Brownell and Kiely (2010), for example, talk about rapid technological advancements and increasingly sophisticated research which offers opportunities for the future education of those excluded within or from the mainstream. They invoke a range of research fields, concluding that new discoveries will surely enable us to structure our interventions so that we can with certainty improve the capacity of the brain to process information. This dream that we have a key to the future seems little different to Langdon Down's conviction that his medical model of management (diet, exercise, sensory simulation and social activities) offered hope to those he identified as being of the mongoloid type; and it seems little different to Alexander Melville Bell's and Alexander Graham Bell's certainty that the Visible Speech System offered the answer for those identified as deaf mutes.

Where does this critique of theoretical and scientific methods in educational contexts leave us, then? Previous chapters have outlined similar challenges in relation to arguments based upon rights and choice. It would seem that all of our dominant arguments and singular ways of thinking lead us to contradictory endings, which may serve the aspirations and beliefs of the thinker but do not provide clear-cut answers for the undecided and uninformed.

There is perhaps a unifying starting position, however. For all our talk, everyday life does not respond to theory, it responds to action … and all human action is social. Take an extreme example: a volcano erupting. The act of the volcano erupting is not social, but the consequences and our responses to it are. They result from where we have built our dwellings, how we have been educated, our networks of support, our cultural response to disaster, the resources we have at our disposal, and so forth … and all of these have in turn resulted from a range of social interactions. Barring the hypothetical possibility of living a life in total isolation, without any interaction with another creature, all we have and know and do is situated within the social. We are influenced by the social decisions and experiences of numerous others not only in the present but from before we were conceived. Our health, our physical and social well-being, our learning all emerges from the interplay with the animate, inanimate, the real and the imagined. This, of course, has a profound impact for all the arguments laid out above. It contradicts the seemingly reasonable premise within the WHO statement (see p. 80), because each of their component parts, the bio, the individual and the social is wrapped up within our wider social capacity. It is only through the social means that the three can be affected. We can only intervene with others through social processes. Figure 4.1 is a very simplistic image which uses some of the theories cited in this chapter in an attempt to encapsulate this.

This is a slightly different position to that which is suggested by Norwich (see p. 79). It does not deny the individual or our need to focus upon the individual's experience, but it acknowledges that there exists a collective reality beyond the life of any one person, that any process involves more than one. It is also not quite the same thing as situating everything within the social model either, for this too is one perspective which is situated within the social whole.

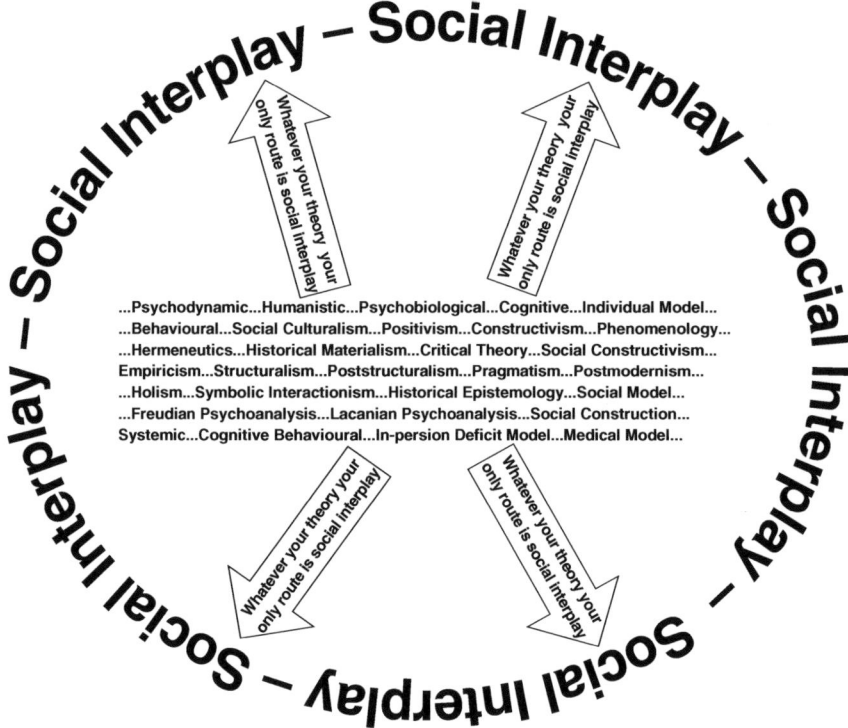

...Psychodynamic...Humanistic...Psychobiological...Cognitive...Individual Model...
...Behavioural...Social Culturalism...Positivism...Constructivism...Phenomenology...
...Hermeneutics...Historical Materialism...Critical Theory...Social Constructivism...
Empiricism...Structuralism...Poststructuralism...Pragmatism...Postmodernism...
...Holism...Symbolic Interactionism...Historical Epistemology...Social Model...
...Freudian Psychoanalysis...Lacanian Psychoanalysis...Social Construction...
Systemic...Cognitive Behavioural...In-person Deficit Model...Medical Model...

FIGURE 4.1 The social interplay through which all theory is enacted.

A more fundamental difficulty in suggesting that the social wraps around or infuses the other theories is that this seems to argue for social construction/constructivist/cultural theories above all others. By acknowledging such a social infusion of theory, we may rummage in the theoretical pickings of history or the cutting-edge dreams of great thinkers, but to understand them we have to begin with the context in which they spoke and in which their ideas and practices were situated. Now this is perfectly acceptable if that happens to be your theoretical starting point, but not if you prioritise others' ways of understanding the world, for example if you believe in objective knowledge.

We will always struggle if we try to demonstrate to people that everything is a social product. For example, is the pleasure I feel after I have been for a run a social product? Surely the individual experience resulting from chemicals released in the body is not social. The chemicals have the potential to be released regardless of who I am. Similarly, running to keep fit is an action I take because of knowledge about fitness I have developed in social situations, but the impact of the action would occur regardless. It seems pedantic to point out that my birth was a social interaction or that my identity emerges within social interactions or that my level of health is allied to my social background, or to question whether our sensory and physical experiences are universal.

Even if we can persuade people that the body is essentially a social product affected by familial circumstances and that our genetic make-up is a consequence of millennia of social and cultural history, and even if they accept, as Abberley (1987) demonstrated, that impairment is frequently a social product, the individual's biological and psychological perception of experience will for many people over-ride arguments about its social cause. We have to recognise that the complexity of our social infusion means that many people will feel that a singular social construction viewpoint does not encapsulate their experiences of complex realities. As William Bagley, a founding father of psychology in education, concluded, a field of study cannot explain the process (Johanningmeier, 1969).

I am convinced that all aspects of our lives are socially infused. However, the more experience I have of living, the less chance I see in the short term of getting the majority to agree with me. Weaning us off our perception of individuality would seem at best a long-term goal, particularly when our culture creates iconic heroes and villains in every walk of life and delineates so much around the individual identity. As a consequence I see less point in trying to resolve an argument such as whether there is a place for the bio-psycho-social lens or whether we should acknowledge that everything is situated by its social construction. Whatever my convictions may be, it would seem that our physical, perceptual and cultural realities mean that life is perceived by a great many of us as being a single individual's experience. This experience is understood in varying biological, psychological, social and spiritual ways. I doubt that we have the capacity to unify people's views on their reality and the 'ways' which dominate their world view.

We might, however, have a better chance of achieving agreement that *social interactions are the means by which we can influence other people's understanding, knowledge and skills*. Many different world views can accept that our means of supporting learning and learners results from our interplay within the social whole. All practice is social. This is a reality which people with very different theoretical starting points can readily understand and which may be widely endorsed.

Part II will consider whether such an approach to the complex weave of competing values and approaches, as well as the tensions between the singular and collective, can provide manageable, regenerative opportunities for education broadly and special and inclusion in particular.

Notes

1 The practitioners were using the Early Years Foundation Stage Profile. The assessment considered six areas of learning at age 5: personal, social and emotional; communication, language and literacy; problem solving, reasoning and numeracy; knowledge and understanding of the world; physical development; and creative development. This will be considered further in Chapter 5.
2 The series editor pointed out that what they choose often lacks any evidence.

3 This is the chance that they will correctly reject the null hypothesis, demonstrating that there was no relationship between the phenomena being measured. This conclusion resulted from analysis of 461 individual studies involved in 41 meta-analyses.
4 They also note the absence of many social costs from previous studies, such as child welfare, research and the pain and suffering and the impact of effective social policies and programmes and preventative care.
5 I have no evidence for this last statement. But you can decide for yourself:

> The main strategies for working with children and young people with FASD were:
>
> - clear, concrete, simple language backed up with visual clues;
> - consistency with language, rewards and routines;
> - being prepared to repeat instructions and rules;
> - implementing and sticking to a routine;
> - providing structure and constant supervision;
> - employing adaptive teaching techniques which focus upon the child's interests, strengths and developmental stage.
>
> (Carpenter, 2011, p. 40)

PART II

Developing a community of provision

5

OUR FOCUS UPON THE INDIVIDUAL AND THE CONTEXT

> He [Harold] had learned it was the smallness of people that filled him with wonder and tenderness, and the loneliness of that too. The world was made up of people putting one foot in front of the other: and a life might appear ordinary simply because the person living it had done so for a long time. Harold could no longer pass a stranger without acknowledging the truth that everyone was the same, and also unique; and this was the dilemma of being human.
>
> (Joyce, 2012, p. 150)

Beneath our smallness

As a parent of a disabled child I frequently find myself in the same space as other parents of disabled children. I am invariably struck by how very different our attitudes can be, even when we seem to be agreeing about something (or largely agreeing about something). On one particular occasion, when my son was ten, I was at a sports club for disabled people that he attended and was chatting to the father of a young man. This father began to talk about his son and the school he went to. He explained how his son was far happier now that he attended a special school. Previously he had been at the bottom of every group and every class, but now that he was attending special school he was experiencing success in various situations. The importance of this made sense to me, because I was always at the bottom of every set of every class of the schools I attended, too … or very close to the bottom. I was also worried about my son's experiences of success. I had frequently asked myself if by keeping him in the mainstream I was condemning him to a life of coming bottom. But my response to these concerns was different. Whereas this other father looked to place his child in a different kind of place, I hoped to encourage my son's schools to acknowledge and recognise success in many different ways. I hoped he might even increase the chance that everyone might experience the allure of achievement.

After having this conversation I wondered why our responses to a similar situation had been so different. Sat in the spectator's gallery I pondered why it was that this other father and I did not reach for the same solution. I was certain neither of us would readily adopt the other's perspective. He would struggle to believe that the school could change, just as I would struggle to accept that certain children should be in certain types of schools. Why would it be so difficult to convince each other?

At first, I settled on the well-worn presumption that we were simply two individuals with different interpretations of the world. But this did not seem to explain the conviction and intensity of the beliefs we had expressed. Looking down at the athletes in training, I began to wonder if our certainties arose not because we were two individuals but because neither the father nor I represented an individual viewpoint. Was it because we represented a myriad of social experiences? From the moment we were born we had both been surrounded by the attitudes and opinions of others. We were part of the things we had seen, heard and felt; we were part of a process emerging from interpretations and understandings, from all that we had witnessed or shared. This life of experience was our version of the world. So when I engaged in an argument with him, I was not engaging in an argument with an individual, but with his entire history and he with mine.

Together or apart, same or unique?

At the end of Chapter 4, I suggested that the social wraps around our individual and communal lives in such a manner that context underpins the processes of theorising and informs any attempt to act upon that theorising. For many people any suggestion that the social is in some way situated around or above other factors would be contentious. The tension between the individual and the social is evident in many fields. For example, a particular emphasis upon individualist understandings of knowledge can be identified within economic theory (Duguid, 2005). There is a tendency amongst some economic thinkers to view social explanations as giving way to variables that are beyond meaningful analysis and depiction. This view contends that our community is fundamentally a network of individuals. It is echoed in comments such as "There is no such thing as society" (Thatcher in interview with Keay, 1987). Individualization, though, is not a universal characteristic which emerges from all industrial and post-industrial societies (Groß, 2003). Others have recognised that both a communal and individualist approach are necessary (Johnson, Lorenz & Lundvall, 2002). There is also a long history, such as in the writings of Marx and Engels, which emphasises the communal nature of economics. Thompson (1971), for example, referred to a moral economy based upon consensus, underpinning not only economic processes but also many collective actions within history.

The tension has also been evident throughout the history of philosophy. Seixas (1993), for example, explored the long heritage of the philosophical idea within the world of academia that individuals alone cannot be trusted. It is only through the collective disputation of ideas amongst those with knowledge and experience in the issue under consideration that we can get closer to something which can be trusted. Even then, collective consensus can only be at best provisional. Arnold (1869) explored how shared ideas could unify the collective. He talked of people as being members of "one great whole" (p. 48), who could not be indifferent to others or have a fulfilling and healthy life "independent of the rest" (p. 48); yet he saw thought and knowledge as "eminently something individual" (p. 131) and the more we made it our own "the more power it has on us" (p. 131). The aim of authority, however, was to make our collective reason act upon individual reason, to give us access to the best ideas of others so that we can reflect upon our "our stock notions and habits" (p. 9).

Within the special and inclusive field the dominant theoretical debates frequently put ideas related to the social and individual in opposition. Many have sought ways to overcome this confrontation. Norwich (2002), for example, suggested that the individual level of analysis is of more relevance to issues such as teaching, learning and assessment, whilst the social level is of more relevance in relation to policy, though both have some relevance in either arena. He concluded that their false opposition resulted from:

- a view that social models relate to values now associated with inclusion (i.e. solidarity and equality), whilst the individual model relates to values associated with market systems (i.e. competition and individualism);
- each model's primary association with the professional cultures of sociology and psychology and their tendency to guard their academic territory.

His perception was that a biological, psychological or social level of analysis may be most appropriate for a particular process but the other levels can still contribute.

This kind of unifying presumption is shared by advocates of the International Classification of Functioning, Disability and Health (ICF). For example, Hollenweger (2011; 2013) suggested that the ICF makes assessment processes more transparent and negotiable, and provides a means to examine practices across policy, enabling discussion between different professional and non-professional perspectives. The focus, however, is still predominantly upon the individual. It is their physical and cognitive identity situated within their context. This brings with it a range of challenges identified in earlier chapters. In particular the focus upon the individual does not seem to provide a mechanism by which to challenge legacy practices or the wider social context.

I would broadly suggest that while the social model is accused of downplaying the experience of 'I' and the medical model too easily ignores the role of 'us', the bio-psycho-social model underplays the cultural history and power balances from which 'I' and 'us' emerge. As a result it may be tempting to pick up on the points being made at the end of Chapter 4 and propose a fourth component to fill this gap in the tripartite model; an expansive model to represent our social and environmental interdependence. This might serve to counterbalance the emphasis upon the individual within the bio-psycho-social model[1] which lends it to being another normative metric. This would enable a richer and more critically alert assessment than is evident in documents such as the ICF. I will avoid exploring such a proposal at this juncture though, because it would serve as a distraction from discussing the fundamental challenge underlying these models: what can be done about this underlying problem of the individual versus the collective, of 'I' versus 'us'?

Starting with a view of our self

Noddings (1996) suggests that we need to find a way which minimises the tendency to see the individual agent and the collective participant as separate. In a detailed commentary on the competing arguments and critiques associated with liberalism and communitarianism,[2] she concludes: "Education for community life requires both self-knowledge and collective-knowledge" (p. 267). She recognises, however, that to achieve this we need to reconceptualise the *self*. This is a particularly tricky cognitive challenge because of the manner in which the self comes to know its self and the degree to which we can reflect upon our self: "'external' or 'objective' reality can only be known by the properties of the mind and the symbol systems on which mind relies" (Bruner, 1996, p. 12).

Bruner describes, for example, how we tend towards seeing our self as a consequence of what we have been before. He points out that our self is experienced as a continuity across time, and that we seem to accept this 'folk belief' despite the arguments of philosophers and findings of researchers which suggest otherwise. He suggests that these kinds of human predispositions create limitations on the meanings we can make and engage with.

There are also cultural predispositions which need to be faced in such a reconceptualisation. Kristjansson (2009), for example, talked about problems in life being increasingly viewed through a "prism of disease".[3] He suggested that the root of our response is the "Western liberal conception of a self". This dominant Western liberal model emerged at a time of industrialisation and secularisation, with fundamental changes in how people worked, lived and communed with each other. As discussed in Chapter 1, it was also a period which saw a culmination in arguments about religious texts and the nature of humanity's relationship with their God. At the heart of this Western liberal model is the notion of self-concept: "the set of distinctive traits and characteristics that persons see as distinguishing them from others and that fuel their self-regarding emotions" (Kristjánsson, 2009, p. 122).

When the American psychologist William James introduced the notion of self-concept in 1890 he ascribed to it two parts; the 'I', which is the self-aware part of consciousness and the 'Me', which arises from our experiences with others (Long, Wood, Littleton, Passenger & Sheehy, 2011). He suggested that the experience of the self operates at different levels, from the physical to the spiritual; the difference between our actual and ideal selves underpins our self-esteem. Kristjánsson (2009) recorded that self-concept includes self-esteem, self-confidence and self-respect, as well as our relationship to the world and other people. It links therefore to our beliefs about our nature and how our self has been formed and developed; it also engages with the aspirations and threats which inform the self's trajectory.

This reading of Western liberal history suggests that since the Enlightenment of the eighteenth century the self has been widely regarded as independent of others. Our roots within social and cultural relationships are subsumed by our conviction of a singular self. The 'I' and 'Me' are set against all others. Kristjánsson pointed out that this is evident within the cultural norms associated with a young person's movement into adulthood. Within this dominant minority-world narrative, we must:

- find ourselves through reflection, planning a direction for our self and creating our own space;
- develop our beliefs and criticality, whilst resisting dependency;
- leave home, if we wish to grow up;
- move beyond the traditions of our upbringing.

This narrative has us moving from a place of comfort to a site of struggle, where through self-examination our self is re-established and reaffirmed.[4]

Wang and Chaudhary (2006), in their extensive review of the underpinning research, confirmed Kristjánsson's description of the Western liberal self. Drawing upon studies across many years they point to a robust pattern between cultures, which has been termed in such ways as independent versus interdependent and autonomous versus collective. They contrast the autonomous, independent, Western liberal model with the emphasis within other cultures, such as those that exist in parts of Asia, Africa, Southern America and Southern Europe. The evidence from communities in these regions emphasises a self which is situated in group solidarity and in maintaining social hierarchies and interpersonal harmony. In these cultures, it would seem that the priority is for a relational self, which focuses upon roles, duties and duties that arise in the social context.

Such cultural understandings of the self are exemplified in diverse ways. Rogoff (2003), for example, pointed to studies which described how adults and children brought up children within social networks in Polynesia, West Africa and India, whilst for a significant proportion of people in the United States this was seen as being the responsibility of parents. This is not to say that the behaviours predominantly associated with collective cultures do not exist within those cultures which emphasise independence and autonomy, or that the characteristics associated with independence and autonomy do not exist in those which emphasise interdependence and collectivity. The characteristic or behaviour may be valued in either culture; however, its relative priority will be different and it may be expressed in a different manner. In an evolving world, therefore, the construction of the self can be seen to be "an ever-complex process during which the individual and the collective interact, negotiate, and accommodate for the development of an adaptive and well-functioning psyche" (Wang & Chaudhary, 2006, p. 350).

The individual and collective models can be regarded as the "idealised developmental pathways" (Greenfield, Keller, Fuligni & Maynard, 2003, p. 463) allied to a universal processes associated with the self. However, just because we cannot say a single process, agent or agency is responsible for our self-conception, this is not the same as saying that no one can be responsible for removing negative influences on the development of that self (Kristjánsson, 2009).

Changing to what?

The last few paragraphs have emphasised that our concept of self is historically situated. It is something which we have changed and can change again. Making changes to our idea of who we are does not simply involve a choice between the two idealised pathways though. Greenfield et al. (2003) suggested that our understanding of the self can be informed by three major theoretical perspectives:[5]

- ecocultural – the influence of interacting with the material environment;
- sociohistorical – the influence of interacting with social and cultural process;
- values – the influence of interacting with the meanings and ideals within our psyche.

This complex interactive self can also be seen to physically operate within us. Within the field of biology, for example, the self is regarded by many as a community organism, a community of cells. Changes in the state of the organism are not seen as a consequence of particular actions but are interconnected interactions as part of the whole (Buchman, 2002).

There is also a long tradition of questioning the existence of the self. Siderits, Thompson and Zahavi (2011) described three broad types of view about the self within Indian and Western philosophy:

1   The Substantialist view is that the self has substance and properties, including consciousness, which are located at one time or different times. The self is an agent and can be morally appraised.
2   The Non-Substantialist view sees the self as being consciousness without agency, being momentary awareness. Agency is seen as the capacity to account past and potential future experiences within a narrative of consciousness.
3   The Non-Self view sees us as having no self. Our struggles emerge because we try to explain our selves. Everything is fleeting. The 'I' may feel like a unity but it is actually evidence of the limitations of our cognition.

Even though the first view is the one which we are most likely to experience (particularly in what is labelled the Western liberal culture), there is a growing body of psychological and neurological research which suggests that it is not the most accurate description of the processes we undergo. Hood (2012), for example, pointed to research which shows that we are not directly in contact with reality. Our experience is always an abstraction and an interpretation of the world; so much so that we experience something as reality even after it has been explained to us that it is illusory. Ramachandran (2003) talked about the illusion of free will. He pointed to studies using PET[6] scans which showed that about a second before you consciously make a decision to move a finger your brain is evidencing 'readiness potential'. These studies suggested that the brain is preparing to move the finger before you have decided to do so. If such scans are correct it suggests that your consciousness is either not aware of itself when it make some decisions, is not involved in making some decisions or is merely a record of a decision made without self-awareness.

My self

So now I must return to the suggestion by Noddings with which I began this section, the recognition that we need to recreate our notion of self. If I am to ask others to take up such a challenge, it seems salient to begin with my own understanding.

I recognise people to be meaningless in relation to the universe, a pattern amongst the patterns of matter.[7] The moment we begin to apply meaning is the moment at which our contextualisation begins. We take up and create a social place. The self does not exist in some substantialist manner, even though we experience it to do so. I therefore question whether there is a notion of 'I' against a notion of 'Us', whether 'I' and 'Us' are two truths. I prefer to see them as two conceits which arise from our deeper notion of just being part of 'Them'. 'I' and 'Us' only exist because our separation requires comparison to others if we are not merely to be part of the mass. The narratives we must use to manage our experiences mean that our sense of separation is most easily described by creating relationships to others.

This notion of a 'self' that creates 'I' and 'Us' as a response to our meaninglessness does not alter the dilemmas, though, which exist because of the dominant cultural narratives. Some people will fill the separation with spiritual or religious notions, some with the almost certainties of science, others with sensory satisfaction or through the challenges of competition or control, and so forth. Nearly all people growing up within the minority-world will not explore this separation as part of their education, though. Whatever explanation emerges to provide a more complete sense of self comes to dominate the narratives they tell about the experiences they have and about the experience of others. This of itself creates the form of a substantial self. We take on the substance of our position. Our routines, our situations, our established practices, our personal and collective experience inform the opportunities we have and our interpretations of them. Like the shapes popularised by Gaetano Kanizsa, where the geometric edges seem real but emerge from our experiences of shapes (see Figure 5.1) or a rows of faces created by their background (see Figure 5.2) our substance emerges from the context around us.

This notion of self does not deny the biological and physical experience of living, but it explains how the self merges and emerges from that experience. We can all have the individual biological and physical experience of an appendicitis, but our narrative and the narrative of those around us will provide the substantial version of our self in that situation.

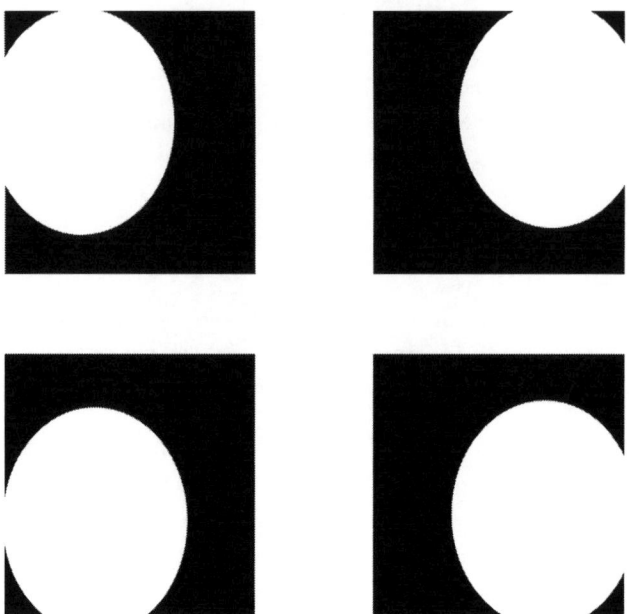

FIGURE 5.1 Do you see ovals, squares and a cross in these shapes?

FIGURE 5.2 Do you see rows of faces emerging from the white background?

But how do I get others to challenge their individualised notions of self? It seems unlikely that many will identify with the notion I have just described. However, many may recognise some of the key factors within that narrative. They may recognise that their self has the capacity to be flexible, that it is context dependent and is established within relationships. This less substantial version might inform the collective reason which acts upon individual reason.

My attempt to influence this process begins by contextualising the role of the 'I' within three examples (assessment, intelligence and development) from schooling, and highlighting why an increased emphasis upon 'Us' might be a better starting point for developing our practices.

Individualised thinking within the social process of education

Bernstein (2000) suggested that school individualises failure and in so-doing legitimises inequalities. The reason a child does not do well is put down to their "inborn facilities (cognitive, affective) or to the cultural deficits relayed by the family which come to have the force of inborn facilities" (Bernstein, 2000, p. xxiv). This pattern of response is evident, for example, in the consistent imbalance around special educational support. In the vast majority of nations there is far more emphasis upon identifying boys and students from families with lower incomes. There is frequently an ethnic aspect to provision too. For instance, data from a 2005 census of 6.5 million English pupils showed under-representation and over-representation of some minority ethnic groups generally within special educational needs (SEN) as well as specifically amongst certain categories (Lindsay, Pather & Strand, 2006). The individualised framing of 'the problem' is evident too across time and policy eras. For example, in their analysis of Scottish policy in relation to additional needs, Tisdall and Riddell (2006) demonstrate how the individualized approach was maintained despite shifts in centres of control. However, what were meant to be experienced as individual approaches were defined by the social processes which governed them. For example, the practices established in policy tended to situate power within bureaucratic processes and bureaucratic rights, as well as within the hands of professional decision-makers.

The prevalent practice of assessing, classifying and categorising individuals within an educational context has been shown to define those who fall both within and outside categories (Waterhouse, 2004; Gillman, Heyman & Swain, 2000). This has consequences for both the individuals and the collective, in terms of bureaucracy and identity. The nature of the funding and support, as well as the relationships between all the members of the school community, is guided by the various groupings which emerge. People find themselves to be insiders, outsiders or somewhere between the two, in a range of formal and informal groupings, and this fundamentally affects how people respond to them. For those who do not have the protection of a category, for example, there can be an authoritarian, punitive response to behaviour. The blame is not laid at the door of the labelled condition but at the door of the non-labelled child (Graham, 2006).

A range of notions which are fundamental to our education systems are frequently associated with individuals, but need not be. Hand (2007), for example, sees the notion of intelligence as a useful everyday concept which provides a background to the expectations a teacher will have about an individual pupil. He suggests that as a concept it is widely understood beyond the highly debatable and widely critiqued technical psychological definitions.[8] Within the same journal there is, however, an article which rebuts Hand's analysis (Gingell, 2007). This article suggests, amongst other things, that intelligence is fundamentally context specific and so cannot be generalised across activities.[9] Clark and Chalmers (1998) demonstrate how ideas of thought go wider still. They talk about the Extended Mind, drawing on a range of literature which positions cognition as a continuous process in relation to the environment. Our cognitive processes are extended into our physical and social situations, and our mental states are to some degree constituted by the states of others.

Notions of distributed cognition and extended mind position our awareness as an ongoing, context-dependent process. Through language and the physicality of communication people think together in creative and productive ways. Our collective communications can be seen to be not merely a process of interaction, but to be interthinking (Littleton & Mercer, 2013). Similarly, there are a range of studies which demonstrate that significant creations either within organisations or by people regarded as individual creators are almost always the result of complex collaborative processes (Sawyer & DeZutter, 2009). It would seem that by individualising notions of intelligence we exclude the rich body of evidence which suggests that it is far more complex than that.

Similarly, models of child development have frequently been one-dimensional, requiring that the child is viewed in isolation (Hedegaard, 2009). In the 1970s and 1980s, critiques of this approach (such as those by Riegel, Bronfenbrenner and Bruner) led to conceptions of development as a complex and dynamic process. These recognised the diverse manner in which we all interact with social conditions and experiences. The individualist mind-set still predominates, however. For example, as mentioned in the last chapter, in England, in the first decade of the twenty-first century, government agencies began to provide developmental journals to parents, which purported to describe typical patterns of development. These included specific editions for parents of deaf babies, babies with Down syndrome and babies with a visual impairment, as well as children and young people with multiple needs. The developmental journal linked to the Early Years Foundation Stage (EYFS) for pre-school children. In the 2013 version the EYFS included 17 early learning goals and lists of developmental statements defining what learners should achieve. Practitioners were supposed to match children to these statements to identify those who fail or exceed them. In so doing these individualised goals and statements defined the nature of learning difficulties, giftedness and additional needs for all[10] (Rix & Parry, 2014).

In contrast, Hedegaard (2009) suggested that a child's development needs to be understood as an institutionalised process. Children are always participating in a dynamic interaction with social structures, practices, traditions, conditions and discourses. She suggested that research needs to examine the traditions of institutional practices and the values and norms of those involved in everyday practices with children. Our research needs to explore the tensions between the demands of different social institutions, be they a kindergarten, family home, playgroup, and so on. It has to ask how these are experienced by the child, how they impact upon their motivations and what conflict is created for the child which can inform their development. This development can be seen as 'a sociocultural trajectory' through diverse institutional practices, affected by variables such as biology, material conditions, and cultural and institutional traditions and norms. I shall return to these ideas in Chapter 6.

Squeezing selected individuals into individualised processes

The consequence of having individualised notions of assessment, intelligence and development coming together in practice creates fundamental contradictions. Much of my thinking around these contradictions emerged from my experiences of delivering the early intervention programme I mentioned in Chapter 2, which I undertook with my son in the first few years of his life. Within a few weeks of him being identified as different, professionals were coming through our door making recommendations. We listened and gladly entered the world of early intervention. The questions we subsequently began to ask led me to undertake a number of research projects with other families.

Through interviews and observation, it became evident that the processes of early intervention were at odds with its aims and values. Its presumption of developmental needs and its focus upon individual deficits and capacities meant that for a great many participants it could not be a fun part of the everyday as the theory intended. Consider this quote from a practitioner (Rix & Paige-Smith, 2011, pp. 34–35):

> As I say with Tim, because of his Down Syndrome he doesn't necessarily learn exactly the same as other children, but by giving that one-to-one help and the experiences he's able to really develop to his full potential, but it is a matter of lots of repetition, starting things at an earlier age than you would do with another child, so as you're laying those foundations for him, and so you're starting you know could be months before another child would be ready for it, for doing that particular thing.

This thoroughly decent and very professional early-years practitioner assumed that having a labelled syndrome changes the way a person learns and needs to be taught; she perceived a thing called 'potential' which can be filled up; and she had a belief that because the child is not ready to do something we need to start teaching them earlier. The practitioner recognised contradictions in her position though (ibid.):

I think sometimes you do get caught up in what you're supposed to be doing, and sometimes it's what the parents expectations of you are as well, that they want to see learning, but I do find myself often saying well you know, trying to get the child to do this I often say to all parents "we wouldn't be doing this with another child, they would just be playing, we would not be expecting them to sit down, do this, it's not a natural thing for children to be doing".

The more I spoke to parents and practitioners, the more unusual it felt that we were encouraging people to be doing something we could agree was "not a natural thing". Some children and families appeared to benefit, but many appeared not to. In the case of my son and me, the hours and hours we spent on early intervention mainly taught him to associate organised learning activities[11] with a failure to learn.

A few years on, I still experience this uncertainty in relation to my son. Very kind and decent people seem to be doing things not because it makes particular sense, but rather because that is their function. They seemed determined to overcome what he cannot do. And I wonder, does this legitimise his inequality to others?

This leads me to extrapolate my experience.

Forcing individualised approaches onto everyone

My son has never made the progress expected in reading and writing. However, the technologies he does make progress with have been little in evidence. We have, for example, rarely seen him being encouraged to use photography, YouTube or typing, though he has shown an affinity for all these approaches. There has been far more focus upon evidence-based techniques, simple reading schemes and more practice.[12] Why have people been so fixated by reading and writing? After all, we are all happy to accept that some people are not particularly good at sport, cooking, friendships, dancing, public speaking, and so forth. We do not expect everyone to reach a particular level in these other important skills.

Literacy is a cornerstone of education. We look to it as a tool of transformation, in terms of knowledge and income. But it seems likely that it has taken up this position not for sound pedagogical reasons, nor to enable equitable outcomes, but because it a key component of the dominant individualist paradigm. We believe we are doing the right thing by imposing it on everyone. Reading and writing are positioned as key skills for individually accessing and creating collective sources of knowledge. It allows our systems to expect independence, to spread messages of choice, to construct us as individuals who can be responsible for our own actions and knowledge.[13]

Text literacy is society's main tool for assessing and ranking us and is widely positioned as an issue for any individual within the education and employment market place. Illiteracy is frequently cited as a cause of low pay and a hindrance to educational training. For example, in a United Nations report, *The Economic and Social Cost of Illiteracy* (Martinez & Fernandez, 2010) the underlying premise is that a professional job is better than a non-professional job because the salary is greater.

Economic value is therefore linked to literacy. This elevates those who have the capacity to read and write and degrades those who do not. The experience of success and failure perpetuate our conviction.

In prioritising this kind of literacy, we have not only come to see it as something essential for schooling but also a means by which to measure the success of schooling and national culture. I have not examined national debates in relation to other languages, but I have sought out papers and online articles in English-speaking countries. It would seem that every time national statistics are released about levels of literacy they are greeted with outpourings from politicians, academics, parents and pundits. There is a wave of articles and speeches which fret about the state of schools, modern teaching, children's interests, television, computers, mobile phones, phonics, reading for meaning, reading for pleasure, dyslexia, the last set of policies, the current set of policies, the next set of policies, funding, parenting, economics, the state of the nation, the state of business, the future, the past, the creation of inequality, the perpetuation of inequality, and so forth.

What is rarely mentioned is just how difficult English is as a language to learn to read and write. For example, a study of European languages (Seymour, Aro & Erskine, 2003) suggested that English is a particularly difficult complex-syllable language. The groups of children[14] in the study found it far harder to read English words and non-words than the children reading other simple-syllable languages and other complex-syllable languages (see Figure 5.3).

In these national debates, there is also little mention made about levels of literacy being relatively consistent across English-speaking countries. For example, international reports suggest that between 10 and 20 per cent of adults are illiterate (level 1 or below)[15] in all English-speaking countries and between 40 and 50 per

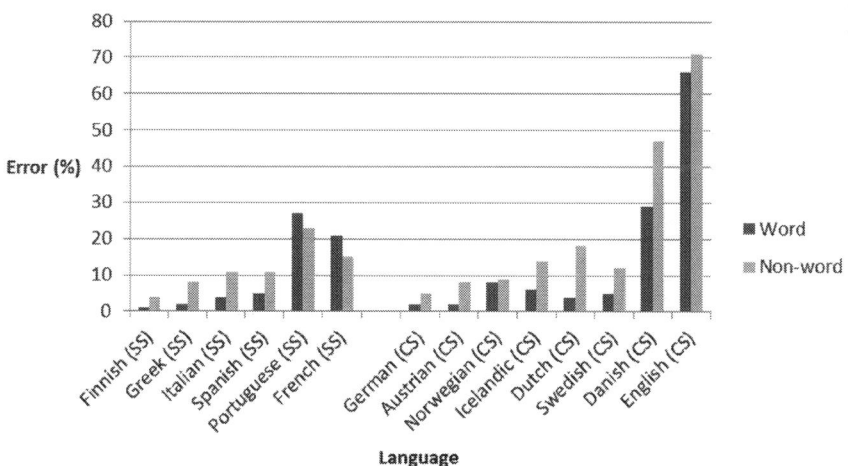

FIGURE 5.3   Error rates (per cent) for familiar word and simple non-word reading by simple syllable (SS) and complex syllable (CS) language groups. (Based on Seymour et al., 2003.)

cent are not deemed suitably competent for marketplace requirements (level 1 & 2 or below) (Australian Bureau of Statistics, 2013; National Center for Educational Statistics, 2006; Satherley, Lawes & Sok, 2008; OECD, 2013a).

This evidence seems to suggest that in English-speaking countries there is a limit to how many people we can expect to read and write at a complex level. So why do we keep on insisting that individuals learn to do it? As our discussion in Chapter 2 demonstrated, it is not as if experts can agree about how best to proceed in relation to reading difficulties/dyslexia. It is, after all, a skill we have come to regard as a universal need only relatively recently. For the vast majority of our history it was something which very few people made use of. Given the ongoing developments of new technologies, it is probably a skill which the majority of people will be able to do without within a few decades. We could already design teaching and assessment methods which did not rely upon it; we could design public information systems which do not rely upon it; we could stop rewarding reading and writing above other socially and economically valuable skills. We could recognise that just because literate jobs have historically been paid more, this does not mean the jobs have a greater social significance or contribute more to individual or communal happiness. It does not mean that there are not many socially significant and fulfilling ways of working which do not require that an individual can read.

Now, I cannot pretend I do not like to read and write, or that they are skills which can be of great benefit to some people, but I know that I could find ways to get my ideas across without them. I know that they are a barrier to understanding just as much as they are a bridge to knowledge. Should we sacrifice so many because we want everyone to access the transformative power of written text or because it serves as a useful tool for selection?

I would not suggest that we should stop helping people to learn to read and write, but it seems sensible to ask, if nearly half the population struggle to use the technology effectively, should we not be putting more emphasis upon alternative tools and valuing them more as inputs and outputs of learning? After all, they involve skills which we have collectively shared in the past and still share in many situations.[16]

Identifying the individual amongst all the others

This capacity to focus upon individual needs to the detriment of many is a theme which re-emerges frequently within education. Education is purportedly premised upon the needs of the individual. We all have a right to be educated, for example, as enshrined in article 26 of the Universal Declaration of Human Rights and article 28 of the Convention on the Rights of the Child. But this blanket requirement to prepare all children to "live an individual life" (OUNHC, 1989, p. 3) often means that the individual has the right to become lost within the mass of individual learners. As will be discussed in Chapter 6, this is partly a consequence of teaching large numbers of people at the same time and of dominant pedagogic approaches, but it is also a consequence of how we focus our support and the political and policy pressures around provision and resources.

The individual model of support was evident globally within our study of 55 administrations. Almost every administration which could afford to do so funded additional in-class support and/or external professional support. This international consensus existed despite:

- a lack of evidence that individual funding was productive;
- its inability to drive change for a wider population;
- its tendency to limit the capacity of teachers and school systems to deal with difference (Slee, 2008).

It was frequently reported that there was a growing demand for funding, as well as bias and inconsistency in its distribution. It was evident that bureaucratic processes dominated proceedings, leading to confrontation and a self-serving need to obtain or maintain resources. It was also reported that the system trapped children in inappropriate provision or failed to provide them with the support they needed (Rix, Sheehy, Fletcher-Campbell, Crisp & Harper, 2013a).

Internationally, a range of support or inclusion plans were in evidence, which operated at different levels of the system. These plans generally focused upon individual children, and very few upon the broader systems and structures for all pupils. By far the most common type of plan, mentioned by the majority of administrations, was the individual education plan (IEP), though there was no discussion of its effectiveness[17] (Rix et al., 2013a). An extensive systematic literature review looking at the international use of IEPs (Mitchell, Morton & Hornby, 2010) concluded that IEPs had unproven efficacy and were produced and used in an inconsistent manner. They also recognised that IEPs were heavily influenced by behavioural psychology and were constrained by having to fulfil multiple educational, legal, planning, accountability and placement purposes.

The tendency of such individual processes to support unreconstructed practices is evident in a Swedish study involving content analysis of 51 IEPs (Isaksson, Lindqvist & Bergström, 2007). Researchers identified the degree to which the difficulties and solutions were associated with the individual or the institution (see Figure 5.4): 34 of the plans were primarily identified as an individual problem to be targeted primarily through individual measures; 15 were primarily identified as an individual problem to be targeted primarily through school practices; and two were primarily identified as a school problem to be targeted through school practices. The researchers' analysis was that despite changes in policy there had been little practical change within schools and that the old traditions still applied to special and mainstream. The problem was still the problem with the child.

The inherent limitation of an individual planning focus is underlined by it being something which we can't do for all students. Within Norway, for example, the notion of individual planning led to an adaptive curriculum for every child (Rix et al., 2013a). This was meant to be a curriculum which was adapted to meet the needs of each student. At one point in time, teachers were expected to create an individualised plan for every student in their class. When we spoke to practitioners in Norway, they told

		Individual problem			School problem		
Individual measures	High		1				
	Middle	1	9				
	Low	1	20	2			
School measures	Low	3	9	2	2		
	Middle	1					
	High						
		High	Middle	Low	Low	Middle	High

FIGURE 5.4 Focus of difficulties and suggested measures within IEPs. (Based upon Isaksson, Lindqvist & Bergaström, 2007.)

us it had been an unrealistic aspiration which they either could not fulfil, could not maintain, or had not attempted. After a few years, the idea was dropped and they returned to focusing upon a few individuals, who frequently had an individualised curriculum, frequently in isolation from their peers in the same classroom.[18]

The argument from inclusionists is not that individuals do not require additional support. As Slee (2008) notes, this is "a basic requirement for educational participation" (p. 110). The argument is about how the resources are deployed and allotted. Individualised assessments simplify the complex multiple relationships out of which individuals, their cultures and cognitions appear. As a consequence they cannot accurately represent that complexity and how it can be supported. There are those who have suggested that such an oversimplification is convenient for the political agenda behind the process. Children become isolated individuals, "units of analysis" (McDermott & Varenne, 1995, p. 337) with the state as record-keeper. This agenda primarily seeks the maintenance of the current social hierarchies; as such, it is not overly concerned that inequalities are recreated through selective measurement against idealized identities or assumptions of normality.

Citing a range of writers, Jóhannesson (2006) suggests that recognised inclusive practices will not be commonly applied whilst students are positioned as individual, diagnosable consumers of services. The individualised approach requires needs to be objectified and quantified in order to fit within managerial systems. There they must compete with other economic priorities within budgets for the school and administrative authority. For example, Jóhannesson describes studies in which Swedish teachers who wished to work more broadly to prevent marginalisation were constrained by head-teachers who had different priorities. More generally, he suggested that the focus upon independent learners and individuals ready for the work marketplace also creates a restricted notion of school effectiveness. Not only does it constrain the vision of education for all students, but it both situates those who cannot meet these aspirations as limited and increases the chance that their performance will reflect badly upon the school (Jóhannesson, 2006).

Jóhannesson (2006) contends that these constraints on inclusion and the focus upon individualisation and learning difficulties restrict a genuine focus upon broader equity issues. He suggests that they are further constrained by the established, individualised, medicalised responses and by the centrality of human rights to international agreements. Vlachou concurs: "Questions of needs, rights and equity include decision-making processes and compromises among unequally competing interest-groups of who gets what, how, when, why, and with what consequences" (2004, p. 6).

As discussed in Chapter 3, arguments associated with individual rights and equality can be used to excuse a wide variety of behaviours and can be seen as detached from everyday social situations. As Vlachou (2004) notes:

- They do not resolve competing policy discourses.
- They do not offer strategies for change.
- They are assumed to exist but do not invoke specific measures.
- They operate as technical issues within bureaucratic practices.
- They function primarily as rhetoric.

She suggests that if they are to be effective they must be grounded in everyday contexts, they must be linked to specific strategies that secure change and they must lead to enforceable sanctions. To be effective the individualist model must be rooted in collectivist, interdependent processes.

Still putting one foot in front of the other

The substance of our rights emerges from the context around us. It is not surprising therefore that a context which is inequitable will prioritise rights inequitably. Similarly, the substance of change in relation to other practices associated with changing education will depend upon the context which situates those practices. Consider the preparation of teachers. As was noted in Chapter 3, the solution to problems associated with special and inclusive is frequently seen to lie in teacher preparation. Brownell and Kiely (2010) suggest that to be effective, teacher preparation depends upon the capacity of systems to change practices and meet the needs of pupils. Their preparation needs to confront beliefs and assumptions about teachers and schools as well as beliefs and assumptions about learning, teaching and the nature of impairment; and it needs to engage people in research and theories about impairment and the effectiveness of different practices. Of course, as previous chapters have explicated, deciding which research, theories, beliefs and assumptions to focus upon is not that simple.

The description Brownell and Kiely provide of teacher preparation in the United States exemplifies the problem. They noted that special education teacher training largely emerged from institutions serving specific impairments, leading to a categorical approach;[19] this gave way to a competency-based view of teacher needs,[20] which increasingly brought them in line with class teachers; and this, in turn, was overtaken by the understanding that teaching and learning was a process of social construction. We might therefore assume that preparation of special and class teachers has arrived at the point at which context is recognised and the significance of collective processes is prioritised. As the paper noted, the complexity of teacher and learner interactions had come to the fore as well as the importance of building on students' values and experiences. However, their recommendations for the future of teacher preparation seems to step back from this broad focus upon context. Their recommended next step is to prepare teachers for response to intervention (RTI).

The RTI approach requires evaluating the child and their learning in relation to the learning situation, then assigning the correct practitioner to an appropriate tier of instruction. The number of tiers can vary between RTI approaches, but the key is that academic intervention increases in intensity as the student moves across tiers, becoming more teacher-centred and explicitly scripted, more frequent, over a longer period. The practitioner must appropriately conceptualise how the child will be worked with at that tier, working with increasingly small groups and having increasing specialisation as they move through the tiers (Fuchs & Fuchs, 2006). In order to deliver RTI, Brownell and Kiely suggest that teachers need to draw from the waves of policy, research and practice which they have identified. They suggest that teachers need:

- a sound grasp of subject content and how it is best taught;
- understanding of specific problems associated either generally or specifically for children with identified impairments in specific subject areas;
- understanding of how technology can mitigate learning barriers or support access;
- understanding of particular assessments and interventions which can enable them to provide explicit, intensive instruction which has meaning within wider curriculum.

Here then is the individual model reframed. Fuchs, Fuchs and Stecker (2010 – Figure 5.5) show how it is little different to the models devised in the 1960s and 1970s, which represented the provision and resources available as education began to accept people who had been previously ignored by schools or had been kept in long-stay institutions (see Figures 5.7 and 5.8). Even advocates of a blurring of special education and mainstream struggle to fit RTI into their arguments. As Figure 5.6 shows, there is still a hierarchy of expertise and implicitly a narrower student base.

These developments suggest that whilst there has been a shift in the collective understanding in relation to learning and teaching for all, special education researchers and practitioners still focused upon individualised notions of need. As discussed in the last chapter, in relation to foetal alcohol syndrome, people still sought to identify certain learners as inherently different and in need of inherently different teaching. So even though Brownell and Kiely could note that

- Special education teachers had moved from being a diagnostic specialist to being a specialist in interventions and curricula.
- Class teachers had shifted towards more generalised teaching and class management skills.
- Both were seen to require having a broad range of skills to hand.

the traditional focus upon the separate child remained.

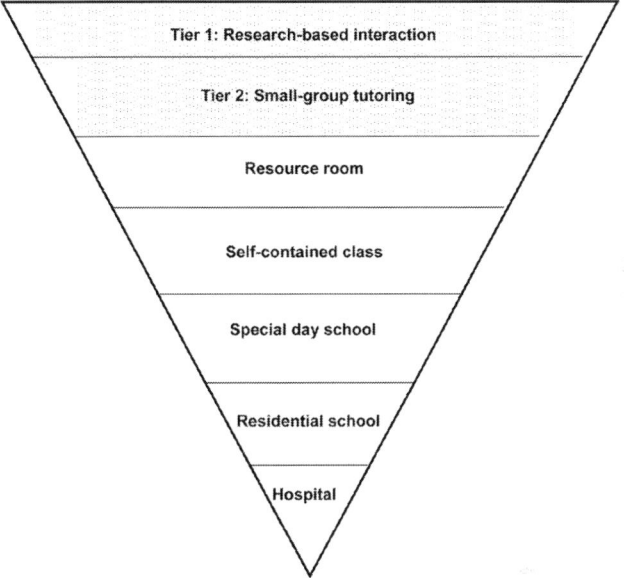

FIGURE 5.5 The continuum taking response to intervention into account (Fuchs et al., 2010).

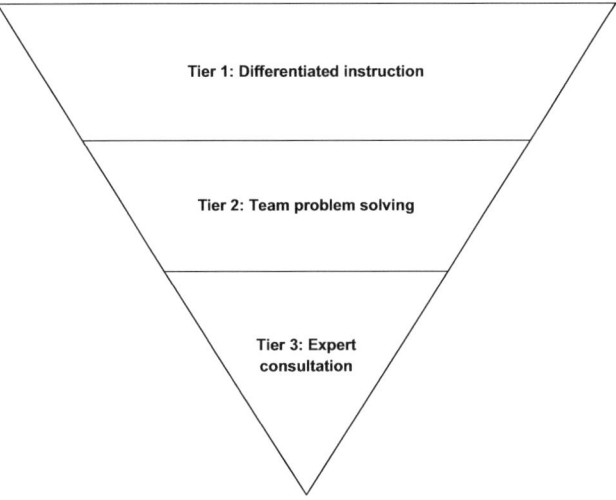

FIGURE 5.6 A new continuum of placements and services (Fuchs et al., 2010).

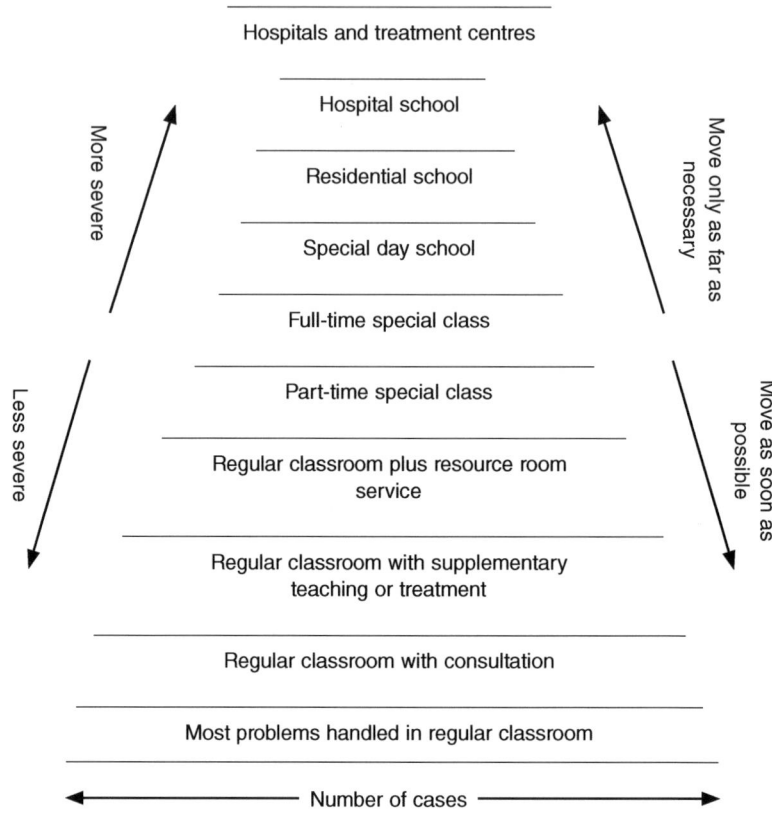

FIGURE 5.7 Reynolds' (1962) hierarchical structure of special education.

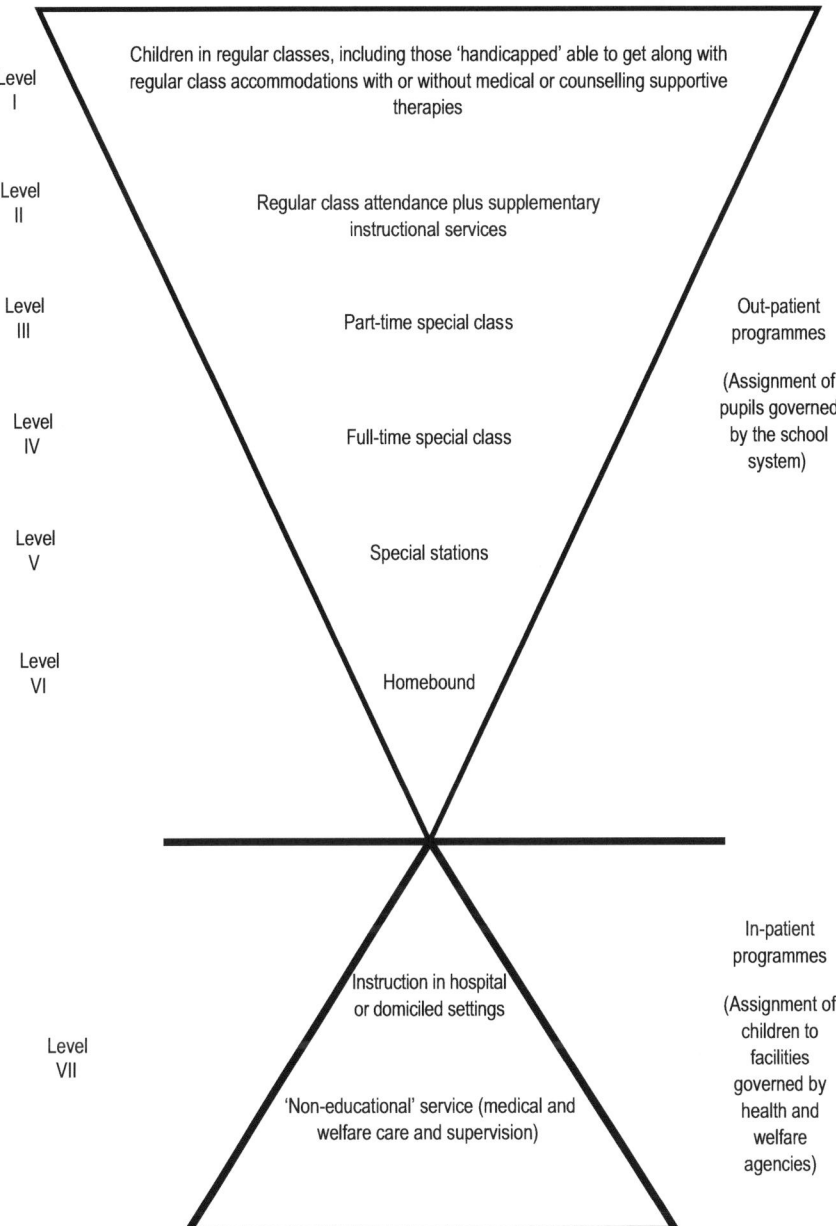

FIGURE 5.8 Deno's Cascade Model of special educational provision (1970).

A life might appear ordinary

At the conclusion to their paper, Brownell and Kiely recognised that delivering RTI through teacher preparation was a lofty aspiration but maintained that it held out hope for the future. However, the model they recommended is not one which is generally associated with all the children within the class. The model they recommended focuses upon exceptions. It is an individualist one. It emerges from the line which runs back to the institutions. It has the potential to be more flexible than its behaviourist, categorical forebears, but it is still about identifying the pupil who is not fitting in. The student who needs intervention is the one who is not responding to the curriculum as the majority of their peers are; their support is provided by practitioners with increasing specialisation. The model therefore contains much the same problems as the ones which their well-written article showed had been so carefully deconstructed over the last few decades. The focus is still upon the curriculum as it is; it is still about how the individual can be changed to fit back in; and if the individual cannot they must be increasingly separated for increasing amounts of time with people whose expertise has increasingly less to do with the mainstream classroom.

I have little doubt that excellent practitioners, well trained within the RTI approach, will feel that they are well positioned to provide expert support and timely intervention. They will feel validated by their training and will feel confident that they can find the answers to the needs they identify in the children with whom they work. I also have little doubt that there will be some pupils who will thrive with this approach and transfer skills learned in their RTI environment into the everyday of life. But I am equally certain that there will be children who do not respond in this manner; that some highly trained professionals will not deliver it as the researchers intended; that it will create a false sense of reliance within those teachers without the right training; that biases and assumptions will still play a part; and that many children who do not stand out from the crowd will continue to be taught in a way which limits their opportunities to learn. This is the lesson from many countries, over many years and in many contexts. Approaches with a tendency to individualise may serve some but they will fail many more.

I am sure that many supporters of RTI would struggle to see how it can be regarded as a barrier to inclusion. At its core is the notion that a teacher looks at how their way of working is impacting upon the children they are teaching. Isn't this at the heart of much writing on the topic? Don't we need teachers to be alert to their practices so that they can avoid marginalising pupils and can maximise their opportunities? The problem with any process which assesses individuals, however, is a tendency towards isolation. The individualised intervention creates a mechanism to remove the individual who doesn't fit into the system. It encourages teachers not to reflect too deeply, and so it does not shift the status quo. As was noted at the start of Chapter 1, a commitment to inclusion within a system which is committed to individualisation may rapidly lead to marginalisation. It does not encourage teachers to engage with alternative methods that may benefit the many.

The study by Snowling (2013) mentioned previously encapsulates this problem. This is a well conducted piece of research, but at its heart are the contradictions explored so far in this chapter. Working with teachers who had used the developmental Early Years Foundation Stage Profile, Snowling confirmed that they correctly identified that 16.4 per cent of the school population involved in the study were behind expectation in relation to reading. This is, of course, the range you would expect based on the international figures cited above. However, as discussed in Chapter 4, the author concludes that teacher assessment of reading using these scales was robust enough to identify those who should receive support, and that this process should be undertaken within an RTI model. The response is not to recognise that this study confirms a problem at the heart of our education system. It is not to call for alternative ways to communicate our learning goals across the curriculum to 1 in 6 of our pupils who we know will not achieve moderate levels of literacy (and to the other 2 in 6 who will be struggling). It is to focus upon an individualised assessment and intervention program which leaves everything as it is. We will be seen to be doing something based upon solid research evidence, but the problem will not have gone away.

Seeking a collective response to the dilemma of being human

There is a fundamental quandary which this chapter is struggling with. How do we shift a cultural norm away from its individualistic conviction to one which puts greater emphasis upon our interdependence, when our sensory experience of being alive may lead some to suggest, in the manner of methodological individualism, that all social experiences can be reduced to the actions of individuals? Our sense that we are individuals first and foremost limits our capacity to focus upon socio-cultural factors which create and are created by our experience of being individuals. Given that the focus of this book is education, the remit for influence is inevitably constrained to the narrow political arena defined by our systems for learning. The next chapter will focus upon pedagogic opportunities and challenges and how context can usefully inform everyday school practices, but this last section will give an example of how three wider social shifts in perception can provide educationalists with the space to create a shift in conceptualisation.

In Chapter 1, the wide range of complex purposes associated with education was outlined. The aspirations driving education's development have represented the values of those in a dominant social position within the relevant community. It would seem reasonable to suggest that in 2014, as I write this, three forces are particularly dominant in the minority-world:

- the advocates of a growth economy;
- the advocates of standards;
- the need to manage the system economically and politically.

Narratives around choice and equality are powerful and can influence decision-makers, but, as discussed previously, they tend to come second-place to the economic, bureaucratic and political priorities. These are evident in the pressures on education:

- to provide a work force suited to the requirements of the marketplace;
- to constantly demonstrate that it is improving its results in relation to others;
- to operate within the available budget.

In order to create a cultural shift we have to find ways of doing so which align with these dominant forces and priorities.

Opportunities for change are always context specific. In England at the time of writing, for example, there was a well-established window of opportunity within the field of business. The headlines which greeted most surveys of business focused upon numeracy and literacy, but it was interdependency skills which business identified as being more urgently needed. They were concerned with life experience and attitudes, team-working skills, communication skills, business and customer awareness, customer-handling skills, foreign language skills and international cultural awareness (e.g. Leitch, 2006; Shury, Winterbotham, Davies, Oldfield, Spilsbury & Constable, 2010; CBI, 2013). Frequently satisfaction levels were half that for literacy and numeracy. A report written by a range of business leaders (Anderson, 2014) included three key recommendations which underlined this tendency. Alongside STEM[21] and language communications skills, there were calls for a focus upon interpersonal and intercultural competencies and attributes such as team-working. These were seen as just as important as core subject proficiency, as was the need to find methods of assessment to evidence these skills. Such calls represent an opportunity to encourage an appreciation of interdependence within education.

The call to assess collective processes within Anderson (2014) was presented alongside an entreaty to understand why England was slipping in International Standards tables, particularly the Programme for International Student Assessment (PISA).[22] This entreaty reflected the fascination amongst the media and politicians the world-over for PISA results. Many had regarded these tests as offering an objective comparison between education systems in relation to numeracy, literacy and science. But the tests had their doubters. For example, evidence suggested that the tests were not of equivalent difficulty within each country and that positions varied according to the statistical approach adopted (Kreiner & Christensen, 2013). The image of PISA as a flawed system was underlined by the national variations in the submission of children identified with SEN. In a sample of 19 countries from the 2009 tests (Smith & Douglas, 2014):

- Five of the 19 countries had less than 1 per cent of children identified with SEN in their submission (Japan,[23] Mexico, Shanghai, Korea, Hong Kong);
- Six of the 19 countries had over 6 per cent[24] of children identified with SEN in their submission (Canada, Ireland, Belgium, Sweden, USA, Iceland).

When this sample was compared with the OECD figures for 65 countries in 2009, it was evident that four of the five countries cited by Smith and Douglas which had less than 1 per cent[25] were in the top six for science, in the top eight for reading, and in the top nine for maths.

There were many other stories which this data told; however, the existence of evidence that questioned the usefulness of these international tests seemed to be largely irrelevant. If the decision-makers had collectively bought into the concept of PISA, as seemed to be the case, then it would have become an accepted truth and be very hard to dislodge. There were opportunities to challenge the status quo, however. For example:

- It had been announced that PISA would measure collaborative problem-solving from 2015 (OECD, 2013b).
- Most of the top countries would be typically defined as collective cultures.
- The most effective European system (Finland[26]) had a comprehensive education system.
- The most effective American system largely had an inclusive education system (Canada[27]) .

These circumstances presented genuine opportunities to change political will within countries dominated by the individualist model and by a focus upon school choice.

A third opportunity was also evident at the time of writing, in relation to funding. Although most countries operated additional funding models based around individual assessment, increasing costs and a recognition of bureaucratic and academic shortcomings meant that administrations were frequently changing or developing new ways of distributing funds. An alternative model beginning to emerge was one based around collective assessment. Tetler (2000) suggested that consideration should be given to evaluation of the whole class or learning group and how it interacts in order to define funding. A model I developed in the context of the English system (Rix, 2009c) was premised upon an assessment of the needs of all those involved in the class situation, including the training and support needs of staff. It gave greater control to schools, reduced bureaucracy and freed up professionals associated with assessment so that they could undertake hands on work within schools. It reduced variation between areas of the country, enabled government to more directly control and be held accountable for expenditure, reduced parental confrontation and encouraged parental collaboration in seeking resources, and moved assessment firmly into the hands of educationalists. The UK parliament's House of Commons Education and Skills Committee (2007) recognised this approach to be "a coherent alternative model" (p. 9).

Other jurisdictions had begun to develop such approaches too. In Norway (Rix et al., 2013a), we were told by a head of service that their intention was to focus more on the class than on the individuals within it. The intention was to shift funding to the class rather than individuals. In Italy, administrators and practitioners described (and critiqued) a range of practices associated with supporting the class. The view held by the principal of a cluster of schools was that teaching staff knew what was needed better than anyone. As a result he made sure resources were allocated taking into consideration not just individuals with certification,[28] but also staff time, staff experience and the wider class context, including the number and diversity of pupils in a class. When the context component of this formula was explained it demonstrated considerable trust in the educational evaluation of need and the role that could be played by other collaborative bodies, such as class councils.[29] Once again, such a shift in funding represented an opportunity to encourage an appreciation of interdependence within education.

It is possible that things will not have changed greatly since the time of writing and that such opportunities still exist in England and in other administrations. These three examples may still suggest ways forward for collective processes if we seek to exploit them. It would be naïve, though, to expect that such pressures and opportunities could alone bring about a shift towards an educational system more focused upon interdependence. They might create a chance for change, creating a downward pressure and policy environment which encourages and supports change, but they will come to nothing if what is being asked of teachers does not fit with how teachers see themselves and understand their role. The next chapter will explore the consequences of the approaches which are currently dominant within schools and the possibilities which might exist within everyday learning situations.

Notes

1 This would be in addition to whether one could or could not reconcile the ICF with the capability approach as some discuss (Bickenbach, 2014; Mitra, 2014), since the need still remains to counterbalance the emphasis upon the individual.

2 In essence, if liberalism is hindered by its emphasis upon individuals with limited social responsibility but presumptions of rights, communitarianism is hindered by the subservience of individuals to collective processes.

3 He explores this with a particular focus upon those whose behaviour is seen to be hyperactive and who do not pay appropriate attention, and questions why our response may be over-medicalised.

4 This trajectory risks a permanent loss of a morally coherent identity. Relationships have to be deconstructed and new ones created, creating vulnerability and an openness to fragmented possibilities. If you get it wrong you can lose control of the self and fail to create your own space. This self is situated in a world where a few values are tenuously agreed; in particular the rule of the majority, individual freedom, fundamental human rights and property rights. Other values are a matter of personal choice, which we aim to express and affirm coherently. Consequently, this dominant interpretation creates a self which always has the potential to be under threat.

5 Which echo the underlying concepts of the bio–psycho–social model.

6 Positron emission tomography.

7 It may be that we have a fundamental unitary association with this metaphorical stardust, perhaps of the sort that quantum mechanics explores or which has been the basis for spiritual explanations of life. This would also reinforce our sense of being part of a metaphorical 'Them'.

8 He attempts to describe intelligence as an aptitude for theorizing. He suggests it is a concept teachers can use to identify effective teaching methods or can use to identify a student who is cheating or has unexpected aptitudes or lacks expected aptitudes.

9 In many ways it does not matter if Gingell or Hand are right or wrong, what is clear is that neither of them can agree about something they are both certain we can all agree exists. One might ask, why they are so certain it exists?

10 This individual focus was evident beyond the early years too, for example in the levels outlined throughout the National Curriculum and in the spread of 'personalisation'

(Leadbetter, 2004) across all childhood and youth services – despite practitioners not really understanding what personalisation involved (Courcier, 2007).

11 We were supposed to weave them into the day so that they just seemed part of everyday life. Nice idea … but it is very hard to disguise an activity as fun play if the child isn't choosing to initiate it or engage in it.

12 I am not excluding myself from this observation … though I have picked up on the oversight.

13 And inaction and ignorance.

14 The UK study used five primary-school classes, with pupils aged 5–7. Equivalent studies were reported as conducted in the other countries.

15 Level 1: the individual has very poor skills and may, for example, be unable to determine the correct dose of medicine to give a child from the label on a package.

Level 2: respondents can only deal with simple, clearly laid-out reading tasks. At this level, people can read but test poorly. They may have developed coping skills to meet every day literacy demands, but they find it difficult to tackle new challenges, such as certain job skills (UNESCO, 2014).

16 For example, in an attempt to properly understand the written word, groups of people have to come together to discuss just exactly what the words might mean (such as in reading groups, courts of law or policy working parties).

17 The term used varied slightly as well, and sometimes a very similar term was used when meaning something different to that envisaged by other administrations.

18 The peers were still purportedly following an adapted curriculum using adaptive pedagogy.

19 Teachers were perceived as requiring particular knowledge about impairment characteristics, assessments and interventions. Much training in the United States, for example, aimed to create teachers who could diagnose needs, prescribe interventions, implement programmes and assess outcomes.

20 Teachers were perceived as active, highly skilled and providing rich opportunities for students within a well-planned and organised setting. Teachers were encouraged to use behavioural and process led strategies.

21 Science, technology, engineering and maths.

22 As organised under the auspices of the Organisation for Economic Co-operation and Development.

23 Japan had 0 per cent.

24 Iceland had 10.6 per cent.

25 Japan, Shanghai, Korea, Hong Kong.

26 Finland's submission included 5.6 per cent of children identified with SEN and they were third in reading, sixth in maths and second in science.

27 Canada's submission included 6.1 per cent of children identified with SEN and they were sixth in reading, tenth in maths and eighth in science.

28 The Italian version of individualised assessment.

29 The class councils met regularly in every type of school. They were made up of all the teachers and support staff who worked with a particular class and parent representatives for that class. The council focused upon the educational activities and teaching approaches for the class, evaluating its progress as a unit as well as the progress of individual pupils.

6

CONFRONTING THE MAINSTREAM CHALLENGE

Adieu, dear amiable youth!
Your heart can ne'er be wanting!
May prudence, fortitude, and truth
Erect your brow undaunting.
In ploughman phrase, God send you speed
Still daily to grow wiser:
And may ya better reck the rede[1]
Than ever did th' adviser.

(Robert Burns, 1786, pp. 91–92)

Daily to grow wiser?

In 1993, Caroline and I spent a month in Albania recording the work of a European Union training project in institutions and the community. During this very powerful experience, we stayed in an orphanage. One morning, on the wards, I saw a little girl I assumed to be around 18 months old, lying in a bed. She had been clearly lying in that bed for a very long time. I went over to her and began to chat. She did not respond to me at all. After a few minutes, I took the girl's hand, but she still did not respond. A few minutes later, I picked the girl up and began to tour the orphanage with her. For over an hour we walked the corridors, but the girl did not respond to me at all. (She turned her face to the light on one occasion as we passed a window. But it was only a slight movement.) Then we came to a plant which had recently been watered. There was a bead of water on a leaf. I reached out her hand and together we touched the droplet. She made the smallest intake of breath … almost a gasp … and turned to look up at me. For the first time our eyes met. This girl did not know how to communicate with another human being because no one had ever bothered to show her how. In this place the plants were more important.

In the 1990s I was teaching in an all-girl comprehensive in Hackney, working with students who used English as an Additional Language.[2] I loved working at this school, but in the end I left because I felt that I was not really helping the students. Two examples stand out.

- A great many of the students were recent arrivals in the country, often refugees from danger or environmental or economic troubles. Part of my work involved supporting sixth-formers studying a vocational Information Technology course. The work of these young women was frequently exemplary, yet they could not get even the most basic school qualifications because they kept failing the written exam, which was in English. Their course work was not enough. They could not have the support of a translator. As a result they repeated a course or left the school with nothing to show for all they had achieved. The system was clearly failing them.

- I was asked to act as a cover teacher for a class which had not had a regular teacher for many months, due to this subject specialist's intermittent health problems. The class was climbing the wall. On my first day with the group, I told them that we were going to read around the class. I did not care if people read one word or a hundred, but we were all going to give it a go. The class refused. They had been told they did not have to do this. It put too much pressure on those who could not read or did not like to read publically. This seemed fair enough if I was going to make great demands, but I knew some of the students. I knew that for them the reading of a couple of words was a triumph we could share. For others, I envisaged the Medieval Ordinary, the person with the book who stood behind the actor and whispered the words so they could deliver their lines. I wanted us all to share in a collective effort. This could be fun. When I sought management support for my request, it was not forthcoming. The head of English clearly felt I was wrong and the policy was right. It seemed clear to me, however, that we were not teaching people the skills to share texts; rather, we were teaching them that not being able to read well was something to hide. By implication, not being good at reading was something shameful.

In the mid 2000s, I was asked to serve as a consultant to Comet, a UK electrical retailer, to assist in the development of their in-house training. This was seven years before the company closed down, and they were still hoping to overcome major shifts in retail patterns by offering the very best customer service. The strategy was to raise the support they offered by providing training and accreditation for all grades of sales staff (at entry, proficient and expert levels). Before I was taken on they had devised a whole series of online activities, which were assessed through end-of-unit multiple-choice questions. I had reservations about this approach, but they felt that this dealt with moving staff from the entry level through to the proficient level. They now wanted a strategy to enable employees to become experts. I spent some time talking with staff and soon realised that many of them had a great deal of knowledge in a particular area of the business which they would be very interested in developing further and sharing with other staff. I proposed a range of strategies which would enable staff to identify their own targets for development and validate their expert status by sharing their deeper understanding with colleagues. The aim was to build on their own interests and create a shop full of staff who were used to helping each other find things out and who were rewarded by the company for doing so. My suggestions were never taken up. It would seem that they did not constitute a definable curriculum or clear categories for assessment. A senior member of the team responsible for the development of the training strategy told me that I really was "just a bit too radical".

The purpose of these tales from three very different learning environments is intended to outline the barriers which emerge not because of any particular 'ism',[3] but because of the underlying nature of working within an institution. Frequently we do not understand the meaning of our habits; we have different priorities; we do not recognise the impact of our actions; we are working in places which require us (or lead us) to be a certain way. Making a difference to such situations can seem impossible even if we might be in a position to be listened to. As a very senior member of a Local Authority support service told me in 2014, the thing that really surprised him about taking on a senior leadership role was how little he could control what went on around him. It is possible that Robert Burns (and my mother) was right, that people are better at telling each other what to do than acting upon their own advice. Certainly in the world of education many of us have very closed minds about learning.

This chapter will consider barriers which marginalise those who we aim to teach within the classroom and then discuss some practical pedagogic responses.

Taken-for-granted experiences

In Chapter 1 we identified various issues associated with marginalisation. The impact of such experience is evident across a range of school activities and is exacerbated by everyday local practices. Consider, for example, background noise in the classroom. Within Scotland it is recognised that a good classroom does not have to equate to a quiet one (Education Scotland, 2014). However, babble has been shown to have a significantly negative impact for some children in the class (Dockrell & Shield, 2006). It can impact not only on students with hearing difficulties or with identified special educational needs, but also those who struggle to concentrate. It impacts too on teachers if they feel a need to be heard. This experience can vary too, between cultures and depending upon the built environment. In Hong Kong, for example, noise levels in special classes were above normal teacher voice levels and above noise standards for United States (Leung & McPherson, 2006).

Well established and well accepted everyday teaching practices can also exclude a variety of pupils. For example, many girls feel marginalised by the physical identities associated with physical education (Goodyear, Casey & Kirk,

2012) and other young women have been marginalised by what they saw as the individual focus of an advanced mathematics syllabus (Abu El-Haj, 2003). Houssart (2002) spent two years looking at the Maths lessons of two classes in two Primary schools. When difficulties arose there was always a possible explanation associated with the nature of the task rather than its conceptual underpinnings. She concluded that children's had preferences for the way in which a concept or task was presented.

> Difficulties in reading and writing were part of this, with copying from the board and drawing charts and tables causing problems. Often children complained about these tasks or asked for help. Some children had a preference for written tasks but had a discrimination to be involved in oral work. One child had difficulties with the keyboard, making computer tasks difficult. Another boy, in contrast, performed better on tasks using the computer than on similar tasks presented in other ways.
>
> (p. 78)

Such findings are in evidence across the full range of subject areas. Bourdieu and Gros suggested, in their evaluation of the French education system (Bourdieu, 1990), that the disciplinary subjects themselves represented one of the biggest barriers to transforming the contents of teaching. One reason is that each subject is situated within a community of users. The language and ideas of a field have particular meanings and nuances to those who work or study within that field. As subject specialists, the role teachers play is remarkably complex. They are situated between a range of communities, trying to serve as a link for their students. Seixas (1993) talks about this challenge in relation to History. He maintains that historical text and analysis systematically excludes most children because they do not have the linguistic and conceptual experience which is required to access those texts. The teacher's mix of subject knowledge and pedagogic knowledge positions them in both the community of historians and the community of students. They sit, however, on the margins of each community. The teacher is, for example, unlikely to be an active participant within the community of historians.

Seixas maintains that overcoming this deficit is a challenge for the historical field. But it is also a challenge to all areas of the curriculum and for those who wish education to resolve any number of issues which have been identified as lacking in young people or society. Teachers are rarely at the heart of the community into which they are aiming to induct students. Given our current educational structures, we cannot expect them to be in this position either.

Subjects do not just constrain what can be taught but also how it can be taught. The notion of subject expertise, for example, is an underlying assumption behind ability grouping.[4] There is fairly robust evidence that ability grouping does not raise standards but merely ensures those in high sets get higher grades and those in low sets get lower grades (Ireson, Hallam & Hurley, 2005). However, summer-born children (who as discussed previously perform less well than peers born earlier in the year) are more likely to find themselves in a bottom set (Hallam & Parsons, 2013) as are working-class students in some schools (Wiliam & Bartholomew, 2004). As a result they will be taught more slowly and cover less of the curriculum (Ireson & Hallam, 1999).[5]

The increasing focus upon subject areas as students move into secondary school is also seen by many as a barrier to inclusion. During our visits to four countries (Rix, Sheehy, Fletcher-Campbell, Crisp & Harper, 2013a) there was a belief that it became harder to work collaboratively and co-operatively as the child moved up the school levels. It seemed that the primary–secondary transition created a clear division in the mind of many practitioners, policy-makers and parents, with an almost resigned acceptance that at this point the curriculum cannot be delivered to as many pupils in the mainstream class. Part of this was framed as a consequence of the increasing focus upon academic and disparate outcomes, part as a consequence of teenagers' purported disinterest in peers with special educational needs,[6] but most prevalent was a lack of belief in the possibility of differentiation to cover all pupils. There was a sense that good teachers were being put in an impossible position.

Common-sense responses

The practices and processes which we feel as practitioners will enable access can frequently constrain. Even seemingly obvious and widely adopted approaches such as the use of images or the simplification of language are problematic. For example, the use of different visual resources to support a question in an exam can have a significant effect on the answers given and the marks received (Crisp & Sweiry, 2006). Not being alert to such an issue can create significant barriers to learning. For instance, a secondary student I was working with could not understand the word *erosion*. She had English as an Additional Language (EAL), so we assumed the problem was her understanding of the words. It transpired that she was confused by the drawing we were using to explain the concept. The hand-drawn picture of reeds protecting a river bank was undermining the words we were using. It was weeks into the project before we considered the image might be the problem (Rix, 2005a).

The use of images is frequently accompanied by simplified language. In a survey of 264 teachers and support staff in England, 87 per cent said that they use simplified language materials (SLMs) and 81 per cent said that they produce them. They used these materials at times across the whole class, and at others with a range of pupils including those with learning difficulties and those who have EAL (J. Rix, 2006). This is despite the value of simplified language being widely contested within the literature (Rix, 2009a) and teachers widely recognising that the use of materials differentiated in this manner causes a wide range of difficulties (see Box 6.1).

Box 6.1 Commonly identified difficulties created by the use of differentiated materials in one Hackney comprehensive

- Students who feel that they are being picked out from the majority unfairly.
- Students not receiving 'easy work' feel that it should be given to them.
- Students who feel the curriculum is not intended for them until 'their materials' appear and so do not become involved in other activities.
- Staff who have produced materials resent student disinterest and disaffection.
- Students who do not feel they can do the work unless it is differentiated.
- Staff who believe students cannot do work unless it is differentiated.
- Students who do not regularly receive differentiated materials soon believe the curriculum is not intended for them at all and so do not attempt the differentiated materials that do come their way.
- Staff who believe that producing and distributing differentiated materials will satisfy the differences of their students.
- Staff uncertainty about the appropriateness of their differentiation in relation to specific students and across ranges of difference.
- Staff uncertainty about how best to produce and use differentiated materials.
- Staff concern over other people using their materials.
- Staff lack of enthusiasm for using other people's materials.
- Staff struggle to produce new materials to meet needs of frequent new arrivals.
- Cost implications in relation to time and money (and who pays).

(Rix, 2004, p. 63)

In a two-stage research project (Rix, 2009a) I looked at the processes involved in producing such materials. Stage 1 of the research involved 35 practitioners designing SLMs based upon a complex text. These materials were analysed and approaches identified. Over 80 per cent of the practitioners produced some variation of rewriting the text, identifying keywords and providing images. Less than 20 per cent suggested using additional activities. In 2007, 43 different practitioners were surveyed to assess which of the four approaches identified in Stage 1 they would use when dealing with a complex text (see Box 6.1). Even though these practitioners said they would be more adventurous than those who had produced materials, less than 45 per cent suggested they would in some way move away from what might be regarded as the traditional SLM. It does seem reasonable to ask whether, in the pressures and culture of current classrooms, many teachers will reach for the kinds of multi-modal, non-print-based strategies identified in Chapter 3.

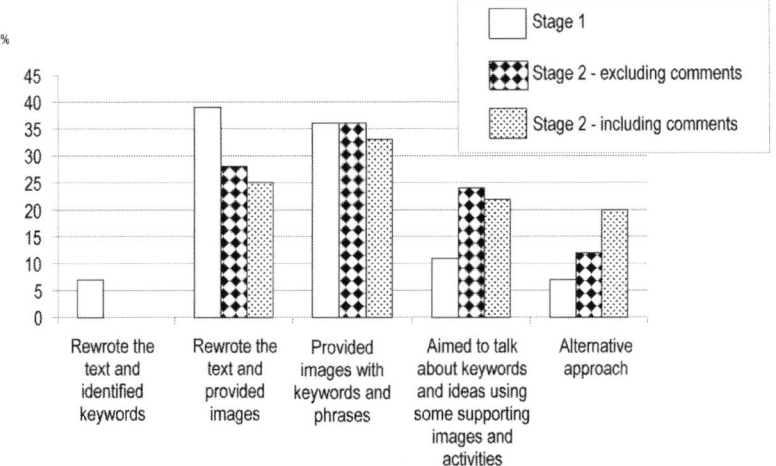

FIGURE 6.1 Percentages adopting each approach in Stages 1 and 2 (Rix, 2009a).

The problem with reliance upon these traditional approaches is that they trap children within a particular educational identity which is framed by those approaches. Méndez, Lacasa and Matusov (2008), for example, describe how a Spanish student is constrained by her teachers' determination to convey knowledge contained within printed material.[7] The teachers did not consider the relevance of the material to the girl, or allow her to "to employ the strategies which she utilises in her daily life when she is not at school" (p. 67). The support class positioned the child as incapable and created "a zone of incapacity" (p. 67). The child's education in this context undermined her learning. Similarly, 12 secondary students in Sweden wished to receive help with their reading and writing, but they felt that the small group support they received resulted in them having labels which served primarily bureaucratic purposes. They also created a greater sense of homogeneity in the class they left behind, encouraging their own exclusion (Mattson & Roll-Pettersson, 2007).

Creating difficulties for ourselves

In their case study of Adam, Mcdermott and Varenne (1995) outlined how learning difficulties are created by the educational context. Outside of school there was much Adam could do, but within school:

> All the people in his class – the teachers, of course, and all the children as well – are involved at various times in recognizing, identifying, displaying, mitigating, and even hiding what Adam is unable to do; if we include his tutors, the school psychologists, the local school of education where he goes for extra help (and his teachers for their degrees), if we include the researchers who show up to study him and the government agencies that finance

them, the number of people found contributing to Adam being highlighted as LD [learning disabilities] grows large. If we add all the children who do well at school because Adam and others like him fail standardized tests, then most of the country is involved in Adam being LD.

(pp. 339–340)

An everyday situation in which this difference can be constructed is school break-time. One of my bleakest memories of my son's primary education was seeing him alone in the playground. The staff always had excuses for why this might be. I know they initiated some activities to overcome this, but I was never convinced that they had made meaningful and consistent efforts to create social situations which would have benefited his communication with his peers. Perhaps it was that they reasonably expected break to be a break for them too?

Research into school play-times also describes situations in which disabled children are kept together at lunch-times and break, or are kept away from the playground at the start of break because they are receiving therapeutic interventions or separate support activities (Woolley, Armitage, Bishop, Curtis & Ginsborg, 2006). This construction of difference was evident when filming in various primary and secondary schools for the modules on which I teach at the Open University too. It was suggested that children were separated for their safety or to avoid distress or to provide relevant activities. However, the values and needs of the practitioners and the institution were clearly being prioritised in these instances. The other children noted the separation too and some told us it was unfair.

The changing nature of schooling in Australia,[8] offers an insight into how practitioners and the wider the education system respond to the energy, interest and enthusiasm which children and young people bring to schools. In this context, Graham (2008b) considered the subjective decisions which teachers are expected to make about children in using criteria associated with gifted and talented (e.g. self-discipline, intensity of attentiveness, length of attention) and with ADHD (e.g. inattentiveness, fidgeting and blurting out incomplete thoughts). How, she asked, are such things to be measured? Whose interpretation is reliable? Such decisions depend upon one's expectations and view of what is normal. And having come to a conclusion it is likely to influence how you subsequently respond to a child. For instance, behaviours which might be discerned in one child as reflecting upon an issue, such as looking out of the window, can come to be interpreted in another child as daydreaming.[9]

Our capacity to overlook everyday practices is exemplified by the factors which are not considered in the diagnosis of ADHD. For example, Davis (2006) points out that the assessments which are carried out to identify ADHD pay little attention to school's social context and the actions and power relationships of teachers, parents and other pupils. We also do not reflect on limitations in the assessment processes themselves. These processes do not require rigorous and sustained observation, they take place in only a few locations and they are carried out by people who often have little experience of qualitative, reflexive research and the analysis of the social context of childhood (Davis, 2006). As a consequence there are a great many things we could be ignoring. Cohen (2006), for example, suggests that we could be ignoring:

- the sensory impact of technology in 'rapid-fire culture';
- cultural obsessions with performance enhancement;
- the lack of any evidence of a neurological basis;
- that the behaviours described are not physical but cultural;
- that describing behaviours is pathologising temperament;
- that diagnosis reframes 'symptoms' as a 'cause';
- the poor quality of research into ADHD;
- that the drugs impact is a side-effect which is only seen as beneficial in settings requiring conformity;
- the poor quality research in drug treatment.

I am not for a moment suggesting that there are not children, young people and adults who do not exhibit behaviours which match up with a diagnosis of ADHD or that these people may find the experience of school and other social institutions very difficult to live with. However, these bullet points position the diagnosis of ADHD not as an issue relating to an individual but as an issue of cultural practices. At the very least we need to be alert to these possibilities. As Armstrong (2006) suggests, children diagnosed as having ADHD can be positioned as "canaries in the coal mine", giving us warning of the impact of a short attention span culture, the disappearance of the freedom to play and the pressure on children to develop as quickly as possible. It may also reflect the changing expectations of education. The economically correct view of education has increasingly come to emphasise the need for classroom-based academic seat-work, preparing young people for a market which has less need for the "unskilled" (Graham, 2008a). Even if it is possible one day to point with certainty to particular genes which lead to behaviours which are subsequently identifiable as ADHD the growth in this individualised diagnosis represents changing values in relation to human energy, interest and enthusiasm.

The manner in which we talk about the diagnosed condition does not help us to resolve the problem either. Graham (2007) identifies the dominant conceptualization of ADHD from academic literature as being a disorder of neurology which the child has no control over, which affects speed of processing, short-term memory, abstract thought, controlling impulses and behaviour – many of the characteristics also used as indicators for other diagnostic categories which label children as having learning difficulties or autistic spectrum disorder or sensory impairments. This in-person deficit is evident in the way which people generally talk about ADHD; however, its imprecise nature is downplayed. Danforth and Kim (2008), for example, analyse the metaphors used in describing ADHD (in particular the brain as a circuit and the person with ADHD as being trapped) and the way in which they encourage belief in a heroic physician who can treat the condition. These popular metaphors steer teachers towards a seemingly authoritative explanation, a singular scientific description of complex social and interactional events. It encourages them away from collective notions and responses and towards separation and an individualised response to a problem. These, however, are not the solutions which emerge from the research literature. The best evidence suggests that solutions for learning are rooted in relationships, routines and participation.

Cooper (2011) in an international review of teacher strategies for young people identified with social, emotional and behavioural difficulties (including ADHD and autistic spectrum disorders) notes that teacher characteristics can initiate, exacerbate or alleviate behaviours associated with this category. Empathy and positive attitudes towards the young people can promote an environment which encourages participation. Certain skills and practices, particularly some developed within the behavioural and cognitive behavioural paradigms can also reduce the behaviours which are seen as problematic. Similarly a meta-analysis of reviews of ADHD treatments, concluded that despite limitations in the research evidence, psychosocial approaches could enhance social and behavioural outcomes (Watson, Richels, Michalek & Raymer, 2012). These researchers do not make a similar claim for academic outcomes. One of their five highly rated reviews (Van der Oord, Prins, Oosterlaan & Emmelkamp, 2008) concluded that whilst both psychosocial and stimulant treatments were effective in improving social and behavioural functioning, neither were effective in improving academic functioning. Another of their highly rated reviews (Purdie, Hattie & Carroll, 2002) concluded that educational interventions had the greatest impact upon educational outcomes.[10] In other words, drug treatments or therapeutic treatments can reduce the behaviours which teachers identify, but they don't help with the learning. That is down to what happens in the classroom.

Who's the adviser? Who's the wiser?

If we accept this view that difficulties associated with learning and behaviour emerge as a consequence of social situations that does not mean we are agreeing that everything about a person's capacity to learn is necessarily constructed by the school environment and our wider systems of support. Neither does it mean that people's behaviours and well-being will not require additional and frequently complex ongoing support. The issue is about how that support frames or exacerbates the challenges some people face. The evident danger is that the education system serves to undermine both the collective belief and the individual belief within a person or a group of people. The lack of achievement undermines our sense of what they can be and their capacity to develop what they might be. As such it undermines our capacity to educate. Success and engagement are closely allied. As Bruner (1966) noted: "We get interested in what we get good at. In general it is difficult to sustain interest in an activity unless one achieves some degree of competence" (p. 118). Such an observation does not just apply to the learner. It is similarly difficult for a practitioner to sustain an interest in someone who makes them feel incompetent or threatens their identity as a practitioner.

The capacity of the teacher to pass their uncertainty onto their relationship with the child is evident in numerous ways. Fox, Farrell and Davis (2004) described a supportive school where staff shared concerns and strategies. In this setting, a child with Down syndrome was viewed as a full class member in one year, with support staff and the class teacher regularly meeting to discuss work, but the next year he had become separated from his peers. His new teacher, a former SEN Co-ordinator saw his planning and support as being the responsibility of support staff.

There is considerable research which shows that teachers' and pupils' attitudes towards processes of inclusion are influenced by their experiences of special needs. For instance, Slovene teachers and pupils had a positive attitude towards pupils with physical impairments but not towards those with emotional and behavioural difficulties. The stress that teachers felt with this latter group was seen to influence the manner in which they worked with them (Cagran & Schmidt, 2011). This process can be understood through a model of knowledge which Norwich and Lewis (2007) identified within their research. This model was seen to influence whether teachers perceived their practice to be special.

Norwich and Lewis identified four kinds of knowledge which teachers drew upon:

1   Knowledge 1 equates to understanding of labelled groups associated with special educational needs.
2   Knowledge 2 equates to understanding of professional identify and of oneself as a teacher.
3   Knowledge 3 equates to understanding of psychological models of learning.
4   Knowledge 4 equates to understanding of areas of the curriculum and pedagogic approaches.

They suggested that Knowledge 1 serves as a filter through which the other three knowledges are subsequently seen. Thus your understanding of 'types' of people will inform how you see your role, the student's learning and how best to approach this. Those people who strongly perceive the child as belonging to a particular group with a particular identity are more likely to see a their role as different from other teachers, and will also regard the way in which the student learns and strategies that are appropriate for them as being inherently different.

As discussed in Chapter 3, teacher's belief structures are linked to how they teach and who they see themselves as being responsible for. The lack of engagement from many teachers is evident in research which reports children with severe impairments working mostly with support staff, whilst the class teachers work with the not-yet-disabled or those who would be identified as having mild impairments (e.g. Cameron, Cook & Tankersley, 2012).

These attitudes of practitioners not only influence their relationships with the pupils, but also the manner in which they work with each other. For instance, Veck (2009) explored the role of learning assistants[11] depending upon the values of a school and class. Drawing upon three perspectives (see Table 6.1) identified by

TABLE 6.1 Attitudes, practices and additional adult role

• Difficulties in learning are seen to proceed from perceived deficiencies within individual students	• Practices arise from and reinforce fixed notions of teaching, behaving and learning • The additional adult must fit in and fulfil a role as devised by others
• Difficulties in learning are seen to proceed from failure to match needs with provision	• Practices may be rigid or flexible with pupils having to meet the requirements of the space or able to negotiate their own place within the whole • The additional adult will adapt materials and link between the teacher and the pupil, fulfilling the role devised by others, and only partially engaging in the space where all children learn
• Difficulties in learning are seen to proceed from the exclusionary nature of the settings as experienced by students	• The space is always developing and those in it are both a participator and contributor to the whole • The additional adult's role must challenge our understandings of efficient practice

Source: Based on Veck (2009).

Ainscow and Hart (1992), he examined the practice of 18 Learning Support Assistants. He was able to find evidence for the first two of these perspectives.

Within these first two perspectives he described how the young person and the additional adult were set apart, frequently seen as default partners for activities. The difficult young person was with the secondary adult. The teacher did not attempt to make the same kinds of encouraging links to this supported child or try to encourage them as they did with other students. The pair became "a segregated teaching unit within the classroom, an exclusionary space within a 'mainstream' space" (p. 48) which rendered invisible the additional adult's teaching. He noted the unfulfilled capacity of the additional adult to contribute insights which would benefit the development of policy and practice within institutions. The exclusionary practice was not a fundamental characteristic of one-to-one support however; it was a consequence of a 'fixed approach' which limited access for those involved, thus reducing the meaningful significance of participation.

Veck also discussed the third perspective, which was not evident in this study. Along with other writers, Veck suggested these third spaces had to be democratic. He noted that even though individuals would not share the same institutional responsibility, they had to have equal worth and their belonging had to be of equal importance. The temptation is to dismiss such a perspective as an outpouring from the aspirational second world of inclusion.[12] But it has more meaning than that. I have spoken to too many practitioners around the world who recognise the power of such an idea to dismiss it out of hand. I have seen enough practitioners, parents and administrators, very much caught up in the third world of inclusion, trying very hard to create an equal space against the odds. They would very much like to move on from the values which perpetuate and are reinforced by those first two perspectives.

It all adds up

The impact of such attitudes is not just relevant to impairment. Teacher's pedagogy can also alter depending upon the predominant social class of the school. Within her study of 12 English primary schools, Hempel-Jorgensen (2009) found evidence of such social class divergence. As a consequence:

- Schools identified as serving children from a predominantly lower social-economic category tended to see academic success as a consequence of appropriate behaviour and the following of rules. Success was evidenced by external measures. The pupils recognised the ideal pupil as someone who conformed to school regulations and followed the perceived wishes of teachers.
- Schools identified as serving children from a predominantly higher social-economic category tended to see academic success as a consequence of student's personal characteristics. The pupils recognised the ideal pupil as someone who took an active role in their own learning and demonstrated personal autonomy.

Reay (2009) referred to young people categorised as working class as the "inferior other" within education. In a project on pupils' perspectives, the pupils described teachers as "a bit snobby" and "putting you down", so pupils "feel left out". They recognised teachers as having favourites: "you are nice to that one, and the rest you don't care about". They felt that teachers needed to learn how to "treat us like humans" with "everyone equal" (quotes from five pupils, p. 25).

Pupils also recognise that teachers have different expectations according to gender. Teachers (particularly male teachers) have been reported as, expecting greater achievement and controlled behaviour from girls whilst treating boys negatively in comparison (Myhill & Jones, 2006). This research suggested that these expectations exacerbated stereotypical assumptions within wider society about certain young men identified as underachieving. Such hidden processes of marginalisation also impact on sexuality, so that studies identify a formal silencing of lesbian and gay sexuality. Those who identify as lesbian and gay have to learn about their own sexuality while they negotiate a culture which is both explicit and implicit in its presentation of heterosexuality as the norm; in which verbal and physical attacks and everyday derogatory turns of phrase go unnoticed and unchallenged (Taylor, 2007). Similarly, stereotypical expressions of extreme-heterosexual femininity have been evident in research looking at urban working-class young women's engagement with schools and education. This research identified links between issues of race, gender and social class, which contributed to the educational exclusion of young working-class women (Archer, Halsall & Hollingworth, 2007).

The impact of race alone, upon practitioner expectations, assumptions and practices, is also well documented. British Asian families, for example, with children identified with complex emotional and behavioural difficulties, described discrimination by professionals working throughout health, education and social care (Bradby, Varyani, Oglethorpe, Raine, White & Minnis, 2007). The negative response of practitioners is frequently evident in the assumptions which they bring to an everyday situation. Consider the comments from a head of year at an English secondary school, who believed that one or two Muslim children in a class will "integrate, make friends", but once there are three, four or more, "then they'll form a little clique or a gang". Even though this teacher recognised there was still "some mixing in", they referred to "gangs" who were "very apparent" and "can be very intimidating" leading to "disputes and confrontations with other groups". The senior staff member concluded that "often it's gang warfare" (Crozier & Davies, 2008, p. 291). The authors of the study, however, noted the lack of evidence to back up these assertions of gang warfare and threatening behaviour. The basis for the teacher's assertions boiled down to pupils hanging around, looking threatening, and being intimidating: "They're threatening because they hang around in a large group and look threatening. They'll hang around and block an exit, or for the toilet and people look and 'well, I'm not going past that lot'" (p. 291).

If such attitudes are widely prevalent then for many teachers the multi-cultural nature of many classrooms must feel disorientating. For example, in England in 2014, 29.5 per cent of primary-school pupils and 25.3 per cent of secondary-school students were classified as being of minority ethnic origin (DfE, 2014). In Scotland, in 2010, there were 35 main home languages identified across all schools, but only six of these categories had more than 1,000 speakers, with 25 having less than 500 (Scottish Government, 2010).

For many of the 6,586 pupils in Scotland who spoke these 25 languages the sense of difference must have been powerful. Certainly for the children, what may seem unimportant to the teachers can have a profound impact. Consider the simple story of Vlora, an Albanian girl, aged 6, entering the schooling system: "When I first went to the nursery I didn't like it and I used to try and run out of the door with my Dad. I didn't know what the food was" (quoted in Rutter, 2001, p. 169).

Marginalisation is rarely expressed so clearly to teachers. Schools mediate the dominant social values and do not encourage critical analysis, rewarding those who conform. Students are aware of this. Students in Sweden, for example, have been seen to go along with the rules even though they secretly disagree with them (Thornberg, 2008).[13]

Many people respond to such tales of marginalisation by pointing to those who have not had such experiences within the school system or who have succeeded despite them. My purpose in sharing these tales is not to excuse the failure of individuals but to highlight the endemic, underlying failings of the system for a wide range of students. It is a system which to a large degree frames who will emerge as 'successful' and the particular identity associated with that success, as well as who will not, along with the identity associated with that failure. This applies as much to what defines a successful teacher, parent, head-teacher, schools administrator or minister for education as it does the pupils.

Bigger than schools

The nature of marginalisation is not just a process of school, of course. For example within Cypriot settings it has been observed how the Turk is constructed as the 'other', reflecting wider social disjunctions. School represents this in a particular way, both through a nationalistic curriculum and teacher–pupil interactions, but it can also provide the alternative voices through which this process could be disrupted (Spyrou, 2006). Education can be seen to reflect the wider social and economic contexts within which schools operate. In the case of England, for example, the system serves as a persistent class mechanism, operating to sustain social segregation in selective, faith and community schools alongside academies, free schools, pupil referral units, special schools and private schools (where nearly 7 per cent attend on the basis of their family income or exceptional exam performance). This is a system where research finds faith schools that have half the national average on free school meals, where grammar schools have a sixth of the national average, and where there is a marked difference within the intake of comprehensive schools both in relation to attainment and social background (Coldron, Cripps & Shipton, 2010). Such class mechanisms operate within other countries too. For example, in many Central and Eastern European countries students from disadvantaged and lower social economic groupings are directed into less prestigious vocational programmes and subsequently into second-tier post-secondary provision (Kogan, Gebel & Noelke, 2012).

Changing the education system does not seem to have much impact upon these wider factors. From the review mentioned in Chapter 3 of studies which had examined funding reforms (Sigafoos, Moore, Brown, Green, O'Reilly & Lancioni, 2010) the researchers could find no legislative reforms which produced better or worse educational outcomes for children identified with SEN.[14] Bunar (2010) noted how after nearly two decades of change in Sweden, with the introduction of 1,000 new independent schools, attended by 150,000 students, there had been little, if any, positive impact upon academic achievement, social segregation and economic costs. This should not perhaps be surprising. Wider socio-economic and politically motivated factors underpin funding. For example, in a study of 46 English primary schools, Lupton, Thrupp and Brown (2010) reported that schools with high numbers of pupils identified with SEN claimed to have greater expertise in identifying and supporting these pupils, attracting children from a wider catchment area.[15] However, the funding system meant that that those in the most disadvantaged schools were less likely to have needs identified and supported, even if the school did claim to have greater expertise. These schools had to divert whole-school funding to provide additional class support. Similarly, in some US administrations whilst the number of trained special education teachers has risen and the requirement to be trained has increased, the role of special education teachers has been taken on by para-professionals, class sizes have increased and caseloads have been seen to require up to 25 per cent fewer special education teachers (Boe, deBettencourt, Dewey, Rosenberg, Sindelar &

Leko, 2013). In Italy too, changes in the economic climate lead to changes in the rules over staffing ratios (Rix et al., 2013a).

It is not necessary at this point to unpack all the possible influences upon the context in which learning support occurs. However, an analysis of interviews I undertook with a colleague, with parents and professionals involved with two families over a five-month period, highlighted the professional and parental awareness of the breadth of issues which influence learning and how we can support it (Rix & Matthews, 2014 – see Table 6.2 and Figure 6.2).

This knowledge, however, does not seem to influence how we assess the child and record our understanding of their learning situation. A subsequent analysis of nine years of paperwork for one child presented a far narrower range of issues than those which emerged in the interviews. Just over 150 pages (12 per cent) of the paperwork made some kind of reference to context. A detailed analysis demonstrated the paucity of consideration given to context even within these documents[16] (see Table 6.2 and Figure 6.3). Context was only evident in:

- a focus on the child's performance in an activity;
- noting the presence of an adult;
- discussing issues of behaviour;
- generalised mentions of other children.

Only once was there a mention of how the child's interaction with his peers supported his learning and only one mention of policy.

There is no suggestion in this research that there was a deliberate decision on behalf of the practitioners to hide problems and issues. Just as has been identified with nurses, the systems used to record information socialises them into a 'thought world' which integrates top down criteria into day-to-day practice (Bowker & Leigh Star, 1999, p. 272). The dominant mind-set in relation to learning difficulties, the nature of funding streams and support networks focus paperwork upon the individual and their support outcomes. The practitioners and parents are bridging between reality and process and are "barely aware" how they are fitting their experiences into "the general schemas of the organization", bringing "the heterogeneous world into line with its processes" (Brown & Duguid, 2000, p. 108).

This should concern us, though. By not recording the negative consequences of practices and systems they are reinforcing those practices and systems. By not chronicling the complexity and contradictions inherent in their workplace, they imply that the struggle lies elsewhere. The status quo is maintained even though its inequities are recognised. From a social model perspective (Oliver, 1983; Finkelstein, 2001) they are failing to describe the ways in which society's construction disables the child. From an educational perspective, because of an expectation that they should assess the child as an individual and not the collective relationships, their focus is away from the context in which inclusive learning opportunities arise.

TABLE 6.2 The contrast between what is said and what is recorded

Consideration of context by professionals and parents in interviews	Consideration of context by professionals and parents in documentation
• Everyday learning opportunities and informal situations • The child's enjoyment and an understanding of their interests • Practitioner priorities (particularly developmental model and parental concerns and/or lack of 'knowledge') • Power balance and relationships between parents, practitioners and children • Relationships with other parents • Parental capacity to prepare a child for professional settings • Parental negativity • Practitioner negativity • Formal assessment processes • Negative impact of therapeutic settings • Automatic assumptions about a child • Child's sensitivity to parental mood • Supportive relationship with parents confronting complex social support systems • How services differ from borough to borough • How access to services depends on local processes • How joined-up services result from investment • A lack of resources • A recognition of other profession's silo thinking	• Descriptive comments focusing child on a task or in a situation, with occasional judgements on his performance • Comments about appropriate activities in relation to a generalised adult (not other children) being in attendance • Comments on child's behaviour and compliance • Brief description of child's interaction with peers (but only five mentions of specific relationship moments with another child) • Strategies which are typically no different to other children's *Only 1 mention in 150 pages:* • Reflection upon how to scaffold his participation and learning *with others* • Child's enjoyment • Activity in a home school context • Policy • Strategy not working

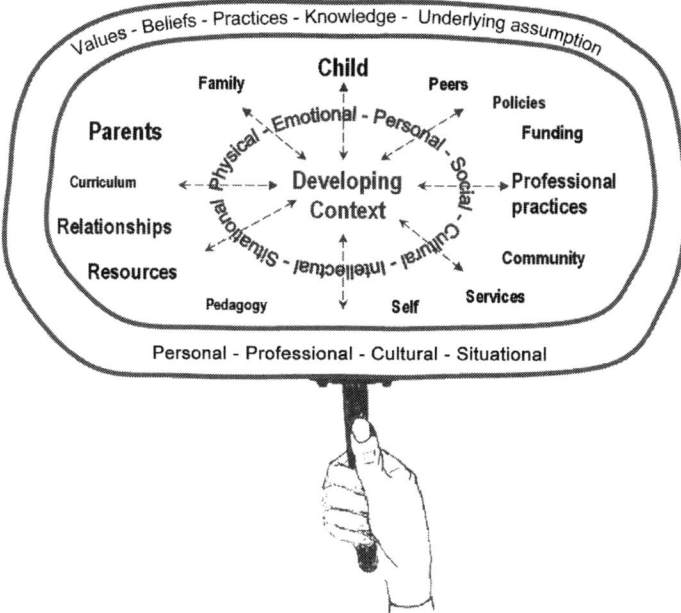

FIGURE 6.2   Issues that emerged from practitioner and parent interviews (the perspective lens (Rix & Paige-Smith, 2011) represents personal reflection and focus) (Rix & Matthews, 2014).

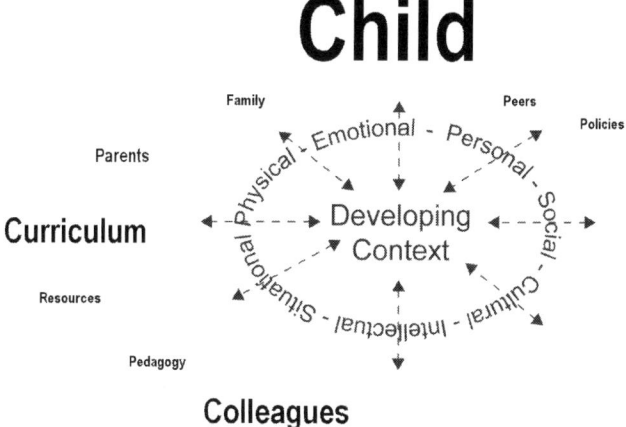

FIGURE 6.3   Issues that emerged from the documents (the perspective lens was not in evidence) (Rix & Matthews, 2014).

We can all start from the same place

In recent years the predominant learning theory for the majority of children has been sociocultural. Notions such as "the zone of proximal development",[17] scaffolding, communities of practice, learning communities and the spiral curriculum have become part of the international school discourse. In Scotland, for example, the new curriculum specifically notes that it is heavily influenced by the work of Vygotsky and by a recognition that learning is a social process. They claim that at the heart of this curriculum is collaborative and co-operative learning (Education Scotland, 2014).

Vygotsky's ideas found their first receptive audience outside of the Soviet Union in 1980s North America (Seixas, 1993). Leading thinkers such as Bruner (1996), Rogoff (2003), Lave and Wenger (1991) came to believe that learning is a fundamentally communal activity, which is situated within a shared culture. Individual's thought is understood to be a social process which depends upon interactions within communities. This shift to a sociocultural understanding was partly as a result of behavioural and process-led strategies proving to be over-simplistic (Brownell & Kiely, 2010) and empirical evidence that higher order cognition emerged more readily from co-operative activities; however, pedagogical methods also arose because people were seeking new ways to encourage learning. The theory reflected practices which were emerging anyway (Resnick & Klopfer, 1989).

As has been discussed in previous chapters, there are many other theoretical perspectives upon learning and development. This is particularly evident in relation to special. In many ways special education is the one field where sociocultural learning has not taken hold. Here behavioural, psychological and therapeutic models have remained to the fore. Ironically, much of Vygotsky's work was with children we would describe as having special educational needs. Vygotsky recognised that impairments are only perceived to be not-normal within social contexts. He saw that social relationships and behaviours alter in response to impairments and their psychological significance varies dependent upon social and cultural environments. It is the social implications which he saw as the primary difficulty. The teacher's job was not to deal with biological factors but with social consequences. Vygotsky was also opposed to the use of terms such as developmental delay or developmental disability. He felt a child was not delayed, but developed in a qualitatively different manner as a result of the social responses to them. However, the need to access the same cultural norms as their peers was equally important to them. As a result, he maintained that disabled children required alternative opportunities to develop equivalent cultural understanding. Vygotsky recognised that different communication modes were needed rather than different information: "Meaning is more important than the sign. Let us change signs but retain meaning" (cited in Gindis, 1999, p. 336).

He particularly advocated the use of collective learning, with peers supporting each other under guidance from an educator. He called for "inclusion based on positive discrimination" (in Gindis, 1999, p. 338). This entails a focus upon the child's social strengths and not their weaknesses and situates them in the same sociocultural environment as their peers.

Seeking some classroom solutions

As mentioned in Chapter 5, good teaching is widely regarded to be active, highly skilled and providing rich opportunities for students within a well-planned and organised setting. The complexity of teacher and learner interactions has come to the fore, as has an understanding of the importance of individual values and experiences and a recognition that learners benefit if the learning process is situated in meaningful contexts which serve a relevant purpose (Brownell & Kiely, 2010).

Along with the editor of this book, I reviewed pedagogic approaches to identify if there were underpinning practices common to *any* learning context (Rix & Sheehy, 2014). We noted a tension between a group-based approach to learning and a direct instruction model which had a possible focus upon individualized teaching and was organized by 'instructional needs'. This tension underlines the kinds of *dilemmas of difference* for people identified with special educational needs and disability which Norwich (2002) noted in relation to their identification, placement and curriculum planning. Whichever choice is made there will be benefits and losses; people's rights will be in conflict; and ambivalence will prevail in many social situations. The temptation therefore is to provide an ordered, hierarchical response which combines both the group-based and individualised processes. This creates a continuum model of delivery (Mcleskey & Waldron, 2011), moving from collective responses to more individualised support:

- universal supports provided in the general classroom (e.g. differentiated instruction or range of materials);
- targeted supports (e.g. explicit and extended instruction in a small group or, peer tutoring);
- specialised supports (e.g. designed for the needs of a small group who do not respond to the first two levels).

Such a model was critiqued within Chapter 5, because of its increasing separation of individual. It is important to underline once again that I am not suggesting that the targeted and specialised supports are all ineffective. Research shows definite advantages for some of these types of teaching approach and a reduction in the identification of students with difficulties (e.g. Fuchs, Fuchs, Craddock, Hollenbeck, Hamlett & Schatschneider, 2008; Torgesen, 2009). The problem is that improvements are small, they are only evident in some students and they are dependent upon consistent delivery of specified teaching programmes.

If we step back from such arguments about how to group and place learners and look at the pedagogy, there are possibilities which can resolve some of these dilemmas. The review we conducted confirmed to us that studies of effective pedagogies were actually describing facets of "good teaching" for all (Sheehy, 2013).[18] It did not really matter which paradigm they emerged from or whether they were traditionally practised in relative isolation, the practices themselves relied upon everyday practices which teachers readily understand.

Some of these everyday teaching practices were discussed in Chapter 3. Consider a couple more examples we identified:

1   In 2010 the Irish National Council for Special Education commissioned an international literature review of best practice models associated with children identified with emotional disturbance/behavioural difficulties (Cooper & Jacobs, 2011). They found high empirical evidence to support only three approaches, and low empirical support for many more of the popular and well-publicised approaches (see Table 6.3). The three approaches which had the strongest evidence base involved collective responses or could be delivered collectively by teachers with relatively little training.

2   Forness (2001) reported on a review of meta-analyses looking at the evidence associated with 20 interventions. The review concluded that unequivocal improvement was associated with those practices which arose from general education, whereas practices involving related services tended to rest between effective and ineffective (with a potential 20 percentile improvement), and those associated with a specific deficit had minimal impact (with less than a 10-percentile advantage for students receiving these interventions) (see Table 6.4).

The everyday nature of many practices is evident in relation to Down syndrome too. Drawing upon my research into accessible audio tours, in which I examined auditory and linguistic research associated with Down syndrome, I identified

TABLE 6.3 Hierarchical summary of main interventions associated with children identified with emotional disturbance/behavioural difficulties

	Teachers' qualities and skills	Whole-school approaches	Small-scale provision	Parental support	Multiagency working
High empirical support	The Good Behaviour Game	FRIENDS	Career academies		
Moderate empirical support	Kernels Student peer support Cognitive behavioural approaches Success For All	School-wide positive behavioural support Coping Power	Nurture groups	Parent management training	Fast Track
Low empirical support	Personal warmth In-service training on SEBD Management of the classroom's physical environment Functional behavioural analysis Instructional strategies	Circle Time SEAL Second Step Restorative practices	Outreach schools Residential provision	Incredible Years Triple P	Gatehouse

Source: Cooper and Jacobs (2011).

TABLE 6.4 Clusters of meta-analyses and mean effect sizes (ES) for Special 'Education', 'Special' Education and 'Related' Services[a]

Special 'Education'	ES	'Special' Education	ES	'Related' Services	ES
Mnemonic strategies	1.62	Psycholinguistic training	0.39	Behaviour modification	0.93
Reading comprehension strategies	0.94	Social skills training	0.20	Cognitive behaviour modification	0.74
Direct instruction	0.84	Modality instruction	0.14	Psychotherapy	0.71
Formative evaluation	0.70	Perceptual training	0.08	Stimulant medication	0.62
Computer-assisted instruction	0.66			Psychotropic medication	0.30
Peer tutoring	0.58			Diet restrictions	−0.12
Word recognition strategies	0.57				
Mean	*0.84*		*0.20*		*0.53*

Source: Forness (2001).

Notes: Effect sizes around 0.20 are considered small, 0.50 are medium and 0.80 are large.

[a] These interventions were categorised according to whether they would be routinely used in general education (Special 'Education'), whether they were focused upon overcoming hypothetical causes of individual deficits ('Special' Education) or whether they involved treatments delivered by or relying upon considerable consultation with other professionals ('Related' Services).

resultant enabling and disabling factors (Rix, 2005b, 2009b) (see Table 6.5). These factors were equally relevant to many other children and would impact upon the learning of any student. They would not be eradicated by shifting this particular population of pupils to a specific setting either.

It is important to recognise that this kind of everydayness is clear across the literature. Consider the findings of a 100 paper, systematic review into best practice for persons with autistic spectrum disorders (Parsons et al., 2009). As with other impairment specific reviews, the key findings supported the notion that best practice requires adapting everyday teaching skills and ways of working. This is my summary:

1   There is some evidence of short-term effectiveness of intensive behavioural approaches but not of their long-term effectiveness.
2   Mixed findings on intensive behaviour programmes suggest that no one approach will be best for all children and there is little evidence of them providing benefits over standard statutory provision.
3   Early intervention around communicative behaviours seems a promising approach.
4   Parents need support to contribute effectively to early intervention but it is stressful and disruptive to families.
5   Practitioners need ongoing training by working with families and young people.

TABLE 6.5 Possible enabling and disabling factors using auditory and linguistic characteristics identified through research with people with the Down syndrome label

Possible enabling factors?

- Use of visual input when teaching
- Encouragement of sub-vocal rehearsal through repetition in text
- Use of repetition to establish names, terms and concepts
- Use of short words and sentences
- Limiting the number of concepts, names etc. discussed per section
- Attempting to have a maximum of two referential concepts, names etc. per text section
- Anticipating possible confusion through pronoun use and considering using the proper noun to refer to the key person or item
- Defining clear, obvious points of reference and limit the need for switching focus
- Use of short sentences – one clause better than two
- Use of simple sentences
- Use of familiar words – but define familiar with care
- Use of words of one or two syllables
- Trying to use single consonant words
- Defining possible new words
- Reinforcing new words through repetition so they become familiar
- Reinforcing the most significant words
- Use of alternative words to explain meaning through context
- Use of alternative words to reinforce meaning through context
- Considering possible alternatives meanings for words, e.g. Cannon/Canon
- Avoiding passive and negative forms
- Using of sign-supported language

Possible disabling barriers?

- Reliance upon auditory input
- Poor diction and clarity of speech
- Presenting information when there are distractions
- Use of complex sentences with a number of different concepts or individuals referred to
- Use of long sentences
- Use of broad vocabulary
- Use of long words
- Complex use of pronouns and proper nouns
- Using negative and passive sentences
- Introducing new words
- Introducing dual tasks
- Introducing a wide number of new skills
- Lack of possibilities to practice skills
- Relying on new skills
- Relying on memory alone
- Unfamiliar situations
- Assumptions about knowledge and vocabulary
- Requiring a rapid response
- Lack of signing

Source: Based on Rix (2009b).

6 Well-known interventions (such as the Picture Exchange Communication System (PECS), Lovaas and applied behavioural analysis) are not as effective as once thought.

7 Structured and less structured approaches, using different modes of presentation (information and communication technology, pictures, videos) have proved useful for promoting specific learning outcomes.

8 Every child identified with autistic spectrum disorder has an individual learning profile.

9 More naturalistic, child-centred and child-led approaches seem more promising than adult-directed, prompt-dependent procedures.

10 Despite a growth in provision focused upon autism, there is a lack of research evidence as to whether separate provision is appropriate and effective.

11 Mainstream settings have to listen to young people with autism about their experiences, which reflect the needs of many who require additional support.

Similarly, Marschark et al. (2011) in the review mentioned previously associated with the deaf in mainstream classrooms noted that teachers generally needed to do more of the same thing rather than something different. The key was to understand what teachers of the deaf do to ensure their pupils gain equally to their peers. They noted strategies and materials which have to be used on an everyday basis,[19] and that regular visits from teachers of the deaf cannot make up for such engagement. The difficulty is not in the strategies themselves, but in being aware of them and how readily they can be incorporated into one's practice. They are far easier to learn than a long list of characteristics associated with an impairment group.

Teachers tend to claim that they lack the skills and knowledge about the nature of the SEN groupings and how to work with them (Scruggs & Mastropieri, 1996; OFSTED, 2004; Ali, Mustapha & Jelas, 2006; Sharma, Forlin & Loreman, 2008; Florian & Black-Hawkins, 2011; Delgado-Pinheiro & Omote, 2010).[20] There is no question that teachers benefit from good initial training but the kinds of skills at the heart of both special and inclusive, are primarily ones which they can develop through experience and practice.[21] Recognising the everydayness of practice and sharing this recognition is one of the biggest challenges school face though. The tensions around its acceptance are evident in it being how practitioners described special pedagogy in Chapter 4 and at the same time being a notion associated with the aspirational second world of inclusion.[22]

Collective autonomy?

Skidmore (2004) suggested that schools which successfully accommodate a diverse range of learners and pupils start from a consideration of the curriculum and subject lessons and from this develop their inclusive teaching practices. My conviction is that these everyday practices will only be widely used to deliver curriculum and subject goals if we can encourage the greater use of open-ended learning activities.

This is the only means by which the full range of student and teacher experiences, skills and capacities can stand a chance of being brought together within a collective learning environment. How, for example, can teachers utilise their pedagogical skills to benefit all children if their study of erosion, cells, shopping in France, use of equations, and so forth has to meet limiting learning outcomes, or students have to achieve a specific predefined level?

It seems very odd to me that open-ended learning is the kind which we encourage in pre-school and post-school but not within school. We want our very young people to play and we want people in their late teens to increasingly take on a research role; but within school we go the other direction. Our requirement that people make the grade and learn specific information or skills restricts what they can achieve, what they can be taught and how that teaching can take place. This does not mean policy-makers cannot construct processes to maintain standards, but it requires recognising that how we define what is to be learned constrains the processes of teaching.

Enabling greater use of open-ended activities is also conducive to the goals identified at the end of Chapter 5, particularly students' capacity to develop the collective and self-regulatory skills identified in relation to workplaces. It also fits effectively within the models of classrooms which researchers suggest are more likely to be inclusive.

Using an immersive research methodology, Florian and Black-Hawkins (2011) looked to identify approaches that included all children through an in-depth study of 'teacher craft' in two Scottish schools. They sought how teachers might avoid thinking about what works for most and what is additional for some, shifting to a focus upon creating rich learning opportunities for the whole community of learners. They talked about creating spaces where children are trusted to make good decisions about how, where, when and with whom they learn. Teachers discuss ideas about teaching and learning with colleagues both inside and outside the class. They create options for learning, consulting students about their assistance, creating situations which support people to work with different groups.[23]

Such an approach reflects the work of Hart, Dixon, Drummond and McIntyre (2004), who argued that educationalists need to focus on the context of the child's experience, setting aside the language of special educational needs and individualized 'outside' support. It echoes too the views of teachers engaged effectively with children identified with social and emotional behavioural difficulties (Goodman & Burton, 2010). They discussed building respectful relationships with students, finding out about their backgrounds and interests, so they could develop collaborative working, with both parties seeking to negotiate rather than confront each other. They sought to give the student responsibilities within the learning situation, as well as encouraging them to manage their own behaviour.

This experience of teachers echoes findings such those of Ryan and Deci (2000), who drew upon a wide range of research from within differing paradigms in developing self-determination theory. They identified that tangible rewards and pressures diminish the intrinsic motivation people feel. In contrast, choice, opportunities for self-direction and acknowledgment of feelings support motivation and encourage interest and the seeking of challenges. Ryan and Deci's notion of autonomous learning environments acknowledges that students in a more controlled environment are less motivated, show less initiative and are less effective learners in comparison to those who are in an autonomy-supportive environment.[24] Students' enjoyment, motivation, perception of challenge, competence and mood have also been shown to be influenced by environments which encourage them to fulfil meaningful tasks (Barkoukis, Tsorbatzoudis & Grouios, 2008). Many children, for example, feel that Physical Education offers a particularly enjoyable time within the school day, because PE teachers and lessons are seen to give them greater autonomy than many other subjects;[25] this provides self-determined reasons for maintaining discipline (Zounhia, Hatziharistos & Emmanouel, 2003).

Within such environments it is easy to see why people might fear the class teacher will lose their position of authority. It is particularly important, however, that this does not happen. The need for the teacher to take responsibility for all students is widely recognised in many countries. For example, in England it is part of the teaching standards. Fox et al. (2004) conclude from their 18 case studies that as well as the effectiveness of inclusion depending upon an accessible curriculum, with the child central to the learning process, it is essential that the class teacher has to centrally manage support and organisation of the child's educational experience on a daily basis. They make it clear that at the heart of this management, and the child's experience, is the how the adult support (teaching assistants) and class teacher work together.

Who's in charge?

The way in which staff work with each other represents a key model of practice to students, framing their understanding of collective working. Unfortunately, the model which is represented is rarely the same collective approach we are seeking in the students. Generally the support teacher will be in a subordinate role to the class teacher (Murphy, 2011). As my experience cited above would suggest, the theory of collaborative or team-teaching processes may also be only partially understood. Our interviews in Italy (Rix et al., 2013a) revealed this similar confusion. Teachers said they were team-teaching but described the hierarchical relationship noted by Murphy.

There are plenty of models for people to follow. Solis, Vaughn, Swanson and Mcculley (2012) reported on six meta-analyses covering 146 studies looking at collaborative models of instruction. They cite research which lists the following forms of co-teaching:

- whole class, teacher led;
- two heterogeneous groups;
- two homogeneous groups;
- station teaching.
- whole class + small group;
- whole class team-teaching.

The findings of this study cannot be considered a ringing endorsement of team-teaching, though. First, only 17 of the studies considered student outcomes; second, the range of variables meant the researchers could only confidently claim a very small positive effect on social and academic outcomes. What seemed to be evident was that team-teaching benefited some more than others. However, across the studies they noted that strategies designed to facilitate peer-to-peer discussion and instruction were consistently reported as popular and potentially effective. This popularity with students and teachers seems significant if you are trying to develop the classroom environment described above. Its capacity to enhance relationships with students and between teachers, along with learning from each other and with each other, has also been recognised in a small Irish study (Murphy, 2011). This examined the working relationship of four team-teaching dyads. These teachers saw team-teaching as the means to reframe withdrawal models of support, providing flexible opportunities to mix and match responses to student learning. Even if there were inconsistencies in its operation, team-teaching provided a degree of adaptability that enabled wider support without the need for specific resource allocation.

The degree to which any kind of team-teaching is used varies considerably. Murphy reported that team-teaching in Ireland was relatively underused, but it has been more prevalent in other countries. Saloviita and Takala (2010), in their study of 434 Finnish practitioners identified that co-teaching was used weekly by 50 per cent of special education teachers, by just over 30 per cent of class teachers and just over 15 per cent of subject teachers, and then for only two to three hours a week. The barriers they identified were lack of planning time (70 per cent), lack of time generally (10 per cent), lack of knowledge (16 per cent) and lack of a teaching partner (29 per cent). Only 5 per cent of participants reported negative experiences with over 90 per cent being positive or very positive about it as a way of working.[26] This echoes my own experiences as a support teacher as well as a parent in discussion with staff at my son's schools.

Given the issues of time raised by practitioners, it is important to note that the amount of time required is not great. Takala and Uusitalo-Malmivaara (2012) working in four Finnish schools over a year, reported views towards team-teaching. Teachers (who co-taught but had no specific training in co-teaching) felt that 15 minutes was enough to plan one lesson. In Italy, teachers at a primary level had a legal right to time for collaborative planning, but this was still a matter of legislative debate at secondary level. The staff we spoke to felt that two hours a week was manageable, but that even one hour would give them an important opportunity to reflect on their teaching activities (Rix et al., 2013a).

There are two strong barriers to an increase in co-teaching; cost and attitudes. Traditionally, people are the greatest cost within the education system. If you double up the number of paid adults within the class or provide them with planning time you invariably increase the cost. Teachers are also very defensive of their territory. For example, when teaching assistant numbers expanded in the UK they were widely regarded as a threat, and there was talk of an unqualified mum's army invading schools (Clark, 2002). In Norway, they talked about the teacher being the king in their class (Rix et al., 2013a).

Our research also suggested opportunities for change, however. We came across some administrations using contracts to define collaborative roles and to require some collaborative working. Models which encouraged collaboration and involved relatively simple reorganisation of staff and teaching groupings were also in evidence, without great cost increases. In Italy and Japan, for example, we found examples of three or four teachers to two classes or a support teacher linked to a subject teacher, or support teachers allocated to a class regardless of identified support needs. During filming in a London school in 2013[27] we also recorded a range of team-teaching arrangements involving a mix of teaching, support staff and students working across a number of classes.

Such models demonstrate there are different ways to provide support and encourage collaboration. Changing assessment practices and opening up the curriculum as discussed elsewhere in the book could also release other personnel to work directly in classes, enabling the spread of their expertise. Cost and traditional class relationship may be constraints but they need not be impermeable barriers to the wider use of collaborative teaching practices.

Yes, but are they learning?

The importance of group collaboration has been outlined in this chapter from a sociocultural theoretical position, but was also highlighted for its economic importance in Chapter 5. A major challenge to its wider usage, however, is its limited role in relation to assessment. It would seem that collaborative assessment or group assessment of learning is not frequently considered an appropriate summative approach. It is very much an additional activity, more commonplace at university level or outside of education or as an occasional class activity. The desire for externally verifiable and comparable data tends to lead us elsewhere. For example, as mentioned in Chapter 5, in 2013 PISA proposed a collaborative problem-solving framework.[28] The framework focuses upon cognitive processes which echo those used for individual problem-solving.[29] They also focus upon measuring the individual learner. It is quite possible to design collective metrics though. Frusciante & Siberon (2010), for example describe a Community Self-Assessment Tool which identifies multiple markers of success.

Early research suggested group assessment could not be relied upon as a predictor of individual performance (Webb, 1993), and given the dominant nature of standardisation processes since then, there has been little to encourage its wider development. Webb (1995) recommended that any collaborative assessment must be clear about its aims, procedures and criteria. All of those involved need to know if the goal is individual student-learning or group productivity and whether the assessment is measuring:

- students' unassisted individual competence;
- students' learning with others;
- group productivity;
- students' capacity to interact and collaborate.

It may or may not be possible to measure all these at once, but this should not be a problem if there is clarity and consistency. Hargreaves (2007) raises other key questions, whilst talking about collaborative formative assessments or assessments for learning:

- Does the assessment lead to learning or other social valued outcomes?
- Does the form of the assessment promote the kind of learning we want to encourage?
- Are students and teachers familiar with collaborative learning situations?
- Is feedback meaningful to the students and the activity undertaken?

For teachers accustomed to traditional classroom activities, encouraging collaborative learning can feel threatening. There is a sense of losing control. A key component in collaborative learning process is that each member has equal value even though they will make different contributions. They should complement each other, constructing a shared understanding by building on each other's contributions. Feedback is less likely to take the traditional summative form. It can take the form of challenges from inside and outside the group, self-regulatory actions or the kinds of support students provide to each other. The teacher however still has a key role to play. They still have to direct the learning, encouraging collaboration as opposed to allowing students to merely share parts of a project or to become competitive with other members of their group (Hargreaves, 2007).

An evaluation of assessment on co-operative learning activities, carried out by a Masters student (Otchoun, 2010) with teachers in France and Norway, noted that the teachers typically relied upon: a range of presentations; self-reflection tasks; and portfolios, seeking to make activities as authentic as possible. They faced challenges in ensuring real participation from each member, in developing a culture of peer-assessment, in timings, costs and resources for tasks, and in relying upon student reports of competence and their awarding of grades. This does not mean that marks (so important within the current education discourse) cannot be given. Hargreaves (2007) described a primary school in England and another in St Kitts. In the former the group divided up 60 marks between them to reflect how each had done; in the latter the group submitted a report, which included a self-assessment and then had to make a presentation to an invited audience and answer questions to explain how the project had been useful.

In the 1990s, a variety of methods were used at the University of Sunderland (Lejk & Wyvill, 1996), involving both participants and tutor. For example, teachers assessed and scored students during a collective activity on the basis of agreed criteria.[30] Other approaches included:

- multiplication of group mark by individual weighting factor;
- distribution of a pool of marks;
- group mark plus or minus contribution mark;
- separation of process (student evaluation) and product (tutor evaluation);

- equally shared mark with exceptional tutor intervention;
- splitting of group tasks and individual tasks;
- yellow and red cards (individual tasks leading to agreed group submission);
- averaged individual assessment;
- deviations from an agreed norm.

What is evident is that we have available to us a diverse range of assessment strategies which can support student learning within collaborative activities, providing both formative and summative opportunities. At the same time, we have a clear desire to enhance the capacity of students to work collaboratively. If we decide to approach these two opportunities using a co-teaching model and open-ended activities, we have a platform to expand practitioner's capacity and self-belief to use their skills to the benefit of all. This of course does not resolve all the difficulties outlined in the opening sections of this chapter, but it does create new possibilities so we can confront them in new ways.

What if I am wrong?

Throughout this book I have attempted to draw upon a wide range of research to support my arguments. I have tended to use more research from meta-analyses or arising from a sociocultural theoretical base, but this has been by no means my only source. I know, though, that the evidence I have presented can nearly all be disputed. A major problem for practitioners is that, whatever people may suggest, the evidence for any teaching approach is equivocal. The scientific evidence is unclear and any theoretical explanation is to some degree an article of faith. The underlying problem is the amount of complex variables which are at play in any given learning context. This presents similar problems to those confronting our understanding of complex environmental systems. This complexity led, in the 1970s, to the development of the precautionary principle. The precautionary principle maintained that decision-makers should act in advance of scientific certainty to avoid environmental damage or social deprivation. Any action likely to cause serious harm was taken to be morally wrong and should be rejected as an option against which other actions could be compared. The principle could be applied with increasing strength depending upon the vulnerability of the environment and the cost envisaged.

Looking across the development of the precautionary principle and the arguments about its nature, O'Riordan and Jordan (1995) outlined seven core elements:

1 *Pro-action.* Taking action prior to having scientific proof or when consequences are unknown.
2 *Cost-effectiveness.* Social and environmental gains have to be examined in relation to costs.
3 *Safeguarding ecological space.* We must avoid irreversible decline or self-reinforcing social injustice.

4   *Legitimising the status of intrinsic value.* It is a moral duty to support vulnerable systems central to regeneration
5   *Shifting the onus of proof.* The proponents of an action need to prove it does not cause harm.
6   *Meso-scale planning.* Decisions have to include consideration of long-term impacts.
7   *Paying for ecological debt.* We exist in a situation in which much damage has occurred, but actions taken in ignorance cannot have responsibility retrospectively applied.

Given the diverse viewpoints upon education and the potential for it to challenge or reassert social inequities and individual marginalisation, such a principle could also be applied to schooling. These core elements can provide educationalists with some useful tools within a complex social system where scientific evidence is limited and frequently contradictory.

3   We should not continue with an action simply because we have always done it that way and there is no clear evidence that it damages learning or learners.
4   We must weigh the benefits of educational approaches for some against the costs for others.
5   We must avoid creating social and physical environments which perpetuate social and personal inequity.
6   We have a moral duty to support marginal and vulnerable members of the community.
7   We should not require evidence that someone is having difficulties but should assume that all actions have the potential to be exclusionary.
8   We need to consider the long-term impact upon children and communities beyond short-term targets.
9   Our systems have perpetuated marginalisation, but we should not seek to blame people for exclusionary practices carried out in good faith.

Such a principle would encourage us to consider the wider processes of education, beyond the everyday pressures of grades and levels of achievement. It may support us in identifying and acknowledging the risks of our long-held assumptions, practices or our latest educational craze. It may help alert us to mundane moments of marginalisation as well as to those which are already obvious. It may make us more attentive to mistakes we have just made, are about to make or have been making for some time. It might also encourage us to consider the wider context.

Looking wider

In Chapter 5 and in our discussion of pedagogy the need to increase our focus upon learning in context has been much in evidence. The importance of researching individual development in context has also been acknowledged for many years.

Bronfenbrenner (1977), for example, said that research in this area had to explore the 'dynamic relation between person and situation' (p. 515). In early years provision such an emphasis has long been in evidence. For example, emphasis is placed upon the family and parents (e.g. Newman, McEwen, Mackin & Slowley, 2009; Mahoney, Perales, Wiggers & Herman, 2006; Bronfenbrenner, 1974) or upon key practitioners working together (e.g. Limbrick, 2010). A range of assessment approaches focus upon the child's perspective in context (e.g. narrative assessment – Cullen, Williamson & Lepper, 2005; a learning story approach – Carr, 2001; the mosaic approach – Clark and Moss, 2001: in-the-picture method – Matthews & Rix, 2013; Parry, 2014). These approaches explore the children's interactions and experiences within a learning situation, encouraging those around the child to challenge their own assumptions and take a more holistic view of the child. Other researchers draw upon the need to understand the child's home, local community and other social institutions. The funds-of-knowledge approach, for example (Gonzalez, Moll & Amanti, 2005) focuses upon the people's competence and knowledge; the strengths and resources which have arisen from and framed their experiences of life. This provides a rich resource for teachers and teaching, since it builds upon student's understanding and the cultural interaction which gives their knowledge meaning.

These approaches all recognise the importance of the social context and are certainly of use in seeking alternative approaches to current dominant priorities. Their influence is limited, however, and they still tend to encourage a focus upon the individual or individuals within context rather than a focus upon collective practices.

A focus upon context needs to become an everyday expectation in relation to wider processes of planning. We need to deliberately consider the wider context when we make decisions about the use of resources and the provision of support. Our documentation and funding mechanisms need to call for such a focus. They need to encourage local discussions about weaknesses and strengths, challenges and opportunities, possible ways forward and barriers to be overcome. They need to be carried out in relation to the whole class. They need to support the range of practitioners, family and community members associated with the learning situation. They need to enable us to reflect and act upon on such variables as:

- peer group interactions;
- learning opportunities and constraints arising from the curriculum or pedagogy;
- teaching relationships between staff;
- people's strengths and limitations;
- training and development possibilities;
- policy and resource constraints;
- school and support service organisation;
- local resources;
- possible programmes of learning;
- research evidence;

- relationships with families and local communities;
- relationships with other professionals and other settings;
- institutional attitudes and expectations.

Appropriate mechanisms could support a growing collective understanding of the challenges which we face. People could better discuss what they cannot do, as well as what they might be able to do and why. Creating an expectation and facilitating such discussions would aim to encourage a more flexible and responsive learning space but it would also facilitate agitation and planning for change.

As with all suggestions in this book, I believe they can be managed in such a way as to ease the workload of those involved, not add another layer of bureaucracy. This is not about producing plans for 30 children in a class or being seen to respond to a tick-list of variables or meeting a target for equity. This is about seeking, together, a better way to achieve the goals of education.

In the final chapter I will attempt to explain how we might come to some agreement about those goals and how we can better describe the process we are going through as we seek to achieve them.

Notes

1 Reck the rede – follow the advice,
2 During this period we were inspected by the Office for Standards in Education (Ofsted) on a number of occasions. In one lesson they observed me teaching grammar to students with English as an Additional Language. This was in response to a request from the students, but the inspector told me such an approach could only ever be deemed satisfactory. The nature of OFSTED's role meant they could not advise me what I should be doing instead; however, they could just point out it was not very good. Later that week I was observed supporting an English teacher in the teaching of Shakespeare's *Macbeth*. Our work was deemed to be outstanding and it was recorded that we were a perfect example of how team teaching should operate. I didn't have a clue what they were talking about. We were just getting on with our job, based on some mutual respect and trust. No one had explained team teaching to me when I was trained.
3 A young person who was a member of a youth theatre group I had just begun to support once had a major shouting match with the youth worker organising the company. This rebuke concluded with the phrase … "'isms, fucking 'isms, we've always got to do fucking 'isms!'". I felt he had identified a problem at the heart of the provision.
4 The language associated with ability underpins a hierarchical view of knowledge too. The better you are, the higher your group. The worse you are, the lower your group.
5 Many schools around the world will use some kind of entry test to allocate children to classes, sets or streams. In earlier chapters we highlighted the limitations of such standardised instruments. There will also be a degree of self-fulfilling prophecy (Brophy & Good, 1974; Rosenthal & Jacobsen, 1968) about such tests. These processes tend to reinforce the status quo too and make it easier for teachers and students to carry on in the traditional teaching roles.
6 I have always found teenagers to be just as caring and sharing as everyone else. Frequently more so. It is a matter of opportunity and expectation.
7 It may be tempting to think that access to online resources changes this, but my experience of education websites is that they are as text heavy as the traditional textbooks. As ever, it is a matter of what you do with the technology.

8 Such as: younger school entry; greater focus upon static, academic tasks; demand for earlier and better reading; an increasingly crowded curriculum; and shorter breaks.

9 Similar problems arise for all conditions which depend upon a behavioural diagnosis. For example, Hilton (2006), in her study of 40 young Scots exhibiting disruptive behaviour and truancy and experiencing exclusion, found that the young people could give consistent and rational explanations for behaviour, frequently situated in the context of school practices and environment.

10 There is also some evidence to support the use of stimulant to reduce subsequent psychiatric disorders and disruptive behaviours in some stimulant responsive children (e.g. Biederman, Monuteaux, Spencer, Wilens & Faraone, 2009; Hechtman et al., 2004). Others point out that in the low doses these drugs are given, the same effect of increased focus and docility would be in evident in anyone, not just children with the ADHD/ASD label (Baughman & Hovey, 2006)

11 One of many terms for the additional adult frequently situated at the heart of what is purported to be inclusive provision.

12 As discussed at the start of Chapter 3.

13 It seems reasonable to ask whether this will encourage a non-critical acceptance of: not questioning rules; lying; deceiving to induce compliance or avoid detection; asymmetric lines of respect within hierarchies. It might also be teaching young people not to expect or value justice.

14 The comparison was made harder by the variation in the processes adopted, as well as difference in research approaches, which rarely measured cost effectiveness or academic achievement.

15 This expertise could not be confirmed by the researchers, but it was evident that they offered a wider range of support programmes.

16 The paperwork was made up of: early intervention activity sheets; teacher and teaching assistant annotated lesson plans; evaluation reports from speech and language therapists, paediatricians, other medical practitioners, portage home visitors, occupational therapists, teachers, nursery workers, educational psychologists and parents; minutes of meetings with all of these individuals; letters to and from practitioners and managers within these support systems.

17 The ZPD was a measure of how much scope there was for educational development. In *Thought and Language,* Vygotsky (1986) describes the "zone of proximal development" as "the discrepancy between a child's actual mental age and the level he reaches in solving problems with assistance" (p. 187). Vygotsky's notion of mental age was not the same as many other twentieth-century psychologists. He rejected the use of the term as a general measure as it is not dynamic. He felt all children are different and working with them according to an assessed level will impede their learning. I once wrote a letter to the *Times Educational Supplement* giving the following reasons why they should not use the term 'mental age' in an article they had published about a person labelled with Down syndrome:

- A mental age suggests we all follow a rigid developmental model – which we do not.
- It ignores the fact that all learning is a response to the opportunities we are presented with in society.
- No two people are the same. We all have different skills and abilities, and we demonstrate intelligences in different ways. One number cannot capture this.
- If we say someone is like a four-year-old we treat them like a four-year-old.
- It is considered an offensive label by many people.
- Very few other people use it any more.
- What does a lifetime of experiences count for?

They chose to dismiss the letter with a heading which suggested I was a political correctness zealot: "Reasons why 'mental age' is an offensive term" and explained that this was the term used by the child's mother and professional carers. The Editors bore no responsibility for language. They did not seem aware of Vygotsky's viewpoint either.

18 This is also how many people have theorised inclusive educational practice (e.g. Hart, 1996; Thomas & Loxley, 2001). Lewis and Norwich (2005) argue that special is an intensification of practice rather than a difference in curriculum design and pedagogic strategies.

19 These strategies were listed in Chapter 3.

20 This is the kind of knowledge which Norwich suggested filters how they see themselves as a teacher, how they understand the way in which children learn and what children should study.

21 Looking at the maths and reading results of Florida students over a five-year period at the start of the twenty-first century, Feng and Marcos (2013) concluded that students with special educational needs do better if their teachers have extensive initial special educational training or if they have greater experience of teaching. In-service training was not seen to have an impact.

22 The three worlds of inclusion were outlined in Chapter 3.

23 As will be discussed in Chapter 7, such approaches do not come without difficulties; they do, however, have a long heritage; e.g. the ideas of A. S. Neill and the free-school movement.

24 Ironically, perhaps the more you are identified as requiring support the greater the control exerted upon you (e.g. previous discussions of response to intervention or schools serving a low socio-economic community).

25 Though maybe not those mentioned earlier in the chapter, who feel marginalised by the body identities associated with PE.

26 These issues echo the wider findings of Solis et al. (2012).

27 This mainstream school had a hugely diverse student intake, including many speakers of English as an additional language and many people identified with serious or profound learning or behavioural difficulties.

28 Unfortunately, a norm-based assumption underpins the PISA approach and they assume that most 15-year-old students will be suitably cognitively and socially "developed" to complete the tasks, rather than the tasks being open ended (OECD, 2013b).

29 Exploring and understanding; representing and formulating; planning and executing; monitoring and reflecting (OECD, 2013b, p. 9).

30 Communication and thinking; relationships; leadership.

7

CHALLENGING THE CONTRADICTIONS WITHIN A COMMUNITY OF PROVISION

'Marooned three years agone,' he continued, 'and lived on goats since then, and berries, and oysters. Wherever a man is, says I, a man can do for himself. But, mate, my heart is sore for Christian diet. You mightn't happen to have a piece of cheese about you, now? No? Well, many's the long night I've dreamed of cheese-toasted, mostly – and woke up again, and here I were.'

'If ever I can get aboard again,' said I, 'you shall have cheese by the stone.'

(Stevenson, 1883)

Living on oysters, dreaming of cheese

Our lives are communal. Some people may not like to think of their lives in this way, but we are always in this together, situated in relationships, living in moments which are negotiated and defined with varying degrees of cognisance and from diverse perspectives. This is not a romantic notion of communal life, however. Community is a complex interplay which marginalises people just as much as it creates a sense of security. It establishes and situates our identities, and the challenges and opportunities which arise because of them.

In the few weeks before I began this final chapter, two friends of the family committed suicide. One attended school with my daughter. He was a lover of music and football and had just finished his GCSE exams. The other was father of my son's best friend, a fine off-road motorbike rider, a skilled painter and decorator and someone whose company our family thoroughly enjoyed. Both of these people carried out an entirely individual act for reasons which at that moment made sense to them; the consequences of their tragic decision however are ours. We scramble to explain, to understand, to find causes and moments of responsibility. We feel sadness and absolute loss, emptiness and loneliness. For those closest to them life seems so bleak. For those who witnessed some aspect of the moment, the shock of the experience must be lifelong. Yet the hope for those who are left is rooted in the responses of those around them. The possibility presented by the support and presence of others (or its denial) will underpin their future. It is not 'time' which will heal the pain, but the accumulation of alternative experiences and ways of understanding themselves within this new situation.

The challenge for us is that life is very rarely black and white. It tends to be very grey indeed. Consider the response of the head-teacher at my daughter's school in trying to deal with their collective grief. He wrote to every family at the school. His letter reflected the complexity of the situation. He asserted that this boy had enjoyed school. He recognised the fundamental decency of the young people in his setting. He did not want them to feel responsible for the death of this member of the community. But he also wanted them to understand that their words and ways of being could have a profoundly negative impact upon people. His tentative comments recognised that the community had had a role to play in how this young man understood himself. Perhaps there were many who without intentional malevolence had placed this young man upon the margins. As I read, I felt sure that the implication of the letter was that none of us was individually responsible, but there was a collective duty in which we may have fallen short.

The greyness of life presents profound challenges for an education system which tends towards absolutes. This is a system which likes to label. It believes in grades and sets, clubs and houses. It teaches that there are correct and incorrect answers. Its conclusions imply that some people are better than others. It inclines to assume that the outcomes of socially infused relationships and understandings can be reliably and consistently measured and described. It is premised upon a vision of life which is factual and subject defined. But this vision is a chimera.

I attended a church service at the turn of the century in which a dying man stood and spoke of his life. He told the congregation that when he began his 'O' levels[1] he thought he knew what an atom was, but as he studied for his exams it became clear what he had been taught before was not the real story. When he arrived to do his 'A' levels he once again thought that he knew what an atom was, but as he studied for his exams it became clear that once more what he had been taught before was not the real story. In his first year at university, and then again in his second year of university, he found his previous convictions overturned. By the time he reached the third year, he said, he had begun to realise the truth, which was that no one knew what an atom was. Subsequently he had spent the rest of his career as a low-orbit astrophysicist struggling with the concept. His point was that we think we know the answers when we don't; but it does not matter that we do not, because it is our relationship with the questions which make life meaningful. Of course the problem for most of us is that we don't get past the first couple of exam levels. Our understanding is stultified. And this stultified understanding is spread across the whole of the curriculum. The knowledge we teach is rarely acknowledged as being ignorance. To do so would risk (for some people) undermining the whole system. Much easier to continue to focus upon the grades, the percentages, the labels, the absolutist measures we have created to divide people up in the belief that we are doing so according to reliable notions of intellect and capacity.

This chapter is an attempt to situate the complex within practices which improve our capacity to understand the complexity of our relationship with each other and with notions of knowledge, skills and personality. It also aims to provide us with a metaphor that we can use to think about our ways of working and being and how best we can support each other.

The problem so far

The previous chapters have outlined a range of factors which serve to marginalise people within education systems and so require the notions of inclusion and special. I will not attempt to list all the issues, but will try to broadly (and briefly) summarise the areas discussed.[2]

Education has emerged from a complex history with multiple competing aims. The traditional processes cannot satisfy this multiplicity and consequently many are failed by the system. However, each of the aims will be understood by different people in different ways, who will support and value it variously and who may fight for its maintenance or wish to downplay its significance. The challenge is to balance the contradictory thrust that consequently emerges from these aims, working towards them whilst overcoming the tendency to marginalise.[3]

Special education also has a complex history which asserts its worth and validates its continuity. Like all social systems it is constituted with vested interests and strong beliefs, playing a key role in creating identity for its population. These represent variable responses to varying social pressures and encourage small fiefdoms of influence. A fundamental role of special is to encourage certainty in the face of the limitations of the mainstream, except that its practices are shown to be uncertain. Similarly, they lack the evidence to suggest that they are essentially different to or less problematic than the mainstream. Attempts to resolve mainstream limitations through the development of inclusion seem to demonstrate the same partial success as special, however. The concept has been interpreted so widely as to undermine its original clarity. For many people within schools, given the workloads, attitudes and policies which dominate settings, there seems to be a big gap between rhetorical possibilities and the practical constraints.

Underlying these tensions is an additional challenge. The only way in which we can institute and deliver the kind of support which will enable more people to benefit from individual or collective processes is social interaction. However, the array of people involved with education have different theoretical views and belief systems. We have a plethora of models to describe practice and people. Sometimes, these discourses have their own terminologies, but even when the languages overlap the meaning we allocate to words and concepts vary. However, the different professions, policy-makers, media pundits, and so forth tend to use these words and concepts as if they are unproblematic. We are frequently seeking agreement whilst using restrictive vocabularies or talking about quite different understandings or possibilities. As a consequence we may find ourselves failing to recognise the disparity between our positions, ironing over the contradictory positions; or we may reject ideas, even if our beliefs are not that far apart, because they seem beyond our control; or we may give up on collaboration because we feel we lack the capacity to build a workable bridge between our discourses.

The challenges of education are also situated within a wider social and cultural context. In many communities this encourages ways of thinking which work against key aspects of learning and the educational goals suggested above. In particular, there is a growing or prevailing emphasis upon individualisation. The recognition and delivery of individual rights is hard fought for. Notions of choice, standards and markets dominate political, organisational and media rhetoric. This emphasis is reflected in the predominant policies. Similarly, our social networks, entertainment and cultural narratives are constructed around aspirational personalities. Our identities and lifestyles are increasingly linked to who we are, in separation from others, or at least they are presented as being so. However, the manner in which we learn, the means by which we establish our place in this world, our capacity to live within it, are far more interdependent than independent.

The established everyday practices of schools frequently create the space in which this discord and these contradictions can be played out. Processes which are meant to better provide support or deliver learning create their own divisions or perpetuate inequities. Curricula, which are intended to frame people's learning, prioritise issues and topics which are more relevant for some, reflecting the dominant voices within our culture. Old ways continue despite much talk of change, professional development and new opportunity. People recognise the contradictions and the challenges, but do not feel able or willing or supported enough to transform their practices and settings. Invariably, there are small changes in some places and larger changes in others, but even dramatic changes to the structure of the systems do not disrupt our tendency to carry on much as before. As a consequence, any shift is glacial. We experience a gradual movement, which hardly feels like change at all, except for the occasional ruptures that graphically illustrate our precariousness amongst the onward creep of generations.

The suggestions so far

The current dominant model cannot overcome the barriers inherent within our socially infused structures. It cannot resolve their underlying inequities. However, any expectation that this dominant model might be dropped seems unrealistic, even if there are strong arguments to do so. Even if we create this shift, many people would seek to adapt their old ways to fit the new discourse. It seems sensible therefore to start from the premise that people do not agree and that our diverse aims, opinions and theories cannot be reconciled. We can and should continue to explain and explore the shortcomings and strengths in our ways of working and thinking. Such reflection should draw upon the kinds of premises which emerge from the precautionary principle; however, this will not produce agreement. It can only serve as a platform for challenging ourselves. Education needs to find a means to counterbalance the emphasis upon the individual, to seek the means to encourage collective skills which focus upon our social interplay and ways of learning and being. This is not simply a reflection of the well-established research into learning processes but also the only means to deliver the kinds of skills which businesses and other key social enterprises repeatedly call for. At its most basic we need to encourage and enable our individualised selves to operate in ways which serve our collective ends.

We need to encourage a political will, media recognition and an enthusiasm within the general public for communal educational aims, which do not deny the historical goals of schooling. We will not drop our belief in subject areas and expert knowledge quickly; however, we need to reduce our emphasis upon their outputs as the markers of a learner's success. We can raise the profile of educational aims associated with: team-working, cultural awareness, people and language skills, diverse life and communication experiences; instilling a desire for the ongoing development of knowledge for ourselves and those around us. In seeking to achieve such aims, we can more meaningfully focus upon our need for social responsibility as well as on an awareness of rights. We can also more readily focus upon the creation of cohesive communities, and do so by enabling people to have a productive and valued role within them.

An increased emphasis upon the collective can also provide space for those involved with education to rethink their ways of working, facilitating a move beyond the problems of special and the barriers to inclusion. It can create opportunities for administrators, funders and practitioners to devise policies and provide resources which enable wider participation within settings. Support for all students could be increasingly situated within: team-teaching and planning, greater curricular autonomy and assessment of collective learning. It would involve collective assessment for funding, a focus upon pupils within context and increased numbers of additional professionals working with pupils in settings. It would be provided through: open-ended activities, as well as more small-group activities and co-operative learning practice, and could more readily involve multi-modal learning and assessment opportunities so as to encourage, recognise and develop diverse literacies.

Some of the more obvious challenges

There is a long history of people calling for fundamental changes to the education system. In 1989 for example, Arthur Costa, President of the Association for Supervision and Curriculum Development, stated that many educators believed "that the passing of the industrial era means the passing of the usefulness of standardization as an organizing educational principle" (p. vii). He was one of many calling for the development of teaching and thinking skills as tools of inquiry. In the intervening years, of course, standardisation has become even more predominant. Similarly, aspects of the key approaches which I have identified have been noted previously. For example, in a report from 15 European countries (Meijer, 2001), five groups of variables were reported as being effective for inclusive education:

1   co-operative teaching/co-teaching/team-teaching;
2   co-operative learning/peer-tutoring;
3   individual planning;
4   collaborative problem-solving;
5   heterogeneous grouping/flexible instruction/differentiation.

Of course, the bullet point which I am suggesting needs to have a reduced emphasis, individual planning, is the only approach which has been widely adopted at national strategy level in many countries. The other issues have not received the same kinds of support, having been introduced spasmodically and without robust policy backing. Without such backing these bullet points and my suggestions can only remain as part of a theoretical second world of inclusion.

As a researcher I also have to acknowledge the limitations of research (where it exists) in convincing people of how to develop practice. For example, a report appeared in *The Guardian* whilst I was writing this chapter which said the UK government was planning to make setting[4] compulsory in English schools. The story was soon denied by government, but it was clear that many politicians supported such an approach. The Prime Minister of the day, Cameron, was quoted from earlier in his career saying: "Parents know it works. Teachers know it works. … a high-quality education means engaging children at the right level" (Wintour, 2014). It was evident too in the 1,147 comments which accompanied the article that setting and selection was exactly what a great many people wanted to see.[5] A prevailing view seemed to be that without selection of some sort, education was dumbing-down society and failing to provide for the high-fliers. These kinds of underlying cultural-assumptions-in-the-face-of-reason even ignore evidence from sources which the culture values. For example, Finnish writers suggest that schools in the United States will not be able to replicate the successful educational processes of Finland[6] despite a will to learn from them, because their political and public focus is upon elite provision and competition rather than upon equity and co-operation (Partanen, 2011).

The belief in competition is predominant in many cultures. It is not necessarily as welcome as some might wish, however. For example, a study was carried out in 2014 for The Cricket Foundation of 1,000 children and 1,000 parents (Chance to Shine, 2014). Nearly 90 per cent of parents said it was important or very important that their child experienced winning and losing in sport, and that winning was important to their child. However, only 27.7 per cent said they would strongly disagree if legislation removed competition, only 38.2 per cent said they would be concerned if there were no winners or losers and only 4.2 per cent felt winning was the most important aspect of children's sport.[7] The children's views were equally clear cut. Over 90 per cent recognised that sport should have winners and losers, but over 70 per cent said they would be relieved, happier or not bothered if winning and losing was not part of sport. The response of those who had commissioned the research was that these findings should be a cause for concern. This reflects a passionate belief in the capacity of competition to serve as a positive driver of economic and social success, as well as educational success. Daley (2008) for example cites the widely held view that boys are doing worse in education because of a decrease in competition within schools. The 18 comments that follow the article concur that the lack of competition is at the heart of a failing education system.[8]

There are other pre-eminent, overlapping ways of thinking which will constrain how people will engage with the approaches outlined above. Mayall (2006) talks about "a set of powerful and interlinked beliefs" that draw "on crude versions of developmental psychology" (p. 13). Through engagement with this developmental view, our educational discourses suggest that our specialised child-focused activities (e.g. school, youth club or play group) should lead to self-control and thoughtful behaviour; it supports a psychological notion that there is a universal reasonable person (Graham, 2007). The child who therefore does not fit in with these specialised activities can be seen to be unreasonable or deficient. These 'crude versions' also lead adults to believe that they 'understand' children and can legitimately draw up a list of their needs. They are encouraged to protect children as opposed to recognise their right of participation in all aspects of society.

Our understanding of participation is further compromised because our notions of freedom and autonomy within educational contexts are strongly linked with therapeutic values and with entrepreneurial values. Brunila (2012) points to the notion of the autonomous-self emerging from psycho-therapeutic roots, and how this informs the educational focus upon self-presentation and self-regulation, defining our understanding of creativity, motivation, flexibility, and so forth. The danger is that people come to believe that we should always be trying to improve ourselves. She warns of young people being "condemned to make a project out of their own identities", "to become obedient to the powers of expertise and to fulfil the needs of working life" (p. 483). These top-down understandings of childhood produce inferred needs[9] which people find it very hard to critique or think beyond. For example, the emphasis upon qualifications and results means that many students are motivated by grades and not by a genuine engaged enjoyment of learning. Noddings (2005) suggests this is a key aspect of contemporary education, which dooms many to failure or limited success, encouraging stress and a sense of disappointment. The curriculum is another example of inferred needs which do not arise from the expressed need of the individual but are established *a priori* and at a distance. So too are the targets, norms and assessments associated with typical and aberrant behaviour and learning.

Practitioners are also likely to engage more readily with different aspects of practice. For example, a survey of 938 Swedish teachers and support staff asked about what they felt was required in order to successfully work with children identified with special educational needs (Lindqvist, Nilholm, Almqvist & Wetso, 2011). The research identified very different priorities amongst different job roles; relatively few saw the child's knowledge and skills as being very important (26.3–48 per cent) or focused upon changing class or group composition (16.2–67.7 per cent). More focused upon mastery exercises and adjustments to materials and the environment (45.9–88 per cent); but the most commonplace statements were about the knowledge, skills, competences and teamwork of the teachers (60.7–96.7 per cent).

Recognition about the need for greater teamwork does not automatically mean that people are well situated to work in that way though. There is frequently a tension over the distribution, management and use of resources. As was evident within our review of international provision (Rix, Sheehy, Fletcher-Campbell, Crisp & Harper, 2013a) practitioners, settings and families can be very protective of resources which they often feel they have had to fight to achieve. The idea of sharing can be very threatening for very understandable reasons. Bureaucratic processes can easily exacerbate these concerns. Problems of communication, of the kind identified above, will also remain. For example, in three studies of senior leaders in English children's services who had to bring together separate health, education and social services, a key concern was the need to establish shared understandings (Edwards, 2012). The service leaders recognised "deeply entrenched professional boundaries" (p. 27) and a need to develop the capacity to relate to others priorities and understandings.

Developing the capacity to relate to each other is not a simple matter, though.[10] For example, in a study examining the characteristics of special education programmes for US teachers (Brownell, Ross, Colón & McCallum, 2005), programmes commonly included extensive experiences in the field, collaboration, programme evaluation, inclusion and cultural diversity. There was variation in how these might be delivered, however. For example, collaboration might be: knowledge of collaborative skills or about faculty to faculty collaboration or school-to-faculty collaboration or student collaboration. Perhaps more significantly there was also clear variation in the underlying philosophies. The researchers framed this as either a positivist or constructivist orientation towards the knowledge of teachers. The former took a competency-based approach, reflecting a belief that special education has a specific set of knowledge and skills which requires dissemination. Slightly more courses (55 per cent) adopted the latter approach, seeking a collective examination of multiple knowledge bases, including claims to specialist fields of knowledge. Such variability within a single field underlines the complex challenge inherent in developing a unified understanding of an issue or situation.[11]

Consideration also needs to be given to the risks associated with greater curricular autonomy. As noted above, autonomy has strong associations with psycho-therapeutic approaches, whilst a great many teachers do not see the child's established knowledge and skills as being significantly important to their support. In addition, greater curricular autonomy does not invariably lead to more equitable outcomes. Consider, for example, a national experiment begun in 1999 in Sweden. Just over 25 per cent of Swedish municipalities offered a flexible timetable when delivering the national curricula within the framework of their national grading criteria. Decisions about what was studied and for how long could be made at a local level by the municipality, the school, individual teaching teams and the students themselves. Ahl (2007) examined the experience of two schools which participated and two which did not over a two and half year period.

Although, initially enthusiastic, the teachers and support staff in the study schools felt that they had lost control over students. The teachers still supported the change because they saw enough benefit in increased student enjoyment and motivation, but they felt a need for more teaching staff and more classrooms. A group of students emerged who needed support because they could not take the initiative and concentrate on key subject areas. Frequently, students focused on what they found enjoyable and interesting; in particular, students with identified difficulties often struggled to plan and carry out their work efficiently. It was recognised that these students needed more guidance time. Teachers did not have more time available, however, if they also wished to challenge and stimulate those who could work autonomously. The teachers' solution was to become more prescriptive for those who struggled. The key difficulty identified within the study was that the national goals for education still drove what was possible. Students and staff were still very aware of the targets they had to achieve. The student's expressed needs were therefore only acceptable if they fitted in with the inferred needs. Evidently, the pedagogy which policy wished to encourage was in conflict with the grading system and required subject outcomes.

Seeking a way to encourage people to think about this differently

If we wish people to widely engage with the ideas discussed in previous chapters, then it seems important to provide them with a conceptual starting point. Theoretical ideas of the kind which have been examined within this book can provide lenses with which to explore the complex social, cultural and historical context of education, its mix of discourses and weave of power and agency (e.g. Dagenais, 2003); but they are of limited appeal to a broader audience. A metaphor, however, can change how people think about social issues, and subsequently how they act, without them necessarily being aware of its influence (Thibodeau & Boroditsky, 2011). How we understand the world is fundamentally bound up with metaphor. As a consequence, metaphors are intentionally used across professions to influence processes and outcomes. Periyakoil (2008), for example, discusses their wide use by medical practitioners:

> It helps us raise the subtext to the text and convert closed awareness to open awareness in a nonthreatening manner. It is a tool to relate to and understand the unknown and the uncertain future by drawing upon past experiences and present knowledge.

> (p. 843)

Lakoff and Johnson (1980) identified how the associations of metaphors can focus our thoughts upon particular details of experience. They can provide a coherence which structures how we understand that experience. The associations which they bring to mind can guide our actions, hiding some aspects of the experience and highlighting others. They can be self-fulfilling, creating a 'truth', by which we describe and know something but they can also provide a platform to summarise complex realities.

The predominant metaphor in relation to special and inclusion has been the notion of the continuum. In Chapters 4 and 5, there was a discussion about how this linear representation of provision underpins much of the thinking in these fields. As part of our international review of special education we conducted an extensive review of the notion of the continuum and its use (Rix, Sheehy, Fletcher-Campbell, Crisp & Harper, in press). Within our systematic review of the literature, we identified 194 associated concepts, 26 of these involving visual representations, which fell into six broad categories:

1   *Continua of space* – concerned with where support takes place.
2   *Continua of students* – concerned with who is being supported.
3   *Continua of staffing* – concerned with who provides the support, where they operate, their values and workload.
4   *Continua of support* – concerned with the quantity, type of support and service providing it.
5   *Continua of strategies* – concerned with the quality of support and how it is developed and reinforced.
6   *Continua of systems* – concerned with issues of governance, the nature of programmes, policy and rules and movement within the system.

The research team were increasingly aware that these categories provided a broad overview of the field of special education but that there were many gaps which emerged in the range of conceptualisations of the continuum. For example, members of the NCSE (National Council for Special Education) advisory group were surprised that there was not a continuum of attitudes (running from the medical model perspective to the social model perspective) or of practitioner qualification (running perhaps from highly specialised to highly generalised, or highly qualified to unqualified). We also noted the absence of a continuum of parental capacity to gain access to networks and resources, or a continuum of marginalisation in relation to gender, ethnicity, class, and so forth. Subsequent to completing the review a number of publications have identified new continua in relation to special education. Evidently the continuum metaphor is only able to describe little bits of the system. As a result it encourages a simplified view of the issues which exist both within the continuum and in relation to it. Even if we suggest a complex weave of flexible, interacting continua (e.g. Norwich, 2008b), at best we are still talking about a series of individual threads. It is perhaps not surprising that people have been calling for a reconceptualisation of provision (Taylor, 1988, 2001; Nisbet, 2004),[12] beyond a linear representation of separated places, people and processes.

In examining our data, it was noticeable that the continuum encouraged a focus upon the individual, yet aspired to provide services which worked in a collective manner. It was frequently framed as encapsulating provision for all at one end and for a select few at the other. It needed to represent shifts in thinking, to describe complex systems, capturing their multi-layered, interconnected nature, engaging with multiple perspectives and offering a platform for flexible, non-linear thinking and for multi-dimensional responses. It was also trying to reflect the context in most countries, where the spirit of legislation was towards inclusion, where the pre-established systems represented a range of public, professional and political communities, where the direction of travel reflected shifting views and complex experiences. Since it was beyond the scope of the continuum to encourage such a non-linear, multi-dimensional understanding, we suggested that *a community of provision* would be a better metaphor. A community of provision encapsulates complex societal support systems. A community is defined by the interweaving characteristics, resources, groupings and priorities of its members. Its internal and external boundaries can be both porous and restrictive; its shape is context dependent and its relationships tenuous. It carries with it a sense of an ideal, but also a warning of insularity, serving to remind its members that they can both welcome and marginalise others from inside and outside the community.

Community history

The notion of *community* is widespread in educational discourse (Pardales & Girod, 2006), gaining popularity during the same period as the term *continuum*. At the outset it was often used to conceptualise the unity of aspects of mainstream experience rather than disparate experiences of segregation and separation. People soon questioned the tendency to romanticise community and the role of formal and informal institutions; they noted that its use often overlooked social structures which may have little in common (Stacey, 1969). There was often a tendency to talk about community in a superficial and idealised way, seeing it almost as a panacea, without suitable consideration being given to the presence of disparate goals, the challenges of sustainability and the experience of exclusion (Bettez & Hytten, 2013). The danger was, and is, that a community comes to be viewed as static, representing sameness and unity. However, there is another strong tradition in the literature which recognises communities as variable, permeable, hard to pin down and mired in the complexity of social contexts. As a result, community remains a powerful concept. It links individuals and institutions; and because it is at the root of many experiences of social inequality it can still stir people to action (Philip, Way, Garcia, Schuler-Brown & Navarro , 2013).

Early reviews of the literature suggested that communities could be defined through four elements: membership or sense of belonging; influence or sense of mattering; integration and fulfilment of needs; and shared emotional connection or common places, histories and experience (McMillan & George, 1986). Subsequently, Garcia, Giuliani and Wiesenfeld (1999) identified its miscellaneous use, referring to such things as:

- neighbourhoods;
- professional organisations;
- religious groups;
- groups of countries;
- populations of varying size;
- diverse social systems.

Communities could be defined though self-identification and a range of structural and functional characteristics; a sense of community both defining that community and serving in its development. Garcia et al.'s review noted that membership was established and maintained through emotional security, belonging, identity and personal investment alongside shared symbols. They noted a capacity to experience emotional connections, to influence or be influenced by others and to integrate and satisfy individual and collective needs. But people also engage with communities purely because of the idea of these relationships, being bonded to others in an *imagined community* (Anderson, 1991) even where they have little knowledge of each other. Significantly though, it is recognised that even within these imagined communities hegemony and ideology are still to the fore and are interwoven with each other (Kanno & Norton, 2009).[13]

The range of uses to which the community has been put is extensive. This demonstrates the breadth of issues to which it is relevant and its potential as a reflective concept (some of these key ideas are noted in Box 7.1).

Box 7.1 An example of the breadth of issues which draw upon the community concept

Issues in the literature have related to:

- the characteristics and powers of a *community of profession* (Goode, 1957);
- the challenges and necessity of sharing interdependent conceptual and linguistic understandings within a *community of knowledge* (Welbourne, 1981);
- understanding the socialisation processes associated with work practices, relationships, boundaries and identity within an *occupational community*, including the failure of occupational labels to encapsulate membership, and the lack of understanding of those outside (Van Maanen & Barley, 1982);
- developing a *democratic and ethically-based community* within schools (Giroux & Mclaren, 1986);
- establishing distributed responsiblities within a *community of leaders* (Barth, 1987);
- identifying how an individual's freedom to make choices is enabled through cooperation within a *community of self-reliance* (Novak, 1990);
- a *community of practice* (Lave & Wenger, 1991),[a] which describes infor-

---

mally connected groups of people, sharing interests and expertise in free-flowing, creative ways (Wenger & Snyder, 2000);

- the processes, communication and relationships which enable a teacher to develop a *learning community* (Peterson, 1992);[b]
- examinations of projects drawing upon the shared experiences and under-standings of *interpretive communities* (Fish in Brown, 1994) and actively seeking dialogue and interpretation between multiple voices within a *community of discourse* (Brown, 1994);
- exploration of the notion of a *community of common interest* including a *community of knowledgeability*, in which people can recognise each other's association, but outsiders cannot (Robinson, 1994);
- a *community of learners* (Rogoff, 1995; Rogoff, Eugene & Cynthia, 1996) which is rooted in a recognition of learning as a consequence of active participation in a community;
- creating a platform for mutual engagement and participation within a *classroom community* through collaborative tasks, personal responsibility and a shared history (Bridges, 1995);
- the possibility of *virtual communities* in which these people do not interact but influence each other as if they do (Hill, Stead, Rosenstein & Furnas, 1995);
- *mythical communities* of common identities and interests (Bernstein, 2000);
- local education systems representing their aim for authentic, collabora-tive, active learning processes as a *community of classrooms,* involving *communities of teachers* and *communities of learners* (Cruz, Gilbert, Harvey, Snowhite, Ybarra, Hudson, Cox, Ybarra-Garcia & Boatsman, 2003);
- electronically mediated communications creating ties with *virtual commu-nities.* without the need to share physical spaces (Wellman, 2005).

Notes

a The community of practice model has been widely associated with schools (as well as many other learning situations) despite Lave and Wenger (1991) advising against it. They recognised that schools constantly engage with far wider communities and that school processes do not match up with the situated learning perspective which they advocated. The notion of the community of practice also struggled to explain the production of new knowledge. It tends to focus upon processes rather than what it is that is learned. For better or worse, our education systems focus upon developing expertise. These systems focus upon learners accessing bodies of knowledge, inculcating their associated values, behaviours, expectations and ways of thinking. Schools struggle to recognise that these are shifting, culturally situated, practices (Edwards, 2005).

b On pages 6-8 of Peterson's book is a table which lists the different attitudes preva-lent in 'traditional' and 'holistic' settings. It perfectly highlights many of the tensions that I have been discussing.

Defining a community of provision

Because of the complexity of the learning and care context, Naraian (2011) concludes that any model of community must practically articulate its unifying constructs in an unambiguous manner. Here then, is a broad definition of a community of provision:

- *A community of provision is made from the settings and services which work together to provide learning and support for all children and young people within their locality.*

By its nature a community of provision includes those who believe in competition and standards, in special pedagogies and separated settings, in core curriculum subjects and exams, in choice and private education, in rote learning and strict discipline, in stages of development and categories of child just as much as it includes those who believe in collaboration and co-operation, in participation for all and inclusion, in democracy and rights for all, in authentic and open-ended learning, and so forth. Most members of any community of provision, however, do not sit entirely within one camp or the other on any of these issues, but have a weave of views which reflect the complex challenges associated with supporting learning.

In an attempt to provide a frame for considering this complex reality, it seems appropriate for the unifying constructs of a community of provision to be based on the evidence gathered in our review of the continuum. A community of provision can therefore be understood as a connected whole within six overarching community perspectives:

1   *Community space* – concerned with where support takes place.
2   *Community staffing* – concerned with who is providing the support.
3   *Community of students* – concerned with who is being supported.
4   *Community support* – concerned with the quantity and type of support.
5   *Community strategies* – concerned with the quality of support.
6   *Community systems* – concerned with issues of governance.

Each perspective must be seen in relation to each other. They are the means by which provision is described but they are also the means by which it is delivered. They do not contain a singular grouping or separate contained aspect of provision. Any and every educational issue will be affected by these six perspectives and needs to be understood through them.

As with all definitions people can interpret the words and phrases in different ways. Arguments can be had about what is meant by "made from", "settings", "services", "work together" and "their locality". It would not seem particularly fruitful to precisely define each word at this juncture however. Broadly speaking this definition is not trying to limit the notion of a community of provision to a boundaried geographical location, but recognises the importance of place. It recognises the current delivery of education, health and care services and the formal relationships between them, the linkages and flows of resources within social groupings. It recognises support as an active process, ongoing in nature, involving formal and informal connections. This is a very broad definition, however; it does not carry with it any particular values or represent a particular underlying philosophy.

Figure 7.1 represents a community of provision as it is frequently experienced, as an interconnected, diffuse collection of practices, services, policies and individuals, in which marginalisation and competing perspectives are everyday experiences. Figure 7.2 shows the community of provision as people might wish it to be, a coherent focused whole, where all the parts work together in effective unity.

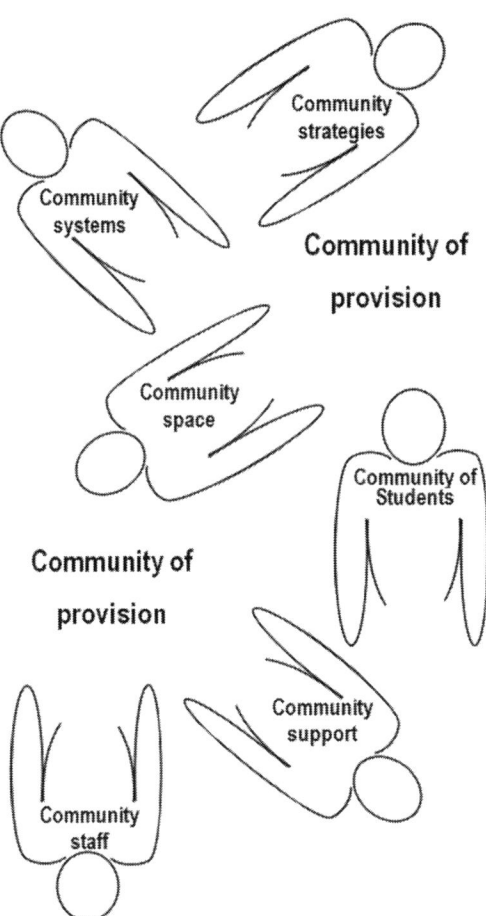

FIGURE 7.1 The community of provision as an interconnected but diffuse collection of practices, services, policies and individuals.

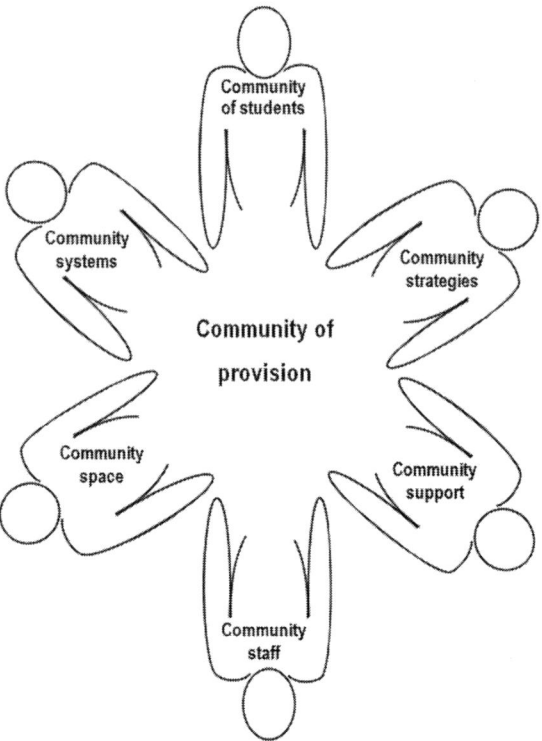

FIGURE 7.2 The community of provision as a focused collection of practices, services, policies and individuals.

Both these figures represent the community of provision at a given moment. They also represent different levels of the system and different locations, requiring different relationships to be established. The reality of any community of provision is that it is constantly interacting with other communities. An appropriate complete image would therefore be three-dimensional, capturing the overlapping nature of communal clusters; it would, by necessity, be open sided (Figures 7.3 and 7.4).

FIGURE 7.3 The multi-dimensions of diffuse, unreconstructed communities of provision.

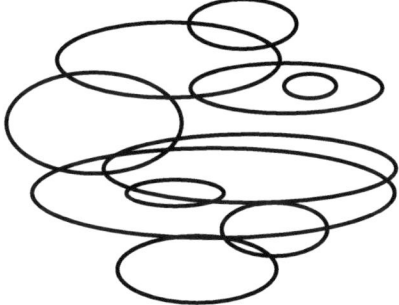

FIGURE 7.4 The multi-dimensions of focused, aspirational communities of provision.

Health warning

We must be wary of how we apply these generalised representations to everyday situations. Any discussion of a community of provision has to be situated within an analysis of issues of social inequality and their production or reproduction. They have to recognise the instable, contradictory nature of practice (Eraut, 2002). The idealised, aspirational, representation in particular can disguise the numerous, diverse difficulties which emerge within communities. When looking at any representation the groupings presented will have a range of goals and processes, whilst their relationships will be defined by a network of formal and informal agreements. A community's identity will depend upon its association with the multifarious professional, political, social and cultural communities which exist around it and their capacity to maintain relationships and share understandings, resources and approaches. It may even be that the practices and the shared values associated with a community are too diffuse or too restrictive to include everyone who might wish to be or might be assumed to be members (Strike, 1999).

We also have to acknowledge a community's capacity to create, maintain and exacerbate negative experiences They are, for instance, sites of loneliness (Pretty, Conroy, Dugay, Fowler & Williams, 1996), often reflecting historically situated or non-negotiable processes of marginalisation (Hodges, 1998). Anzaldua (1999) describes experiences of cultural tyranny, where actions are condemned by the dominant value systems, leading to individuals being identified as "deviants". Their welfare comes to be less important than the welfare of wider groups within the community; less important than the social conventions, rules and categories which control relationships. Levels of participation within a community or people's positions relative to the margins may also change across time and in different places, or they may be fixed, perhaps requiring people to deny aspects of their self. Some may be disinterested in being part of the community in which they are being expected to participate and negotiate their position and identity (Linehan & McCarthy, 2001). Communities of resistance (Sivanandan, 1990)[14] can also emerge to challenge top-down approaches as people seek to create experiences of non-hierarchical, locally controlled struggle (Van der Velden, 2004). At the same time, some people may come to prize and value their isolation (Brodsky, 1996).

These kinds of issues go to the heart of special and inclusion just as much as the ideas of co-operation, collaboration and reflection which are evident across the community models. The position which the community of provision should take upon them still needs to be clarified, however.

Developing a prescriptive, aspirational definition

This book has attempted to demonstrate the great many barriers which emerge from our support systems. If we wish to transform them in the spirit of much national and international discourse then we need to be encouraging many of the practices outlined in earlier chapters: collaboration, participation, access, inclusion and equity. The idea of the community of provision would have to encourage a shift in the status quo by drawing upon these values. With this in mind, as part of the NCSE research project we arrived at the following prescriptive, aspirational definition for a community of provision:

- *The collective delivery of services broadly related to learning, health and welfare involving a range of providers within a network of agreements. It is within this community of provision that support for children, families and practitioners is negotiated, mediated and experienced. It is within this community that needs, challenges and opportunities arise and are met. The community of provision requires leadership which coheres and supports practices and strategies which emerge from and enhance collaborative working and planning. It aims, as a whole and within its constituent parts, for the community and organisational structures of each setting and service to be representative and inclusive of a full cross-section of their local communities in all aspects of their provision.*

We recognised that not everything can involve everybody and nor should it. However, segregation has been defined by the European Agency for Development in Special Needs Education (2011) as any setting in which children are separated in special provision for the largest part (80 per cent) or more of the day. Using this international figure as our basis we can specify that the aim of representation and inclusion in all aspects of provision means that at least 20 per cent of the time individuals or groups are brought together with their peers. The nature and quality of participation can subsequently be assessed with some certainty on the basis of individuals' own recognition of its effectiveness for them, and more tentatively can be surmised on the basis of individuals choosing to engage or showing levels of satisfaction on being engaged. This would, for example, offer a point of reflection both for the special education student in general education classes without sufficient support and the student within segregated provision who is overly supported. It would also apply to the capacity of different practitioners and family members to engage with the whole community or its constituent parts; and would provide a strong reminder to reflect upon – and confront – cultural and social aspects of services which can marginalise others within the community.

The boundaries of each community are invariably porous and at times imprecise; however, for reasons of transparency and practicality, we advocated two defining criteria: a defined geographical spread and a network of agreements. The former needs to be flexible in relation to rural and urban contexts and settings of different sizes; the latter needs to recognise that membership within most administrations will be constrained by professional and administrative boundaries and processes. A profound challenge for aspirational communities is how they can localise control, so that it reflects priorities of those it aims to serve and enables practitioners to meaningfully design services that reflect these priorities. The community of provision has to pay attention to the negotiation, mediation and experience of support and be aware of the ongoing creation of identities and relationships from all six overarching community perspectives. The priorities should be evident within the actions of leaders and other members of the community, so that their roles and practices reflect the community's inclusive aspirations. They should also support communication across the range of discourses and be alert to the challenges and opportunities which emerge from shifting boundaries and forms of resistance.

This more prescriptive, aspirational, definition is still a very flexible beast. However, it creates a framework which can be placed upon all provision regardless of its professional background and whether it is currently badged as independent, special, specialist, mainstream, and so forth. It could provide policy mechanisms by which funding decisions could encourage change within disparate services. For example:

- A private setting could lose tax breaks unless it operated as part of a community of provision.
- A segregated setting could receive additional funds or protect resources if it shared its facilities and support time as part of a community of provision.
- A mainstream service which segregated a small part of its population could be directly challenged by a national inspectorate.
- A national system which traditionally streamed students at an early age could maintain a collective ethos even if it maintained an emphasis upon subject-based and vocationally based learning.

The community of provision would also provide an accessible explanation for the transformation of practice and a clear goal for all.

A possible ending

Throughout this book I have laid out reasons why people may not do things or may choose to stick with their old ways and beliefs. It is clear though that people can and do change their social structures. In many situations we can see a movement away from tradition and towards social reflection (Halpin, 1999). This reflection cannot simply be top-down or bureaucratically guided; it has to allow a diverse, critical examination of who is privileged or harmed, legitimated or disqualified (Cannella

& Lincoln, 2009) and how this happens. This can be a very uncomfortable process for people. But with the right kinds of support, even top-down and bureaucratically guided, the relevance, ease and reward from engaging in such a process can make it possible and worthwhile.

The six community perspectives are intended to support reflection. So, let's consider a situation at the heart of supporting children and young people – the class. The class is where virtually all formal education begins. McLeskey and Waldron (2011), in a literature analysis mentioned in Chapter 3, suggest that resourced classes are ineffective in providing appropriate instruction and that mainstream classes are not flexible enough. Many schools recognise these limitations. In the UK, for example, particularly outside of secondary education, the class is already a far more fluid institution than when I was a child; consequently, in many places the kinds of flexibility mentioned in Chapter 6, by the teachers in Murphy (2011), are within reach. The aspirational vision of the community of provision could support classes to become even more adaptable.

The *community space* needs to allow for individual, small-group and large-group work as well as online virtual-world work. It needs to allow for privacy and public sharing. A class should be accustomed to working in different places within a setting and outside of that setting. Every member of the class ought to feel that at different times they will work with other people because:

- They share an interest.
- They like each other.
- They need to get on with each other.
- Life throws up random combinations.
- They can support the other person(s).
- The other person(s) can support them.
- They can learn from each other.
- They are trying to achieve the same standard in something.
- They need some very specific support.
- They need some very regular support.
- They need to practice something.
- They need time to work on something in privacy.
- They need time to work on something without distraction.

The *community of students* would reflect the local geographical area or those linked to the setting through wider community relationships. The learners may be associated with a particular age range, and might spend more time than others in a particular space; they could also work with other learners from other classes or settings, who might be older or younger;[15] but for a sizeable part of the day all students would be working with a broad range of peers linked to the same class. As a consequence they may increasingly work with groups from other classes or with multiple teachers and other practitioners or with adults and children from outside the more immediate setting.

The *community staffing* should also represent a cross-section of the local community. It would involve a mix of teachers, support staff, outside professionals, members of the wider school community, members of the local community, 'critical friends' from universities, local authority and an inspectorate. Staff would be encouraged to recognise their responsibility for all children in the class and would be supported to work with them in different circumstances. The practitioners might also experience alternative staffing arrangements, aiming to create and support opportunities for new collaborative partnerships; these might include working with other teachers with equal responsibility for another classes, or having specific links with a support teacher, regardless of the children in the class. Maybe they would also be contractually required to work collaboratively, or be rewarded for doing so effectively, or be provided with specific time for collaborative planning.

The *community support* would include all those associated with the class. As was evident in our NCSE study, there would be a place for professionals trained to work between education, health and social care, and there would be a focus upon providing additional support to staff and classes which particularly needed it. The nature of support provided to individual and groups of children would be defined within the whole class context, but invariably this context would sometimes include individual needs which require specific additional professional input. Simple, formal agreements between services with a few significant agreed deadline dates and principles about services to be delivered, to which they can be held accountable, could provide the parents and practitioners with clear, accessible guidelines.

The *community strategies* would be underpinned by a wide range of pedagogical approaches. These would invariably reflect the views and experiences of the professionals within the community spaces. This means that interwoven within the day can be programmes and strategies which emerge with a strong evidence base; however, to achieve the aims discussed earlier, there would need to be a strong focus upon collective planning, collaborative teaching, assessment of collective learning involving more than one practitioner, open-ended activities, recognition and use of multiple literacies, alongside opportunities for multi-modal learning and assessment. There would also be a place for greater support of self-direction within the curriculum, seeking to ensure that learners recognise the valid purpose to any activity and that they recognise that they will be supported to achieve useful learning outcomes. There would be recognition that planning for the social aspects of learning is essential.[16] The strategies would also focus upon professional training and the need for professionals to experience a wide range of cultural and social needs.

The *community systems* would seek to promote the development of the practices outlined above, through its funding, administrative and political processes, policies and plans. Evidence from our NCSE study suggests that classes could benefit from head-teachers who direct a cluster of schools (from early years to secondary) tasked with building networks, and overseeing assessment, planning, staff co-ordination and the equitable allocation of funding. They would have staff allocated to support collaboration and scheduled to train colleagues. The practitioners' understanding and collaboration could be supported through having opportunities to work alongside staff from and within other settings, including having access to sabbatical training years. They could be encouraged to develop in-class research and build links with local universities. Practitioners could benefit from mechanisms such as shared class co-ordinators, assessment of the class context for funding purposes,[17] funding for shared planning, the development of class councils, and extended teacher exchange programmes. Their understanding and expectations could also be informed by a policy commitment to share resources, knowledge and skills. If they were new to the profession they would have experienced far greater emphasis upon collaborative processes within initial teacher-training, both experiencing effective team-teaching and gaining insights into working with a broad range of professionals.

A final assessment

In seeking to build aspirational communities of provision there are a great many practices already evident across the globe which can give us reasons for hope. However, if we wish the communities of provision of which we are all part to be more equitable and to produce the collective understanding and responsibility required by workplaces, economies and social fellowship then a great many of us have to shift our ways of working. These shifts need to encourage and enable teachers to share their traditional control, to more readily trust in the ideas of the children and other adults with whom they work, recognising the wide range of priorities and capabilities that exist in each setting. In turn, they need to be trusted so that the standards, objectives and evaluations which underpin educational processes increasingly emerge from within the class, school and community context.

Despite the critical tone of much of this book, I am convinced that the major barrier to this change is not people who are wedded to separate provision for particular groups or who believe in a special pedagogy or campaign for full inclusion or battle for their children's rights or those who love their subject area. The vast majority of these views can be accommodated within the kind of community of provision discussed in this chapter. I am convinced instead, that two fundamental practices stand in our way; two practices which largely go unquestioned; one which has its roots deep in our collective educational history and the other in the bureaucratic processes which developed alongside the emergence of professions. Policy-makers need to find a way to shift from the final assessment, subject-based model of validating learning[18] and the individualised model of assessing and funding additional support. The flexibility that we require can only take place when we release learning from these bureaucratic shackles; so that our education system stops primarily serving as a selection process open to accusations of divide and rule.

Until we can recognise the constraints which arise from these top-down assessment processes our education systems will be unable to escape the past. We will continue with practices which inevitably marginalise a great swathe of children, young people and adults. We will claim that change is not possible and continue to blame the characteristics of individuals or the structure of secondary education or skills of practitioners or the social processes of schools or people's attitudes or competing policies. We will continue to rely upon special and call for inclusion.

A shift away from these dominant mechanisms of sorting and selecting would not remove the other challenges discussed in this book. But it would create the latitude for ways of working which may accommodate our differences and build on our strengths. In developing a space for collective actions we could move beyond the problem of inclusion and special, so that learning[19] which required an additional time and place might be embraced as a fundamental part of every community of provision. We owe it to each other to develop such spaces. A community of provision is our history, our present and our future. It provides our context for supporting one another in who we are and may become. It is the means by which all of us can shape ourselves for the better.

Notes

1 'O'levels were a subject-based UK qualification taken at age 15–16, 'A' levels were taken at 17–18.
2 When writing a report for the NCSE, a reviewer said it would be useful to have a summary of all the key issues raised. I sat down and produced a list which ran for eight pages and had 165 bullet points, each identifying a factor which had emerged from the interviews, vignette studies, literature review or policy analysis. It was a fascinating list, but everyone apart from me felt it would just send people to sleep. The list for this book would be considerably longer I fear. It would exemplify the multiple variables at work, however!
3 The kinds of aims mentioned in the opening chapter were: controlling particular groups within society; creating a respect for rules and social hierarchy; producing a workforce; supporting the spread of skills for communication and learning; creating a nation or sense of nationhood; developing social cohesion; meeting individual needs and desires; delivering individual choice; developing democratic processes; creating equitable learning experiences and outcomes.
4 Setting involves putting children in groups within a specific subject area according to an assessment of ability.
5 This was despite the article presenting research findings from the Education Endowment Foundation which stated that setting may benefit some high-achieving students but has a negative impact on the results and attitudes of the mid-range and low-achieving students.
6 As discussed in Chapter 5, Finland has a very successful history in the international PISA tests.
7 Just over 75 per cent saw teamwork (42.7 per cent) and exercise (33.8 per cent) as most important.
8 I do not have the experience to comment on other cultures or other countries, but I would suggest that within the UK there is a fundamental tension between those who are motivated by competition and those who are demotivated by it. I think it is very likely that it is the minority who actually benefit from being competitive; however, the concept is firmly situated within the economically correct notion of personal and national development and so in direct tension with any proposal which builds upon a co-operative ethos.
9 An inferred need is externally identified and taken to be a requirement. An expressed need is something which comes from an individual or group and is expressed in words or actions. Most educational needs are of the former, particularly with younger learners.
10 Ironically, of course, a key aim of the changes suggested in this book is to develop this capacity in future generations.

11 In their conclusions. Brownell et al. noted that research into special education teacher training was virtually non-existent and so we cannot know how the different approaches impact on practice and which is most effective. It is also worth noting that Brady and Woolfson (2008) found there was no relationship between training and how practitioners regarded the attributes of disabled people. The key factors were: Teacher efficacy, experience of teaching students with support needs, attitudes towards disabled people, and teachers' role.

12 Taylor (1988, 2001) identified that the concept of the continuum had fallen into disrepute. He said that it legitimised restrictive environments and the denial of human rights; it prioritised professional decision-making, assumed people needed to be ready for mainstream participation and linked intensity with segregation; it shifted the focus away from redeveloping mainstream provision, underpinning many people's ongoing conceptualisation of services, so that new approaches just become additional slots; it worked against self-determination, integration and independence and focused upon the extremes of need. Nisbet (2004) reaffirmed these views, noting that despite changes in policies and practices, the notion still underpinned financial structures and incentives, maintaining restrictive settings, and the identification of new groups for exclusion whilst moving some others into the mainstream.

13 I would suggest that the unifying features of communities are frequently a perception and remain unspoken. We often attempt to encapsulate them within a name, a word or a phrase; for example, 'He is Welsh', 'a primary school pupil', 'a black man', 'a conservative', 'she was a woman', 'they are Catholic' or 'I am an educational psychologist'.

14 This term was also used by feminist theologist Sharon Welch in 1985.

15 The evidence around the impact of age groupings is equivocal. Wilkinson and Hamilton (2003) for example showed that slightly lower reading performance in "composite" classes was down to the nature and quality of instruction.

16 The need for planning is exemplified by a study which found that children grouped as low–middle ability demonstrated significantly more high-quality exploratory talk than those grouped as low–high ability. However, when those grouped as low–high were assigned roles the quality of their exploratory talk notably improved (Schmitz & Winskel, 2008).

17 Interviewees in all countries talked about wanting to have dynamic assessment of students' needs which was rooted in the practices of teaching and learning.

18 For example, getting rid of the national GCSE exams at 16 in England would save huge resources. It would also provide an opportunity to support a greater shift to collective assessment, encourage a focus upon student and staff interests and expertise, enable people to be assessed as and when they are ready, raise the status of vocational activity and make vocational opportunities available to more learners. With a bit of effort we could also encourage exam boards, employers and universities to develop more creative final assessment processes which reflected their needs. This might even involve a system of references from communities of provision. After all, if references are good enough in the workplace, why can we not trust them as an output of education?

19 Our experience of learning brings together our past, present and future whether we are alert to this or not. It is always relational, in that it involves the learner in relation to anything which might offer an opportunity for learning. Learning is relevant to all the senses, sensibilities and capacities associated with being alive. It is about changing our understanding and our means for accessing, sharing or enacting our understanding. Understanding is an interweaving of information, knowledge, skills, experiences, interpretations, imaginings, feelings, physical and emotional responses, opinions, beliefs, certainties, uncertainties, identity and agency. Learning and understanding are context dependent processes. They involve participation in communication. These communications operate within individual and collective cultural parameters, developing or reinforcing them in the process (for example, certain aspects of learning and understanding are prioritised within the different discourses surrounding education).

These communications reflect power relations which prevail or have traditionally prevailed and their asymmetries, biases and inequities. Learning, understanding and communication are always experienced individually but are always socially situated and socially constructed. They can only be mediated, shared and supported through social means. They are intentional and unintentional processes and the meaning attached to them is inferred, of limited transferability and cannot be guaranteed to be equivalent. We can therefore only come to know the learner through a process of learning. Knowing the learner is part of the process of learning, understanding and communication. It begins with the social processes of being human.

BIBLIOGRAPHY

Abberley, P. (1987). The concept of oppression and the development of a social theory of disability, *Disability, Handicap & Society*, 2, 1, 5–19.

Abbott, L., McConkey, R., & Dobbins, M. (2011). Key players in inclusion, *European Journal of Special Needs Education*, 26, 2, 215–231.

Abel, E. (1995). An update on incidence of FAS, *Neurotoxicology and Teratology*, 17, 4, 437–443.

Abel, E. (1998). Fetal alcohol syndrome – The 'American paradox', *Alcohol & Alcoholism*, 33, 3, 195–201.

Abel, E., & Sokol, R. (1987). Incidence of fetal alcohol syndrome and economic impact of FAS-related anomalies, *Drug and Alchohol Dependence*, 19, 51–70.

Abu El-Haj, T (2003). Challenging the inevitability of difference, *Curriculum Inquiry*, 33, 4, 401–425.

Adams, J., Swain, J., & Clark, J. (2000). What's so special? Teachers' models and their realisation in practice in segregated schools, *Disability & Society*, 15, 2, 233–245.

Ahl, A. (2007). Equality and the freedom to choose the 'what and when' of schooling, *European Journal of Special Needs Education*, 22, 2, 183–197.

Ainscow, M. (1998). Would it work in theory? Arguments for practitioner researcher and theorising in the special needs field. In C. Clark, A. Dyson, & A. Millward (Eds) *Theorising special education*, London: Routledge.

Ainscow, M. (2000). Profile. In P. Clough & J. Corbett (Eds) *Theories of inclusive education: A students' guide* (pp. 39–42), London: Paul Chapman.

Ainscow, M., & Hart, S. (1992). Moving practice forward, *Support for Learning*, 7, 3, 115–120.

Ainscow, M., Booth, T., & Dyson, A. (2006). Inclusion and the standards agenda, *International Journal of Inclusive Education*, 10, 4–5, 295–308.

Ali, M. M., Mustapha, R., & Jelas, Z. M. (2006). An empirical study on teachers' perceptions towards inclusive education in Malaysia, *International Journal of Special Education*, 21, 3, 36–44.

Allan, J. (2008). *Rethinking inclusive education*, Dordrecht: Springer.

Allor, J., Mathes, P., Champlin, T., & Cheatham, J. (2009). Research-based techniques for teaching early reading skills to students with intellectual disabilities, *Education and Training in Developmental Disabilities*, 44, 3, 356–366.

Ambitious About Autism (2014). Ruled out: Sign up for our new campaign. http://www.ambitiousaboutautism.org.uk/page/who_we_are/news/article/index.cfm?articleId= 334, accessed 14 February.

Anderson, B. (1991). *Imagined communities* (revised), London and New York: Verso.

Anderson, R. (2014). *Making education work*, London: Pearson.

Anney, R., Klei, L., Pinto, D., Almeida, J., Bacchelli, E., Baird, G., et al. (2012). Individual common variants exert weak effects on the risk for autism spectrum disorders, *Human Molecular Genetics*, 21, 21, 4781–4792.

Anzaldua, G. (1999). *Borderlands/la frontera: The new mestiza* (2nd ed.), San Francisco: Aunt Lute.

Appleton, M., Buckley, S., & MacDonald, J. (2002). Early reading skills of preschoolers with Down syndrome and their typically developing peers, *Down Syndrome News and Update*, 2, 1, 9–10,

Archer, L., Halsall, A., & Hollingworth, S. (2007). Class, gender, (hetero)sexuality and schooling, *British Journal of Sociology of Education*, 28, 2, 165–180.

Armstrong, T. (2006). Canaries in the coal mine. In G. Lloyd, J. Stead, & D. Cohen (Eds) *Critical new perspectives on ADHD* (pp. 34–44), Abingdon, UK: Routledge.

Arnold, M. (1869). *Culture and anarchy* (1st ed.), e-text, Project Gutenberg.

Australian Bureau of Statistics (2013). National Year of Reading. http://www.abs.gov.au/ausstats/abs@.nsf/Lookup/by%20Subject/1301.0~2012~Main%20Features~The%20National%20Year%20of%20Reading:%20libraries%20helping%20to%20make%20Australia%20a%20nation%20of%20readers~206, accessed 8 May 2014.

Bakker, N. (2012). Making a mess in the mud, *Paedagogica Historica*, 48, 1, 37–41.

Ball, S. (2009). Privatising education, privatising education policy, privatising educational research, *Journal of Education Policy*, 24, 1, 83–99.

Ballet, K., & Kelchtermans, G. (2008). Workload and willingness to change, *Journal of Curriculum Studies*, 40, 1, 47–67.

Barbara Priestman (2003). http://www.barbara-priestman.org.uk/home.htm and http://www.barbara-priestman.org.uk/pages/camp.htm, accessed 19 February 2014.

Barbara Priestman (2014). Head teacher's welcome. http://www.barbara-priestman.org.uk/?page_id=8, accessed 19 February 2014.

Barkoukis, V., Tsorbatzoudis, H., & Grouios, G. (2008). Manipulation of motivational climate in physical education, *European Physical Education Review*, 14, 3, 367–387.

Barron, I., Holmes, R., MacLure, M., & Runswick-Cole, K. (2007). *Primary schools and other agencies*, Cambridge: University of Cambridge.

Barth, R. (1987). School: A community of leaders. Paper presented at the Annual Spring Conference of the Georgia State University Principals' Institute, 4–5 March.

Barton, L., & Armstrong, F. (Eds). (2007). *Policy, experience and change* (Vol. 4), Dordrecht: Springer.

Baughman, F. & Hovey, C. (2006) *The ADHD fraud: How psychiatry makes 'patients' of normal children*, Bloomington, IN: Trafford Publishing.

BBC (2010). 'Cage' for autistic Nicolson Institute pupil removed, 1 November.

Beckmann, A., & Cooper, C. (2005). Conditions of domination, *British Journal of Sociology of Education*, 26, 4, 475–489.

Bell, L., Long, S., Garvan, C., & Bussing, R. (2011). The impact of teacher credentials on ADHD stigma perceptions, *Psychology in the Schools*, 48, 2, 184–198.

Benavot, A., Resnik, J., & Corrales, J. (2006). *Global educational expansion*, Cambridge, MA: American Academy of Arts and Sciences.

Bernstein, B. (2000). *Pedagogy, symbolic control, and identity*, Lanham, MD: Rowman & Littlefield.

Betteney, M. (2010). All for one, and one for all, *Literacy*, 44, 2, 91–97.

Bettez, S., & Hytten, K. (2013). Community building in social justice work, *Educational Studies*, 49, 1, 45–66.

Bickenbach, J. (2014). Reconciling the capability approach and the ICF, *ALTER – European Journal of Disability Research*, 8, 1, 10–23.

Bickman, L., Wighton, L., Lambert, W., Karver, M., & Steding, L. (2012). Problems in using diagnosis in child and adolescent mental health services research, *Journal of Methods and Measurement in the Social Sciences*, 3, 1, 1–26.

Biederman, J., Monuteaux, M. C., Spencer, T., Wilens, T. E., & Faraone, S. V. (2009). Do stimulants protect against psychiatric disorders in youth with ADHD? A 10-year follow-up study, *Pediatrics*, 124, 1, 71–78.

Birdsall, N. (2001). Why inequality matters, *Ethics & International Affairs*, 15, 2, 3–28.

Black, A., & Norwich, B. (2014). *Contrasting responses to diversity*, Bristol: Central Studies for Inclusive Education (CSIE).

Blackburn, C., Carpenter, B., & Egerton, J. (2010). Shaping the future for children with foetal alcohol spectrum disorders, *Support for Learning*, 25, 3, 139–145.

Black-Hawkins, K., Florian, L., & Rouse, M. (2007). *Achievement and inclusion in schools*, Abingdon, UK: Routledge.

Blatchford, P., Bassett, P., Brown, P., Koutsoubou, M., Martin, C., Russell, A. et al. (2009). Deployment and impact of support staff in schools, Research Report No. DCSF-RR148, Department for Children, Schools and Families.

Boe, E., deBettencourt, L., Dewey, J., Rosenberg, M., Sindelar, P., & Leko, C. (2013). Variability in demand for special education teachers, *Exceptionality*, 21, 2, 103–125.

Booth, T., Ainscow, M., Black-Hawkins, K., Vaughan, M., & Shaw, L. (2002). *Index for inclusion*, Bristol: Centre for Studies on Inclusive Education.

Borthwick, C. (1996). Racism, IQ and Down's syndrome, *Disability & Society*, 11, 3, 403–410.

Boseley, S. (2009). Is autism screening close to reality?, *The Guardian*, Monday 12 January.

Bourdieu, P. (1990). Principles for reflecting on the curriculum, *Curriculum Journal*, 1, 3, 307–314.

Bourne, J. (2001). Doing 'what comes naturally', *Language And Education*, 15, 4, 251–268.

Bowker, G., & Leigh Star, S (1999). *Sorting things out*, Cambridge, MA: MIT Press.

Bradby, H., Varyani, M., Oglethorpe, R., Raine, W., White, I., & Minnis, H. (2007). British Asian families and the use of child and adolescent mental health services, *Social Science & Medicine*, 65, 12, 2413–2424.

Brady, K., & Woolfson, L. (2008). What teacher factors influence their attributions for children's difficulties in learning?, *British Journal of Educational Psychology*, 78, 4, 527–544.

Breen, R., Luijkx, R., Müller, W., & Pollak, R. (2010). Long-term trends in educational inequality in Europe, *European Sociological Review*, 26, 1, 31–48.

Bridges, L. (1995). *Creating your classroom community*, New York: Stenhouse Publishers.

Bridle, L., & Mann, G. (2000). Mixed feelings. Paper presented at the National Conference of Early Childhood Intervention, June, Brisbane, Australia.

British Psychological Society's Division of Clinical Psychology (BPS-DCP) (2013). *Position statement on the classification of behaviour and experience in relation to functional psychiatric diagnoses.*

Brodsky, A. (1996). Resilient single mothers in risky neighborhoods: Negative psychological sense of community, *Journal of Community Psychology*, 24, 4, 347–363.

Bronfenbrenner, U. (1974). *Is early intervention effective?*, Washington, DC: Department of Health, Education, and Welfare, Office of Child Development.

Bronfenbrenner, U. (1977). Toward an experimental ecology of human development, *American Psychologist*, 32, 7, 513–531.

Brophy, J., & Good, T. (1974). *Teacher–student relationships. Causes and consequences*, New York: Holt, Rinehart, and Winston.

Brown, A. (1994). The advancement of learning, *Educational Researcher*, 23, 8, 4–12.

Brown, J. & Duguid, P. (2000). *The social life of information*, Boston: Harvard Business School Press.

Brown, T. (2005). *Attention deficit disorder*, New Haven, CT: Yale University Press.

Brownell, M., & Kiely, M. (2010). Special education teacher quality and preparation, *Exceptional Children*, 76, 3, 357–377.

Brownell, M., Ross, D., Colón, E., & McCallum, C. (2005). Critical features of special education teacher preparation, *The Journal of Special Education*, 38, 4, 242–252.

Bruner, J. (1966). *Towards a theory of instruction*, Cambridge, MA: Harvard University Press.

Bruner, J. (1986). *Actual minds, possible worlds*, Cambridge, MA: Harvard University Press.

Bruner, J. (1996). *The culture of education*, Cambridge, MA: Harvard University Press.

Brunila, K. (2012). A diminished self, *European Educational Research Journal*, 11, 4, 477–486.

Buchman, T. G. (2002). The community of the self, *Nature*, 420, 6912, 246–251.

Buckley, S. (2008). Precise descriptions of Down syndrome, *Down Syndrome Research and Practice*, 12, 2, 90–90.

Buckley, S., Bird, G., Sacks, B., & Archer, T. (2006). A comparison of mainstream and special education for teenagers with Down syndrome, *Down Syndrome Research and Practice*, 9, 3, 54–67.

Bunar, N. (2010). Choosing for quality or inequality, *Journal of Education Policy*, 25, 1, 1–18.

Burch, P. (2006). The new educational privatization, *Teachers College Record*, 108, 12, 2582–2610.

Burgoyne, K., Duff, F., Clarke, P., Buckley, S., Snowling, M., & Hulme, C. (2012). Efficacy of a reading and language intervention for children with Down syndrome, *Journal of Child Psychology and Psychiatry, and Allied Disciplines*, 53, 10, 1044–1053.

Burns, J. (2013). Private tuition boom for wealthy 'risks learning gap'. http://www.bbc.co.uk/news/education-23973213, accessed 8 November.

Burns, R. (1786). Epistle to a young friend. In J. Logie Robertson (Ed.) *The poetical works of Robert Burns* (1910), Oxford: Oxford University Press.

Butler, J. (1990). *Gender trouble: Feminism and the subversion of identity*, New York: Routledge.

Button, K., Ioannidis, J., Mokrysz, C., Nosek, B., Flint, J., Robinson, E., et al. (2013). Power failure: Why small sample size undermines the reliability of neuroscience. Nature Reviews, *Neuroscience*, 14, 5, 365–376.

Čagran, B., & Schmidt, M. (2011). Attitudes of Slovene teachers towards the inclusion of pupils with different types of special needs in primary school, *Educational Studies*, 37, 2, 171–195.

Cambian Group (2013). *Finding a special needs school*, CAM076, Cambian Group.

Cameron, D., Cook, B., & Tankersley, M. (2012). An analysis of the different patterns of 1:1 interactions between educational professionals and their students with varying abilities in inclusive classrooms, *International Journal of Inclusive Education*, 16, 12, 1335–1354.

Canadian Council on Learning (2009). *Lessons in learning: Does placement matter?*

Cannella, G., & Lincoln, Y. (2009). Deploying qualitative methods for critical social purposes. In N. Denzin & M. Giardina (Eds) *Qualitative inquiry and social justice* (pp. 53–80), Walnut Creek, CA: Left Coast Press.

Carpenter, B. (2007). Developing the role of schools as research organisations, *British Journal of Special Education*, 34, 2, 67–76.

Carpenter, B. (2011). Pedagogically bereft! Improving learning outcomes for children with foetal alcohol spectrum disorders, *British Journal of Sociology of Education*, 38, 1, 37–43.

Carpenter, L., & Austin, H. (2008). How to be recognized enough to be included?, *International Journal of Inclusive Education*, 12, 1, 35–48.

Carr, M. (2001). *Assessment in early childhood settings: Learning stories*, London: Paul Chapman.

CBI (2013). *Changing the pace*, London: Pearson.

Ceci, S., Scullin, M., & Kanaya, T. (2003). The difficulty of basing death penalty eligibility on IQ cut-off scores for mental retardation, *Ethics & Behavior*, 13, 1, 11–17.

Chabbott, C. (2003). *Constructing education for development*, New York: Routledge Falmer.

Chance to Shine (2014). It's only a game? Competition in school sport under threat. http://www.chancetoshine.org/news/it-s-only-a-game-competition-in-school-sport-under-threat, accessed 9 September 2014.

Chappell, M. (2003). Weaving a tale. In M. Nind, J. Rix, K. Sheehy, & K. Simmons (Eds) *Learning from each other: Diverse perspectives on inclusive education*, London: David Fulton.

Christensen, L., Fraynt, R., Neece, C., & Baker, B. (2012). Bullying adolescents with intellectual disability, *Journal of Mental Health Research in Intellectual Disabilities*, 5, 1, 49–65.

Cirrin, F., Schooling, T., Wolf Nelson, N., Diehl, S., Flynn, P., Staskowski, M., et al. (2010). Effects of speech-language pathology service delivery model on communication outcomes for elementary school-age children, *Language, Speech, and Hearing Services in Schools*, 41, 3, 233–264.

Clark, A., & Chalmers, D. (1998). The extended mind, *Analysis*, 58, 1, 7–19.

Clark, A., & Moss, P. (2001). *Listening to young children: The Mosaic approach*, York, UK: Joseph Rowntree Foundation.

Clark, L. (2002). 'Mums army' will wreck standards, claim teachers. http://www.dailymail. co.uk/news/article-107792/Mums-army-wreck-standards-claim-teachers.html# ixzz37YlY4eJF, accessed 15 July 2014.

Clifford, D., Geyne-Rahme, F., & Mohan, J. (2012). Variations between organisations and localities in government funding of third-sector activity, *Urban Studies*, 50, 5, 959–976.

Clifford, J., Hamblin, J., & Theobald, C. (2011). *Comparative cost review of non-maintained and independent special schools with local authority maintained special schools*, National Association of Independent Schools and Non-Maintained Special Schools.

Cobbett, W. (1830). Rural rides, Wednesday, 26 October 1825, London: The Political Register.

Coe, R (2013). Improving education: A triumph of hope over experience, Inaugural Lecture of Professor Robert Coe, University of Durham, 18 June, accessed from http://www. cem.org/attachments/publications/ImprovingEducation2013.pdf.

Cohen, D. (2006). Critiques of the 'ADHD' enterprise. In G. Lloyd, J. Stead, & D. Cohen (Eds) *Critical new perspectives on ADHD* (pp. 12–33), Abingdon, UK: Routledge.

Cohen, J., Bloom, D., & Malin, M. (2006). Preface. In A. Benavot, J. Resnik, & J. Corrales (Eds) *Global educational expansion*, Cambridge, MA: The American Academy of Arts and Sciences.

Coldron, J., Cripps, C., & Shipton, L. (2010). Why are English secondary schools socially segregated?, *Journal of Education Policy*, 25, 1, 19–35.

Cole, T. (1989). *Apart or a part?*, Milton Keynes, UK: Open University Press.

Coles, C., Platzman, K., Raskind-Hood, C., Brown, R., Falek, A., & Smith, I. (1997). A comparison of children affected by prenatal alcohol exposure and attention deficit, hyperactivity disorder, *Alcoholism, Clinical and Experimental Research*, 21, 1, 150–161. Retrieved from http://www.ncbi.nlm.nih.gov/pubmed/9046388

Connolly, P. (2006). The effects of social class and ethnicity on gender differences in GCSE attainment, *British Educational Research Journal*, 32, 1, 3–21.

Connor, D., & Ferri, B. (2007). The conflict within, *Disability & Society*, 22, 1, 63–77.

Connor, F. (1976). The past is prologue, *Exceptional Children*, 42, 7, 366–378.

Connor, R. (1999). How responsive are charities to market needs?, *International Journal of Nonprofit and Voluntary Sector Marketing*, 4, 338–348.

Contact a Family (CAF) (2013) Falling through the net – illegal exclusions, the experiences of families with disabled children in England and Wales, http://www.cafamily.org.uk/ media/639982/falling_through_the_net_-_illegal_exclusions_report_2013_web.pdf, accessed 2 June 2013.

Cooper, P. (2011). Teacher strategies for effective intervention with students presenting social, emotional and behavioural difficulties, *European Journal of Special Needs Education*, 26, 1, 87–92.

Cooper, P., & Jacobs, B. (2011). *An international review of the literature of evidence of best practice models and outcomes in the education of children with emotional disturbance/behavioural difficulties*, Trim, Ireland: National Council for Special Education.

Copeland, I. (2001). Integration versus segregation: The early struggle, *British Journal of Learning Disabilities*, 29, 1, 5–11.

Corbett, J. (1997). Include/exclude, *International Journal of Inclusive Education*, 1, 1, 55–64.

Corbett, J. (1999). Inclusive education and school culture, *International Journal of Inclusive Education*, 3, 1, 53–61.

Costa, A. (1989). Foreword. In L. B. Resnick & L. E. Klopfer (Eds) *Toward the thinking curriculum*, Washington, DC: ASCD.

Courcier, I. (2007). Teachers' perceptions of personalised learning, *Evaluation & Research in Education*, 20, 2, 59–80.

Crisp, V., & Sweiry, E. (2006). Can a picture ruin a thousand words?, *Educational Research*, 48, 2, 139–154.

Crozier, G., & Davies, J. (2008). The trouble is they don't mix, *Race Ethnicity and Education*, 11, 3, 285–301.

Cruz, E., Gilbert, G., Harvey, J., Snowhite, M., Ybarra, N., Hudson, G., et al. (2003). A survey of effective practices in basic skills. Report to the Academic Senate for California Community Colleges.

Cullen, J., Williamson, D., & Lepper, C. (2005). Exploring narrative assessment to promote empowerment of educators and parents of children with special educational needs. Paper presented at ISEC 2005, Glasgow.

Curcic, S. (2009). Inclusion in PK-12, *International Journal of Inclusive Education*, 13, 5, 517–538.

Dagenais, D. (2003). Accessing imagined communities through multilingualism and immersion education, *Journal of Language, Identity & Education*, 2, 4, 37–41.

Daley, J. (2008). White working class boys need structure and competition to succeed, *The Daily Telegraph*, 16 December. http://blogs.telegraph.co.uk/news/janetdaley/5983638/White_working_class_boys_need_structure_and_competition_to_succeed/, accessed 9 September 2014.

Danforth, S., & Kim, T. (2008). Tracing the metaphors of ADHD, *International Journal of Inclusive Education*, 12, 1, 49–64.

Davis, J. (2006). Disability, childhood studies and the construction of medical discourses. In G. Lloyd, J. Stead, & D. Cohen (Eds) *Critical new perspectives on ADHD* (pp. 45–65), Abingdon, UK: Routledge.

Davis, P., & Florian, L. (2004). *Teaching strategies and approaches for pupils with special educational needs*, London: DfE.

Delgado-Pinheiro, E., & Omote, S. (2010). Conhecimentos de professores sobre perda auditiva e suas atitudes frente á inclusão, *CEFAC* [online], 12, 4, 633–640.

Deno, E. (1970). Special education as developmental capital, *Exceptional Children*, 37, 2, 229–237.

Department for Children, Schools and Families (DCSF) (2008). Secretary of State report on progress towards disability equality across the children's and education sector. http://www.dcsf.gov.uk/ des/ docs/ 2008SecretaryofStateReport_a.doc.

Department for Education (DfE) (2011). *Support and aspiration*, London: Her Majesty's Stationery Office.

Department for Education (DfE) (2013a). *Permanent and fixed period exclusions from schools and exclusion appeals in England, 2011/12*, London: DfE.

Department for Education (DfE) (2013b). *Statistical first release, special educational needs in England*, January 2013, London: DfE.

Department for Education (DfE) (2014). Schools, pupils and their characteristics, January. https://www.gov.uk/government/uploads/system/uploads/attachment_data/file/319028/SFR15_2014_main_text_v2.pdf, accessed 9 July 2014.

Devecchi, C., Dettori, F., Doveston, M., Sedgwick, P., & Jament, J. (2012). Inclusive classrooms in Italy and England, *European Journal of Special Needs Education*, 27, 2, 37–41.

Dey, S. (Ed.) (2011). Genetics and etiology of Down syndrome, InTech, accessed from www.intechopen.com.

Dockrell, J., & Shield, B. (2006). Acoustical barriers in classrooms, *British Educational Research Journal*, 32, 3, 509–525.

Dorn, S., & Johanningmeier, E. (1999). Dropping out and the military metaphor for schooling, *History of Education Quarterly*, 39, 2, 193–198.

Duguid, P. (2005). The art of knowing, *The Information Society*, 21, 2, 109–118.

EASPD (2012). *Analysis of the use and value of the Index for Inclusion (Booth & Ainscow 2011) and other instruments to assess and develop inclusive education practice in P2i partner countries*, Brussels/Tilburg: Fontys OSO.

Ecker, C., Spooren, W., & Murphy, D. G. M. (2013). Translational approaches to the biology of autism, *Molecular Psychiatry*, 18, 4, 435–442.

Education Scotland (2014). Co-operative and collaborative learning. http://www.educationscotland.gov.uk/learningteachingandassessment/approaches/collaboration/index.asp, accessed 27 June 2014.

Edwards, A. (2005). Let's get beyond community and practice, *Curriculum Journal*, 16, 1, 49–65.

Edwards, A. (2012). The role of common knowledge in achieving collaboration across practices, *Learning, Culture and Social Interaction*, 1, 1, 22–32.

Elliott, J. G., & Gibbs, S. (2008). Does dyslexia exist?, *Journal of Philosophy of Education*, 42, 3–4, 475–491.

Eraut, M. (2002). Conceptual analysis and research questions: Do the concepts of 'learning community' and 'community of practice' provide added value? Paper presented at the Annual Meeting of AERA, New Orleans, 1–5 April.

European Agency for Development in Special Needs Education (2011). Special needs education country data 2010. Retrieved from http://www.european-agency.org/publications/ereports/special-needs-education-country-data-2010/specialneeds-education-country-data-2010.

Evans, J., & Lunt, I. (2002). Inclusive education: Are there limits?, *European Journal of Special Needs Education*, 17, 1, 1–14.

Evans, P. (2003). Aspects of the integration of handicapped and disadvantaged students into education: Evidence from quantitative and qualitative data, OECD/CERI. http://www.oecd.org/edu/school/27141224.pdf, accessed 20 June 2013.

Exley, B. (2008). Staying in class so no one can get to him, *International Journal of Inclusive Education*, 12, 1, 65–80.

Farrell, P. (2012a). Inclusive education for children with special educational needs. In D. Armstrong & G. Squires (Eds) *Contemporary issues in SEN* (pp. 35–47), Maidenhead, UK: Open University Press.

Farrell, P. (2012b). *New perspectives in special education*, Abingdon, UK: Routledge.

Farrell, P., & Venables, K. (2009). Can educational psychologists be inclusive? In P. Hick, R. Kershner, & P. Farrell (Eds) *A psychology for inclusion*, London: Routledge (cited in Sheehy, 2013).

Farrell, P., Dyson, A., Polat, F., Hutcheson, G., & Gallannaugh, F. (2007). Inclusion and achievement in mainstream schools, *European Journal of Special Needs Education*, 22, 2, 131–145.

Fein, D., Barton, M., Eigsti, I., Kelley, E., Naigles, L., Schultz, R., et al. (2013). Optimal outcome in individuals with a history of autism, *Journal of Child Psychology and Psychiatry, and Allied Disciplines*, 54, 2, 195–205.

Feng, L., & Marcos, S. (2013). What makes special-education teachers special?, *Economics of Education Review*, 36, 122–134.

Fidler, D. (2006). The emergence of a syndrome-specific personality profile in young children with Down syndrome, *Down Syndrome Research and Practice*, 10, 2, 53–60.

Finkelstein, V. (2001). *The social model of disability repossessed*, Manchester coalition of disabled people.

Flem, A., & Keller, C. (2000). Inclusion in Norway, *European Journal of Special Needs Education*, 15, 2, 188–205.

Flippin, M., Reszka, S., & Watson, L. (2010). Effectiveness of the Picture Exchange Communication System (PECS) on communication and speech for children with autism spectrum disorders: A meta-analysis, *American Journal of Speech language Pathology American Speech Language Hearing Association*, 19, 2, 178–195.

Florian, L., & Black-Hawkins, K. (2011). Exploring inclusive pedagogy, *British Educational Research Journal*, 37, 5, 813–828.

Florian, L., Hollenweger, J., Simeonsson, R. J., Wedell, K., Riddell, S., Terzi, L. et al. (2006). Cross-cultural perspectives on the classification of children with disabilities, *Journal of Special Education*, 40, 1, 36–45.

Flynn, J. R. (2000). The hidden history of IQ and special education, *Public Policy, and Law*, 6, 1, 191–198.

Forness, S. (2001). Special education and related services, *Exceptionality*, 9, 4, 185–197.

Foucault, M. (1994). The subject and power. In J. Faubion (Ed.) *Power* (pp. 326–348), London: Penguin.

Fox, M. (2003). Opening Pandora's box – evidence-based practice for educational psychologists, *Educational Psychology in Practice*, 19, 2, 37–41.

Fox, S., Farrell, P., & Davis, P. (2004). Factors associated with the effective inclusion of primary-aged pupils with Down's syndrome, *British Journal of Special Education*, 31, 4, 184–190.

Frances, A., & Widiger, T. (2012). Psychiatric diagnosis, *Annual Review of Clinical Psychology*, 8, 109–130.

Frusciante, A., & Siberon, C. (2010). Constructing collaborative success for network learning, *The Foundation Review*, 2, 1, 53–71.

Fuchs, D., & Fuchs, L. (2006). Introduction to response to intervention, *Reading Research Quarterly*, 41, 1, 93–99.

Fuchs, L., Fuchs, D., Craddock, C., Hollenbeck, K., Hamlett, C., & Schatschneider, C. (2008). Effects of small-group tutoring with and without validated classroom instruction on at-risk students' math problem solving, *Journal of Educational Psychology*, 100, 3, 491–509.

Fuchs, D., Fuchs, L., & Stecker, P. (2010). The 'blurring' of special education in a new continuum of general education placements and services, *Exceptional Children*, 76, 3, 301–323.

Gallagher, D. (1998). The scientific knowledge base of special education, *Exceptional Children*, 64, 4, 493–502.

Garcia, I., Giuliani, F., & Wiesenfeld, E. (1999). Community and sense of community, *Journal of Community Psychology*, 27, 6, 727–740.

Geddes, L. (2009). Gene variant found in 65% of autism cases, *New Scientist*, 28 April, accessed from http://www.newscientist.com/article/dn17041–gene-variant-found-in-65-of-autism.

Gellner, E. (1983). *Nations and nationalism*, New York: Cornell University Press.

Gewirtz, S. (2008). Give us a break!, *European Educational Research Journal*, 7, 4, 414–424.

Gewirtz, S., Ball, S. J., & Bowe, R. (1995). *Markets, choice, and equity in education*, Buckingham, UK: Open University Press.

Giangreco, M. (1996). The stairs didn't go anywhere! (an interview with Norman Kunc), *Physical Disabilities: Education and Related Services*, 14, 2, 1–12.

Gillborn, D., Rollock, N., Vincent, C., & Ball, S. (2012). You got a pass, so what more do you want?, *Race Ethnicity and Education*, 15, 1, 121–139.

Gillman, M., Heyman, B., & Swain, J. (2000). What's in a name? The implications of diagnosis for people with learning difficulties and their family carers, *Disability & Society*, 15, 3, 389–409.

Gindis, B. (1999). Vygotsky's vision, *Remedial and Special Education*, 20, 6, 333–340.

Gingell, J. (2007). The concept of intelligence: A reply to Michael Hand, *London Review of Education*, 5, 1, 47–49.

Giota, J., & Emanuelsson, I. (2011). Policies in special education support issues in Swedish compulsory school, *London Review of Education*, 9, 1, 95–108.

Giroux, H., & Mclaren, P. (1986). Teacher education and the politics of engagement, *Harvard Educational Review*, 56, 3, 213–239.

Godsland (2013). Dyslexia myths and facts. http://www.dyslexics.org.uk/dyslexia_myths.htm, accessed 23 September 2014.

Goldacre, B. (2013). Teachers! What would evidence based practice look like? 15 March. http://www.badscience.net/2013/03/heres-my-paper-on-evidence-and-teaching-for-the-education-minister/, accessed 27 November 2013.

Gonzalez, N., Moll, L., & Amanti, C. (Eds). (2005). *Funds of knowledge*, Abingdon, UK: Routledge.

Goode, W. J. (1957). Community within a community: The professions, *American Sociological Review*, 22, 194–200.

Goodey, C. (2011). *A history of intelligence and 'intellectual disability'*, Farnham, UK: Ashgate.

Goodman, R., & Burton, D. (2010). The inclusion of students with BESD in mainstream schools, *Emotional And Behavioural Difficulties*, 15, 3, 223–237.

Goodyear, V., Casey, A., & Kirk, D. (2012). Hiding behind the camera, *Sport, Education and Society*, 19, 6, 712–734.

Graham, L. (2006). Caught in the net, *International Journal of Inclusive Education*, 10, 1, 3–25.

Graham, L. (2007). Out of sight, out of mind/out of mind, out of site, *International Journal of Qualitative Studies in Education*, 20, 5, 585–602.

Graham, L. (2008a) ADHD and schooling, *International Journal of Inclusive Education*, 12, 1, 1–6.

Graham, L. (2008b) From ABCs to ADHD, *International Journal of Inclusive Education*, 12, 1, 7–33.

Greenfield, P., Keller, H., Fuligni, A., & Maynard, A. (2003). Cultural pathways through universal development, *Annual Review of Psychology*, 54, 1, 461–90.

Groß, M. (2003). Educational systems and perceived social inequality, *European Societies*, 5, 2, 193–225.

Gruner Gandhi, A. (2007). Context matters, *International Journal of Disability, Development and Education*, 54, 1, 91–112.

Gulliford, R. (1971). *Special educational needs*, London: Routledge & Kegan Paul.

Hallahan, D. (1998). International perspectives on special education reform, *European Journal of Special Needs Education*, 13, 1, 37–41.

Hallam, S., & Parsons, S. (2013). The incidence and make up of ability grouped sets in the UK primary school, *Research Papers in Education*, 28, 4, 393–420.

Halpin, D. (1999). Democracy, inclusive schooling and the politics of education, *International Journal of Inclusive Education*, 3, 3, 225–238.

Hampden-Thompson, G. (2013). Family policy, family structure, and children's educational achievement, *Social Science Research* 42, 3, 804–817.

Hand, M. (2007). The concept of intelligence, *London Review of Education*, 5, 1, 35–46.

Hargreaves, E. (2007). The validity of collaborative assessment for learning, *Assessment in Education*, 14, 2, 185–199.

Hart, C. (2011). *Poverty and history*, Milton Keynes, UK: AuthorHouse.

Hart, S. (1996). *Beyond special needs: Enhancing children's learning through innovative thinking*, London: Paul Chapman.

Hart, S., Dixon, A., Drummond, M., & McIntyre, D. (2004). *Learning without limits*, Maidenhead, UK: Open University Press.

Harvey, D. (2006). Neo-liberalism as creative destruction, *Geografiska Annaler*, 88B, 2, 145–158.

Heath, N., McLean-Heywood, D., Rousseau, C., Petrakos, H., Finn, C., & Karagiannakis, A. (2006). Turf and tension, *International Journal of Inclusive Education*, 10, 4–5, 335–346.

Hechtman, L., Abikoff, H., Klein, R., Weiss, G., Respitz, C., Kouri, J., et al. (2004). Academic achievement and emotional status of children with ADHD treated with long-term methylphenidate and multimodal psychosocial treatment, *Journal of the American Academy of Child and Adolescent Psychiatry*, 43, 7, 812–819.

Hedegaard, M. (2009). Children's development from a cultural-historical approach, *Culture and Activity*, 16, 1, 64–82.

Hedges, A. (2007). Service user empowerment in a disability charity: The rhetoric and reality, Voluntary Sector Working Paper 6, The Centre for Civil Society.

Hempel-Jorgensen, A. (2009). The construction of the 'ideal pupil' and pupils' perceptions of 'misbehaviour' and discipline, *British Journal of Sociology of Education*, 30, 4, 435–448.

Hevey, D. (1992). *The creatures time forgot: Photography and disability imagery*, London: Routledge.

Hill, W., Stead, L., Rosenstein, M., & Furnas, G. (1995). Recommending and evaluating choices in a virtual community of use. In *Proceedings of the SIGCHI conference on human factors in computing systems – CHI '95* (pp. 194–201), New York: ACM Press.

Hilton, Z. (2006). Disaffection and school exclusion: Why are inclusion policies still not working in Scotland?, *Research Papers in Education*, 21, 3, 295–314.

Hirsch Jr, E. (2002). Classroom research and cargo cults, *Policy Review*, 115, 51–69.

Hodges, D. (1998). Participation as dis-identification with/in a community of practice, *Mind, Culture, and Activity*, 4, 5, 272–290.

Hodkinson, A. (2005). Conceptions and misconceptions of inclusive education – one year on, *Research in Education*, 76, 43–56.

Hollenweger, J. (2011). Development of an ICF-based eligibility procedure for education in Switzerland, *BMC Public Health*, 11, 4, S7.

Hollenweger, J. (2013). Developing applications of the ICF in education systems, *Disability and Rehabilitation*, 35, 13, 1087–1091.

Hood, B. (2012). Re-creating the real world, *Scientific American Mind*, 23, 4, 42–45.

Hornby, G., Atkinson, M., & Howard, J. (1997). *Controversial issues in special education*, London: David Fulton.

Horton-Salway, M. (2013). Gendering attention deficit hyperactivity disorder, *Journal of Health Psychology*, 18, 8, 1085–1099.

House of Commons Education and Skills Committee (2007). *Special educational needs: Assessment and funding tenth report of session 2006–07*, London: Her Majesty's Stationer.

Houssart, J. (2002). Count me out: Task refusal in primary mathematics, *Support for Learning*, 17, 2, 75–79.

Howe, M. (1997). *IQ in question*, London: Sage.

Hughes, V. (2012). Genetic tests for autism debut amid concerns about validity. http://sfari. org/news-and-opinion/news/genetic-tests-for-autism-debut-amid-concerns-about-validity, accessed 23 October 2013.

Ireson, J., & Hallam, S. (1999). Raising standards: Is ability grouping the answer?, *Oxford Review of Education*, 25, 3, 343–358.

Ireson, J., Hallam, S., & Hurley, C. (2005). What are the effects of ability grouping on GCSE attainment?, *British Educational Research Journal*, 31, 4, 443–458.

Isaksson, J., Lindqvist, R., & Bergström, E. (2007). School problems or individual shortcomings?, *European Journal of Special Needs Education*, 22, 1, 75–91.

Jans, M. (2004). Children as citizens, *Childhood*, 11, 1, 27–44.

Jóhannesson, I. (2006). Strong, independent, able to learn more…, *Studies in the Cultural Politics of Education*, 27, 1, 103–119.

Johanningmeier, E. (1969). William Chandler Bagley's changing views on the relationship between psychology and education, *History of Education Quarterly*, 9, 1, 3–27.

Johnson, B., Lorenz, E., & Lundvall, B. (2002). Why all this fuss about codified and tacit knowledge?, *Industrial and Corporate Change*, 11, 2, 245–262.

Johnson, L. (1991). Tings an times. In *Tings an times, selected poems*, Newcastle upon Tyne: Bloodaxe Books.

Jones, R. (2003). The construction of emotional and behavioural difficulties, *Educational Psychology in Practice*, 19, 2, 147–157.

Jordan, A., & Stanovich, P. (2001). Patterns of teacher–student interaction in inclusive elementary classrooms and correlates with student self-concept, *International Journal of Disability, Development and Education*, 48, 1, 33–52.

Jordan, A., Glenn, C., & McGhie-Richmond, D. (2010). The supporting effective teaching (SET) project, *Teaching and Teacher Education*, 26, 2, 259–266.

Joyce, R. (2012). *The unlikely pilgrimage of Harold Fry*, London: Doubleday.

Kalambouka, A., Farrell, P., Dyson, A., & Kaplan, I. (2005). The impact of population inclusivity on student outcomes, DfES/Institute of Education.

Kanno, Y., & Norton, B. (2009). Imagined communities and educational possibilities, *Journal of Language, Identity & Education*, 2, 4, 241–249.

Kay, E., Tisdall, M., & Riddell, S. (2006). Policies on special needs education, *European Journal of Special Needs Education*, 21, 4, 363–379.

Keay, D. (1987). Margaret Thatcher interview for *Woman's Own*, 23 September. http://www. margaretthatcher.org/document/106689, accessed 19 May 2014.

Kirmayer, L. (2001). Cultural variations in the clinical presentation of depression and anxiety, *The Journal of Clinical Psychiatry*, 62, 13, 22–28.

Kirp, D. (1982). .Professionalisation as a policy choice, *World Politics*, 34, 2, 137–174.

Kitchin, R. (2000). The researched opinions on research, *Disability & Society*, 15, 1, 25–47.

Kiuppis, F. (2013). Why (not) associate the principle of inclusion with disability?, *International Journal of Inclusive Education*, (ahead-of-print), 1–16.

Kogan, I., Gebel, M., & Noelke, C. (2012). Educational systems and inequalities in educational attainment in central and eastern European countries, *Studies of Transition States and Societies*, 4, 1, 69–83.

Kreiner, S., & Christensen, K. B. (2013). Analyses of model fit and robustness, *Psychometrika*, 1–22.

Kristjansson, K. (2009). Medicalised pupils: The case of ADD/ADHD, *Oxford Review of Education*, 35, 1, 111–127.

Lakoff, G., & Johnson, M. (1980). Conceptual metaphor in everyday language, *Journal of Philosophy*, 77, 8, 453–486.

Lave, J., & Wenger, E. (1991). *Situated learning*, New York: Cambridge University Press.

Laws, G., Byrne, A., & Buckley, S. (2000). Language and memory development in children with Down syndrome at mainstream schools and special schools, *Educational Psychology*, 20, 4, 447–457.

Leadbetter, C. (2004). *Learning about personalisation: How can we put the learner at the heart of the education system?*, Nottingham, UK: DfES.

Leitch, S. (2006). *The Leitch review of skills. Class skills*, London: The Stationery Office.

Lejk, M., & Wyvill, M. (1996). A survey of methods of deriving individual grades from group assessments, *Assessment & Evaluation in Higher Education*, 21, 3, 267–281.

Leung, S., & McPherson, B. (2006). Classrooms for children with developmental disabilities, international journal of disability, *Development and Education*, 53, 3, 287–299.

Lewis, A., & Norwich, B. (Eds). (2005). *Special teaching for special children: Pedagogies for inclusion*, Maidenhead, UK: Open University Press.

Liasidou, A. (2012). Inclusive education and critical pedagogy at the intersections of disability, race, gender and class, *Journal for Critical Education Policy Studies*, 10, 1, 168–184.

Liggett, H. (1988). Stars are not born, *Disability & Society*, 3, 3, 263–275.

Limbrick, P. (2010). Team around the child, *Interconnections Quarterly Journal*, 3, 35–45.

Lindqvist, G., Nilholm, C., Almqvist, L., & Wetso, G.-M. (2011). Different agendas?, *European Journal of Special Needs Education*, 26, 2, 143–157.

Lindsay, G. (2007). Educational psychology and the effectiveness of inclusive education/mainstreaming, *British Journal of Educational Psychology*, 77, 1–24.

Lindsay, G., Pather, S., & Strand, S. (2006). Special educational needs and ethnicity, *Education*, 27, 1, 36–40.

Linehan, C., & McCarthy, J. (2001). Reviewing the 'community of practice' metaphor, *Mind, Culture, and Activity*, 8, 2, 129–147.

Littleton, K., & Mercer, N. (2013). *Interthinking: Putting talk to work*, London: Routledge.

Long, M., Wood, C., Littleton, K., Passenger, T., & Sheehy, K. (2011). *The Psychology of Education* (2nd ed.), London: Routledge.

Lundstro, S., Larsson, H., & Anckarsa, H. (2012). Autism spectrum disorders and autistic-like traits, *Archives of General Psychiatry*, 69, 1, 46–52.

Lupton, C., Burd, L., & Harwood, R. (2004). Cost of fetal alcohol spectrum disorders, *American Journal of Medical Genetics*, 127C, 42–50.

Lupton, R., Thrupp, M., & Brown, C. (2010). Special educational needs: A contextualised perspective, *British Journal of Educational Studies*, 58, 3, 267–284.

Macbeath, J., Galton, M., Steward, S., Macbeath, A., & Page, C. (2006). *The costs of inclusion*, University of Cambridge, Faculty of Education.

MacInnes, J., & Diaz, J. (2009). The reproductive revolution, *The Sociological Review*, 57, 2, 262–284.

Mackintosh, N. J. (1998). *IQ and human intelligence*, Oxford: Oxford University Press.

Mahoney, G., Perales, F., Wiggers, B., & Herman, B. (2006). Responsive teaching, *Down Syndrome Research and Practice*, 11, 1, 18–28.

Mangan, J., & Galligan, F. (2011). Militarism, drill and elementary education, *The International Journal of the History of Sport*, 28, 3–4, 568–603.

Mangan, J., & Ndee, H. (2003). Military drill – Rather more than 'brief and basic'. In J. Mangan (Ed.) *Militarism, sport, Europe* (pp. 65–96), London: Frank Cass.

Marschark, M., Spencer, P., Adams, J., & Sapere, P. (2011). Evidence-based practice in educating deaf and hard-of-hearing children, *European Journal of Special Needs Education*, 26, 1, 3–16.

Martinez, A., Western, M., Haynes, M., Tomaszewski, W., & Macarayan, E. (2014). Multiple job holding and income mobility in Indonesia, *Research in Social Stratification and Mobility*, 1–17.

Martinez, R., & Fernandez, P. (2010). *The social and economic impact of illiteracy: Analytical model and pilot study*, UNESCO, United Nations.

Mason, M., & Rieser, R. (1994). *Altogether better*, London: Comic Relief.

Matthews, A., & Rix, J. (2013). Early intervention: Parental involvement, child agency and participation in creative play, *Early Years*, 33, 3, 239–251.

Mattson, E., & Roll-Pettersson, L. (2007). Segregated groups or inclusive education?, *Scandinavian Journal of Educational Research*, 51, 3, 239–252.

May, P., Fiorentino, D., Gossage, P., Kalberg, W., Hoyme, E., Robinson, L., et al. (2006). Epidemiology of FASD in a province in Italy, *Alcoholism: Clinical and Experimental Research*, 30, 9, 1562–1575.

Mayall, B. (2006). Values and assumptions underpinning policy for children and young people in England, *Children's Geographies*, 4, 1, 9–17.

McCrone, K. (1984).Play up! Play up! And play the game!, *Journal of British Studies*, 23, 2, 106–134.

McDermott, R., & Varenne, H. (1995). Culture as disability, *Anthropology & Education Quarterly*, 26, 3, 324–348.

McInerney, D. M. (2005). Educational psychology – theory, research, and teaching: A 25-year retrospective, *Educational Psychology*, 25, 6, 585–599.

McLeskey, J., & Waldron, N. (2011). Educational programs for elementary students with learning disabilities, *Exceptional Children*, 26, 1, 48–57.

McMenamin, T. (2011). The tenacity of special schools in an inclusive policy environment, *Support for Learning*, 26, 3, 97–102.

McMillan, D., & George, D. (1986). Sense of community, *Journal of Community Psychology*, 14, 1, 6–23.

Meijer, C. (Ed.) (2001). *Inclusive education and effective classroom practices*, European Agency for Development in Special Needs Education.

Meijer, C., & De Jager, B. (2001). Population density and special needs education, *European Journal of Special Needs Education*, 16, 2, 143–148.

Mencap. (2007). *Bullying wrecks lives*, London: Mencap.

Méndez, L., Lacasa, P., & Matusov, E. (2008). Transcending the zone of learning disability, *European Journal of Special Needs Education*, 23, 1, 63–73.

Mendick, H., & Francis, B. (2012). Boffin and geek identities, *Gender and Education*, 24, 1, 15–24.

Miles, S., & Singal, N. (2010). The education for all and inclusive education debate: Conflict, contradiction or opportunity?, *International Journal of Inclusive Education*, 14, 1, 1–15.

Mirza, H. S. (1998). Race, gender and IQ, *Race Ethnicity and Education*, 1, 1, 109–126.

Mitchell, C. (1999). Building learning communities in schools, *Interchange*, 30, 3, 283–303.

Mitchell, D., Morton, M., & Hornby, G. (2010). *Review of the literature on individual education plans* (p. 109), Wellington: Ministry of Education.

Mitra, S. (2014). Reconciling the capability approach and the ICF: A response, *ALTER – European Journal of Disability Research (Revue Européenne de Recherche Sur Le Handicap)*, 8, 1, 24–29.

Mittler, P. (2000). *Working towards inclusive education*, London: David Fulton.

Molteno, C. (2008). Foetal alcohol spectrum disorder, *Journal of Intellectual Disability Research*, 52, 8, 640.

Murphy, F. (2011). Team-teaching for inclusive learning, PhD thesis, University of Cork.

Myhill, D., & Jones, S. (2006). She doesn't shout at no girls, *Cambridge Journal of Education*, 36, 1, 99–113.

Naraian, S. (2011). Seeking transparency, *International Journal of Inclusive Education*, 15, 9, 955–973.

National Center for Educational Statistics (2006). A first look at the literacy of America's adults in the 21st century. http://nces.ed.gov./NAAL/PDF/2006470.PDF, accessed 9 May 2014.

Neary, M. (2013). Viewpoint: 10 jargon phrases used for my autistic son, posted 24 July. http://www.bbc.co.uk/news/blogs-ouch-23423541, accessed 26 November 2013.

Newman, T., McEwen, J., Mackin, H., & Slowley, M. with Morris, M. (2009). *Improving the wellbeing of disabled children up to age 8 and their families through increasing the quality and range of early years interventions*, London: The Centre for Excellence and Outcomes in Children and Young People's Services.

Nisbet, J. (2004). Caught in the continuum, *Research and Practice for Persons with Severe Disabilities*, 29, 4, 231–236.

Noddings, N. (1996). On community, *Educational Theory*, 46, 3, 245–267.

Noddings, N. (2005). Identifying and responding to needs in education, *Cambridge Journal of Education*, 35, 2, 147–159.

Norton, B. (2001). Non-participation, imagined communities and the language classroom. In M. Breen (Ed.) *Learner contributions to language learning: New directions in research*, Harlow, UK: Pearson Education.

Norwich, B. (2002). Inclusion and individual differences, *British Journal of Educational Studies*, 50, 4, 482–502.

Norwich, B. (2008a) *Dilemmas of difference, inclusion and disability*, Abingdon, UK: Routledge,

Norwich, B. (2008b). What future for special schools and inclusion? Conceptual and professional perspectives, *British Journal of Special Education*, 35, 136–143.

Norwich, B., & Lewis, A. (2007). How specialized is teaching children with disabilities and difficulties?, *Journal of Curriculum Studies*, 39, 2, 127–150.

Novak, M. (1990). A community of self-reliance, *Journal of Legislation*, 16, 173–189.

O'Riordan, T., & Jordan, A. (1995). The precautionary principle in contemporary environmental politics, *Environmental Values*, 4, 3, 191–212.

Odom, S., Parrish, T., & Hikido, C. (2001). The costs of inclusive and traditional special education preschool services, *Journal of Special Education Leadership*, 14, 1, 33–41.

OECD (2009). *What students know and can do: Student performance in reading, mathematics and science*. http://www.oecd.org/pisa/46643496.pdf, accessed 9 May 2014.

OECD (2012). *CX3.1 Special Educational Needs (SEN)*. http://www.oecd.org/social/family/50325299.pdf, accessed on 16 February 2013.

OECD (2013a). *OECD Skills Outlook 2013*, OECD.

OECD (2013b) *PISA 2015 – Draft collaborative problem solving framework*. http://www.oecd.org/pisa/pisaproducts/Draft%20PISA%202015%20Collaborative%20Problem%20Solving%20Framework%20.pdf, accessed 19 May 2014.

Office of the United Nations High Commissioner for Human Rights (OUNHC)(1989). *Convention on the rights of the child*, Geneva: Office of the United Nations High Commissioner for Human Rights.

OFSTED (2004). *Remodelling the school workforce*, HMI 358, London: Office for Standards in Education.

Oliver, M. (1983). *Social work with disabled people*, Basingstoke, UK: Macmillan.

Oliver, M. (1996). User involvement in this voluntary sector. Paper prepared for submission to the Commission on the Future of the Voluntary Sector.

Osler, A. (2006). Excluded girls, *Gender and Education*, 18, 6, 571–589.

Otchoun, A. (2010). *Teachers' educators' perceptions of authentic assessment tasks in cooperative learning groups*, Université de Reims Champagne-Ardenne & Akershus University College.

Pardales, M. J., & Girod, M. (2006). Community of inquiry: Its past and present future, *Educational Philosophy and Theory*, 38, 3, 299–309.

Parry, J. (2014). Making connections and making friends: Social interactions between two children labelled with special educational needs and their peers in a nursery setting, *Early Years* (ahead-of-print), 1–14.

Parry, J., Rix, J., Sheehy, K., & Simmons, K. (2013). The journey travelled, *British Journal of Educational Studies*, 61, 4, 385–399.

Parsons, C. (2008). Race relations legislation, ethnicity and disproportionality in school exclusions in England, *Cambridge Journal of Education*, 38, 3, 401–419.

Parsons, S., Guldberg, K., Macleod, A., Jones, G., Prunty, A., & Balfe, T. (2009). *International review of the literature of evidence of best practice provision in the education of persons with autistic spectrum disorders*, Trim, Ireland: National Council for Special Educational Needs.

Partanen, A. (2011). What Americans keep ignoring about Finland's school success, *The Atlantic*, 29 December. http://www.theatlantic.com/national/archive/2011/12/what-americans-keep-ignoring-about-finlands-school-success/250564/2/, accessed 8 September 2014.

Patrick, H., Anderman, L., Bruening, P., & Duffin, L. (2011). The role of educational psychology in teacher education, *Educational Psychologist*, 46, 2, 71–83.

Peadon, E., Freemantle, E., Bower, C., & Elliott, E. J. (2008). International survey of diagnostic services for children with FASD, *BMC Paediatrics*, 8, 12, 1–8.

Periyakoil, V. (2008). Using metaphors in medicine, *Journal of Palliative Medicine*, 11, 6, 842–844.

Peters, S. (2007). Education for all?, *Journal of Disability Policy Studies*, 18, 2, 98–108.

Peterson, D. (1992). *Life in a crowded place*, Portsmouth: Heinemann.

Philip, T., Way, W., Garcia, A., Schuler-Brown, S., & Navarro, O. (2013). When educators attempt to make 'community' a part of classroom learning, *Teaching and Teacher Education*, 34, 174–183.

Pijl, S-J. (2013). Steps towards inclusive education in the Netherlands. Paper presented at the European Conference of Educational Research, 10–13 September, Istanbul.

Pijl, S-J., Frostad, P., & Flem, A. (2008). The social position of pupils with special needs in regular schools, *Scandinavian Journal of Educational Research*, 52, 4, 387–405.

Podsakoff, P., MacKenzie, S., Lee, J., & Podsakoff, N. (2003). Common method biases in behavioral research, *The Journal of Applied Psychology*, 88, 5, 879–903.

Popova, S., Stade, B., Bekmuradov, D., Lange, S., & Rehm, J. (2011). What do we know about the economic impact of fetal alcohol spectrum disorder?, *Alcohol and Alcoholism*, 46, 4, 490–497.

Pratchett, T. (2002), *Nightwatch*, London: Doubleday,

President's Commission on Excellence in Special Education (2002). *A new era: Revitalising special education for children and their families*. https://education.ucf.edu/mirc/Research/President's%20Commission%20on%20Excellence%20in%20Special%20Education.pdf, accessed 14 February 2014.

Pretty, G., Conroy, C., Dugay, J., Fowler, K., & Williams, D. (1996). Sense of community and its relevance to adolescents of all ages, *Journal of Community Psychology*, 24, 4, 365–379.

Purdie, N., Hattie, J., & Carroll, A. (2002). A review of the research on interventions for attention deficit hyperactivity disorder, *Review of Educational Research*, 72, 1, 61–99.

Rae, A. (1996). *Survivors from the special school system*, Bolton Institute of Higher Education.

Ramachandran, V. (2003). Lecture 5: Neuroscience – the new philosophy, Reith Lectures, *The Emerging Mind*, BBC Radio 4.

Read, J., & Walmsley, J. (2006), Historical perspectives on special education, 1890–1970, *Disability & Society*, 21, 5, 455–469.

Reay, D. (2009). Making sense of white working class educational underachievement. In K. Sveinsson (Ed.) *Who cares about the white working class?*, London: Runnymede Trust.

Resnick, L., & Klopfer, L. (1989). Toward the thinking curriculum: An overview. In L. Resnick & L. Klopfer (Eds) *Toward the thinking curriculum: Current cognitive research*, Washington, DC: ASCD.

Reynolds, M. (1962). A framework for considering some issues in special education, *Exceptional Children*, 28, 7, 267–370.

Richardson, J., & Powell, J. (2011). *Comparing special education*, Stanford, CA: Stanford University Press.

Richardson, T., & Johanningmeier, E. (1997). Intelligence testing, *International Journal of Educational Research*, 27, 8, 699–714.

Riddell, S., & Weedon, E. (2013). Understanding the expansion of ASN in Scotland. Paper presented at the European Conference of Educational Research, Istanbul, September 2013.

Riddell, S., Tisdall, K., Kane, J., & Mulderrig, J. (2006). Literature review of pupils with additional support needs. Final report to the Scottish Executive Education Department Centre for Research in Education Inclusion and Diversity (CREID).

Rieffer, B.(2003). Religion and nationalism, *Ethnicities*, 3, 2, 215–242.

Rix, B. (2006). *All about us*, London: Mencap.

Rix, J. (2004). Building on similarity, *Westminster Studies in Education*, 27, 1, 57–68.

Rix, J. (2005a). Creating and using inclusive materials, collaboratively and reflectively. In M. Nind, K. Simmons, K. Sheehy, & J. Rix (Eds.) *Values into practice: Curriculum and pedagogy in inclusive education*, London: RoutledgeFalmer.

Rix, J. (2005b). Checking the list, *International Journal of Heritage Studies*, 11, 4, 341–356.

Rix, J. (2006). Simplified language materials – their usage and value to teachers and support staff in mainstream settings, *Teaching and Teacher Education*, 22, 8, 1145–1156.

Rix, J. (2009a). A model of simplification: The ways in which teachers simplify learning materials, *Educational Studies*, 35, 2, 95–106.

Rix, J. (2009b). Educating a syndrome?, Seeking a balance between identifying a learning profile and delivering inclusive education, *Perspectives on Language Learning and Education*, 16, 3, 97–103.

Rix, J. (2009c) Statutory assessment of the class?, *International Journal of Inclusive Education*, 13, 3, 253–272.

Rix, J. (2010). 21st century skills ... all dressed up in the technology of the knowledge age. In K. Sheehy, R. Ferguson, & G. Clough (Eds) *Controversies at the frontier of education*, New York: Nova Science.

Rix, J. (2011). Repositioning of special schools within a specialist, personalised educational marketplace, *International Journal of Inclusive Education*, 15, 2, 263–279.

Rix, J., & Matthews, A. (2014). Viewing the child as a participant within context, *Disability & Society* (ahead-of-print), 1–15.

Rix, J., & Paige-Smith, A. (2008). A different head?, *Disability & Society*, 23, 3, 211–221.

Rix, J., & Paige-Smith, A. (2011). Exploring barriers to reflection and learning, *Journal of Research in Special Educational Needs*, 11, 1, 30–41.

Rix, J., & Parry, J. (2014). Without foundation: The EYFS framework and its creation of needs. In J. Moyles, J. Payler, & J. Georgeson (Eds) *Early years foundations*, Maidenhead, UK: Open University Press.

Rix, J., & Parry, J. (in press) Ongoing exclusion within universal education. In F. Kiuppis & R. Haußstätter (Eds) *Inclusive education twenty years after Salamanca*, New York: Peter Lang.

Rix, J., & Sheehy, K. (2014). Nothing special. In L. Florian (Ed.) *Sage handbook of special education*, 2nd ed. (pp. 459–474), London: Sage.

Rix, J., Hall, K., Nind, M., Sheehy, K., & Wearmouth, J. (2009). What pedagogical approaches can effectively include children with special educational needs in mainstream classrooms? A systematic literature review, *Support for Learning*, 24, 2, 86–94.

Rix, J., Paige-Smith, A., & Jones, H. (2008). Until the cows came home, *International Journal of Contemporary Issues in Early Childhood*, 9, 1, 66–79.

Rix, J., Sheehy, K., Fletcher-Campbell, F., Crisp, M., & Harper, A. (2013a). *Continuum of education provision for children with special educational needs: Review of international policies and practices* (Vols 1 & 2), Trim, Ireland: National Council for Special Education.

Rix, J., Sheehy, K., Fletcher-Campbell, F., Crisp, M., & Harper, A. (2013b). Exploring provision for children identified with special educational needs: An international review of policy and practice, *European Journal of Special Needs Education*, 28, 4, 375–391.

Rix, J., Sheehy, K., Fletcher-Campbell, F., Crisp, M., & Harper, A. (in press) Moving from a continuum to a community, *Review of Educational Research*.

Robbins, T. (2002). *Fierce invalids home from hot climates*, Harpenden: No Exit Press.

Robinson, A. (1994). It takes one to know one, *Critical Enquiry*, 20, 4, 715–736.

Robson, C. (2005). *Students with disabilities, learning difficulties and disadvantages*, Paris: OECD.

Rockwell, E. (2002). Learning for life or learning from books, *Paedagogica Historica: International Journal of the History of Education*, 38, 1, 113–135.

Rogers, C. (2007). Experiencing an 'inclusive' education, *British Journal of Sociology of Education*, 28, 1, 55–68.

Rogoff, B. (1995). Observing sociocultural activity on three planes. In J. Wertsch, P. del Rio, & A. Alvarez (Eds) *Sociocultural studies of mind* (pp. 139–164), Cambridge: Cambridge University Press.

Rogoff, B. (2003). *The cultural nature of child development*, New York: Oxford University Press.

Rogoff, B., Eugene, M., & Cynthia, W. (1996). Models of teaching and learning. In D. Olson & N. Torrance (Eds) *The handbook of education and human development* (pp. 388–414), Cambridge: Blackwell.

Rolph, S., Atkinson, D., Nind, M., Welshman, J., Brigham, L., Chapman, R., et al. (2005). *Witnesses to change*, Kidderminster: British Institute of Learning Disabilities.

Rosenthal, R., & Jacobsen, L. (1968). *Pygmalion in the classroom: Teachers' expectations and pupils' intellectual development*, New York: Holt, Rinehart, and Winston.

Ruijs, N., & Peetsma, T. T. D. (2009). Effects of inclusion on students with and without special educational needs reviewed, *Educational Research Review*, 4, 2, 67–79.

Rutter, J. (2001). *Supporting refugee children in twenty first century Britain*, Stoke-on-Trent: Trentham Books.

Ryan, R., & Deci, E. (2000). Self-determination theory and the facilitation of intrinsic motivation, social development, and well-being, *The American Psychologist*, 55, 1, 68–78.

Saloviita, T., & Takala, M. (2010). Frequency of co-teaching in different teacher categories, *European Journal of Special Needs Education*, 25, 4, 389–396.

Sammons, P., Sylva, K., Melhuish, E., Siraj-Blatchford, I., Taggart, B., Toth, K., et al. (2012). *Effective Pre-School, Primary and Secondary Education Project (EPPSE 3–14). Influences on students' attainment and progress in Key Stage 3: Academic outcomes in English, maths and science in Year 9*. Department for Education.

Sampson, P., Streissguth, P., Bookstein, F., Little, R., Clarren, S. Dehaene, P., et al. (1997). Incidence of fetal alcohol syndrome and prevalence of alcohol-related neurodevelopmental disorder, *Teratology*, 56, 5, 317–26.

Satherley, P., Lawes, E., & Sok, S. (2008). The Adult Literacy and Life Skills (ALL) survey: Overview and international comparisons. http://www.educationcounts.govt.nz/__data/assets/pdf_file/0010/19495/Overview-and-International-Comparisons.pdf, accessed 9 May 2014.

Sawyer, R. K., & DeZutter, S. (2009). Distributed creativity: How collective creations emerge from collaboration, *Psychology of Aesthetics, Creativity, and the Arts*, 3, 2, 81–92.

Schmitz, M., & Winskel, H. (2008). Towards effective partnerships in a collaborative problem-solving task, *British Journal of Educational Psychology*, 78, 4, 581–596.

Schmitz, M. F., Filippone, P., & Edelman, E. M. (2003). Social representations of attention deficit/hyperactivity disorder, 1988–1997, *Culture & Psychology*, 9, 4, 383–406.

Scottish Government (2009). *Pupils in Scotland, 2009*, Statistical Bulletin, Edinburgh: Scottish Government.

Scottish Government (2010). *Exclusions from schools 2008/09 statistics publication notice*, Education Series, National Statistics, London: Thomas Coram Research Unit, Institute of Education, University of London.

Scruggs, T., & Mastropieri, M. (1996). Teacher perceptions of mainstreaming/inclusion, 1958–1995, *Exceptional Children*, 63, 1, 59–74.

Scruggs, T., Mastropieri, M., & McDuffie, K. (2007). Co-teaching in inclusive classrooms, *Exceptional Children*, 73, 4, 392–416.

Scull, B., & Winkler, A. (2011). *Shifting trends in special education*, Dayton, OH: Thomas Fordham Institute.

Seixas, P. (1993). The community of inquiry as a basis for knowledge and learning, *American Educational Research Journal*, 30, 2, 305–324.

Seymour, P., Aro, M., & Erskine, J. (2003). Foundation literacy acquisition in European orthographies, *British Journal of Psychology*, 94, 2, 143–174.

Shah, S. (2007). Special or mainstream?, *Research Papers in Education*, 22, 4, 425–442.

Sharma, U., Forlin, C., & Loreman, T. (2008). Impact of training on pre-service teachers' attitudes and concerns about inclusive education and sentiments about persons with disabilities, *Disability & Society*, 23, 7, 773–785.

Sharma, Y. (2013). Asia's parents suffering 'education fever'. http://www.bbc.co.uk/news/business-24537487, accessed 8 November 2013.

Sheehy, K. (2009). Teaching word recognition to children with severe learning difficulties, *Educational Research*, 51, 3, 379–391.

Sheehy K., (2013). Educational psychology and inclusive education. In A. Holliman (Ed.) *Educational psychology: An international perspective*, Abingdon, UK: Routledge.

Sheehy, K., & Duffy, H. (2009). Attitudes to Makaton in the ages of integration and inclusion, *International Journal of Special Education*, 24, 2, 91–102.

Shunit, R., & Lapidot-Lefler, N. (2007). Bullying among special education students with intellectual disabilities, *Intellectual and Developmental Disabilities*, 45, 3, 174–181.

Shury, J., Winterbotham, M., Davies, B., Oldfield, K., Spilsbury, M., & Constable, S. (2010). *National employer skills survey for England 2009*, Wath Upon Dearne: UK Commission for Employment and Skills.

Siderits, M., Thompson, E., & Zahavi, D. (2011). *Self, no self?: Perspectives from analytical, phenomenological, and Indian traditions*, Oxford: Oxford University Press.

Sigafoos, J., Moore, D., Brown, D., Green, V., O'Reilly, M. F., & Lancioni, G. E. (2010). Special education funding reform, *Australasian Journal of Special Education*, 34, 1, 17–35.

Sindelar, P., Dewey, F., Rosenberg, S., Denslow, D., & Lotfinia, B. (2012). Cost effectiveness of alternative route special education teacher preparation, *Exceptional Children*, 79, 1, 25–42.

Sivanandan, A. (1990). *Communities of resistance*, New York: Verso.

Skaalvik, E., & Skaalvic, S. (2005). *Skolen som læringsarena*, Oslo, Norway: Universitetsforlaget (cited in Pijl et al., 2008).

Skidmore, D. (2004). *Inclusion: The dynamic of school development*, Maidenhead, UK: Open University Press.

Slee, R. (2006). Limits to and possibilities for educational reform, *International Journal of Inclusive Education*, 10, 2–3, 109–119.

Slee, R. (2008). Beyond special and regular schooling?, *International Studies in Sociology of Education*, 18, 2, 99–116.

Smith, E., & Douglas, G. (2014). Special educational needs, disability and school accountability, *International Journal of Inclusive Education*, 18, 5, 443–458.

Snowling, M. (2013). Early identification and interventions for dyslexia, *Journal of Research in Special Educational Needs*, 13, 1, 7–14.

Solis, M., Vaughn, S., Swanson, E., & Mcculley, L. (2012). Collaborative models of instruction, *Psychology in the Schools*, 49, 5, 498–511.

Sowa, J. (2008). The collaboration decision in nonprofit organization, *Nonprofit and Voluntary Sector Quarterly*, 38, 6, 1003–1025.

Spaulding, L. (2009). Best practices and interventions in special education, *Teaching Exceptional Children Plus*, 5, 3, 2–13.

Spyrou, S. (2006). Constructing 'the Turk' as an enemy, *South European Society and Politics*, 11, 1, 95–110.

Stacey, M. (1969). The myth of community studies, *The British Journal of Sociology*, 20, 2, 134–147.

Stein, J. (2009). Why dyslexia does exist, Saturday 5 September. http://www.dystalk.com/talks/90–why-dyslexia-does-exist, accessed 12 November 2013.

Stevenson, R. (1883). *Treasure Island*, London: Cassell & Co.

Stiker, H. (1999). *A history of disability* (W. Sayers, Trans.), Ann Arbor: University of Michigan Press.

Strike, K. (1999). Can schools be communities?, *Educational Administration Quarterly*, 35, 1, 46–70.

Sunfield (2012). Statement of purpose. http://www.sunfield.org.uk/wp-content/uploads/2011/11/SUNFIELD-Statement-of-Purpose-2012.pdf, accessed 12 November 2012.

Tadema, A., Vlaskamp, C., & Ruijssenaars, W. (2005). The development of a checklist of child characteristics for assessment purposes, *European Journal of Special Needs Education*, 20, 4, 403–417.

Takala, M., & Uusitalo-Malmivaara, L. (2012). A one-year study of the development of co-teaching in four Finnish schools, *European Journal of Special Needs Education*, 27, 3, 373–390.

Taylor, S. (1988). Caught in the continuum: A critical analysis of the principle of the least restrictive environment, *The Journal of The Association for the Severely Handicapped*, 13, 1. In *Research & Practice for Persons with Severe Disabilities* (2004), 29, 4, 218–230.

Taylor, S. (2001). The continuum and current controversies in the USA, *Journal of Intellectual and Developmental Disability*, 26, 1, 15–33.

Taylor, Y. (2007). Brushed behind the bike shed, *British Journal of Sociology of Education*, 28, 3, 349–362.

Tempelaar, W., Otjes, C., Bun, C., Plevier, C., van Gastel, W., MacCabe, J., et al. (2014). Delayed school progression and mental health problems in adolescence, *BMC Psychiatry*, 14, 1, 244–252.

Tetler, S. (2000). *Den inkluderende skole: Fra vision till virkelighed*, København, Denmark: Gyldendal Uddannelse.

Therrien, W., Zaman, M., & Banda, D. (2010). How can meta-analyses guide practice?, *Remedial and Special Education*, 32, 3, 206–218.

Thibodeau, P. H., & Boroditsky, L. (2011). Metaphors we think with, *PloS One*, 6, 2, e16782.

Thomas, G. (1997). Inclusive schools for an inclusive society, *British Journal of Special Education*, 24, 3, 103–7.

Thomas, G. (2000). Doing injustice to inclusion, *European Journal of Special Needs Education*, 15, 3, 307–310.

Thomas, G., & Glenny, G. (2002). Thinking about inclusion, *International Journal of Inclusive Education*, 6, 4, 345–369.

Thomas, G., & Loxley, A. (2001). *Deconstructing special education and constructing inclusion*, Buckingham, UK: Open University Press.

Thomas, G., & Vaughan, M. (2004). *Inclusive education*, Maidenhead, UK: Open University Press.

Thompson, E. (1971). The moral economy of the English crowd in the eighteenth century, *Past and Present*, 50, 76–136.

Thornberg, R. (2008). It's not fair! Voicing pupils' criticisms of school rules, *Children & Society*, 22, 6, 418–428.

Tisdall, E., & Riddell, S. (2006). Policies on special needs education, *European Journal of Special Needs Education*, 21, 4, 363–379.

Tomlinson, S. (1982). *A sociology of special education*, London: Routledge & Kegan Paul.

Tomlinson, S. (1985). The expansion of special education, *Oxford Review of Education*, 11, 2, 157–165.

Torgesen, J. K. (2009). The response to intervention instructional model, *Child Development Perspectives*, 3, 1, 38–40.

Treehouse® (n.d.) *Schools from scratch*.

UNESCO (2007). *From exclusion to equality, disabilities handbook for parliamentarians.* http://www.un.org/disabilities/documents/toolaction/ipuhb.pdf, accessed June 2013.

UNESCO (2013). World inequality database on education. http://www.education-inequalities.org/, accessed on 2 July 2013.

UNESCO (2014). LAMP – Literacy Assessment and Monitoring Programme. http://www.uis.unesco.org/Literacy/Pages/lamp-literacy-assessment.aspx, accessed 9 May 2014.

UNESCO IBE (2008). Inclusive education: The way of the future. *Conclusions and recommendations of the 48th Session for the International Conference on Education (ICE)*, Geneva, 25–28 November. http://www.ibe.unesco.org/National_Reports/ICE_2008/brazil_NR08_es.pdf, accessed 1 November.

Van der Oord, S., Prins, P., Oosterlaan, J., & Emmelkamp, P. (2008). Efficacy of methylphenidate, psychosocial treatments and their combination in school-aged children with ADHD, *Clinical Psychology Review*, 28, 5, 783–800.

Van der Velden, M. (2004). From communities of practice to communities of resistance: Civil society and cognitive justice, *Development*, 47, 1, 73–80.

Van Maanen, J., & Barley, S. (1982). *Occupational communities: Culture and control in organizations*, No. TR-ONR-10, Cambridge, MA: Alfred P. Sloan School of Management.

Vanlaar, G., & Van Damme, J. (2012). A propensity score matching analysis of the effects of mainstream versus special education on math learning. Paper presented at ECER 2012 Cádiz, The European Conference on Educational Research, 18–21 September.

Veck, W. (2009). From an exclusionary to an inclusive understanding of educational difficulties and educational space, *Oxford Review of Education*, 35, 1, 41–56.

Vislie, L. (2003). From integration to inclusion, *European Journal of Special Needs Education*, 18, 1, 17–35.

Visser, J., Cole, T., & Daniels, H. (2002). Inclusion for the difficult to include, *Support for Learning*, 17, 1, pp. 23–6.

Vlachou, A. (2004). Education and inclusive policy-making, *International Journal of Inclusive Education*, 8, 1, 3–21.

Vygotsky, L. S. (1986). In A. Kozulin (Ed.) *Thought and language*, Cambridge: MIT Press.

Waitoller, F. & Kozleski, E. (2015). No stone left unturned: Exploring the convergence of new capitalism in inclusive education in the U.S., *Education Policy Analysis Archives*, 23, 18.

Waltz, M. (2012). Images and narratives of autism within charity discourses, *Disability & Society*, 27, 2, 219–233.

Wang, P., & Spillane, A. (2009). Research-based techniques, *Education and Training in Developmental Disabilities*, 44, 3, 318–342.

Wang, Q., & Chaudhary, N. (2006). The self. In K. Pawlik & G. d'Ydewalle (Eds) *Psychological concepts: An international historical perspective* (pp. 325–358), Hove: Psychology Press.

Warren Little, J. (2003). Inside teacher community, *Teachers College Record*, 105, 6, 913–945.

Waterhouse, S. (2004). Deviant and non-deviant identities in the classroom, *European Journal of Special Needs Education*, 19, 1, 69–84.

Watson, S., Richels, C., Michalek, A., & Raymer, A. (2012). Psychosocial treatments for ADHD, *Journal of Attention Disorders* (OnlineFirst).

Webb, N. (1993). Collaborative group versus individual assessment in mathematics, *Educational Assessment*, 1, 2, 131–152.

Webb, N. (1995). Group collaboration in assessment, *Educational Evaluation and Policy Analysis*, 17, 2, 239–261.

Wedell, K. (2008). Evolving dilemmas about categorization. In L. Florian & M. McLaughlin (Eds) *Disability classification in education: Issues and perspectives*, London: Sage.

Weiner, M. (1991). *The child and the state in India*, Princeton, NJ: Princeton University Press.

Welbourne, M. (1981). The community of knowledge, *The Philosophical Quarterly*, 31, 125, 302–314.

Wellman, B. (2005). Community: From neighborhood to network, *Communications of the ACM*, 48, 10, 53–55.

Wenger, E., & Snyder, W. (2000). Communities of practice, *Harvard Business Review*, 78, 1, 139–146.

West Sussex (2013). Cabinet Members for Education and Schools, Children and Families, Finance and Resources Ref: ES27 (12.13). *January 2013 school funding reform 2013/14 – high needs.* http://www2.westsussex.gov.uk/ds/mis/060213es27.pdf.

White, C., de Burgh, H., Fear, N., & Iversen, A. (2011). The impact of deployment to Iraq or Afghanistan on military children, *International Review of Psychiatry*, 23, 2, 210–217.

White, J. (2010). The coalition and the curriculum, *Forum*, 52, 3, 299–310.

White, S. (1996). Depoliticising development, *Development in Practice*, 6, 1, 6–15.

Whitehurst, T. (2007). *Evaluation of features specific to an ASD designed living accommodation*, Sunfield Research Institute.

Wiliam, D., & Bartholomew, H. (2004). It's not which school but which set you're in that matters, *British Educational Research Journal*, 30, 2, 279–293.

Wilkinson, I., & Hamilton, R. (2003). Learning to read in composite (multigrade) classes in New Zealand, *Teaching and Teacher Education*, 19, 2, 221–235.

Williams, J., Pazey, B., Shelby, L., & Yates, J. (2013). The enemy among us, *NASSP Bulletin*, 97, 2, 139–165.

Williams, K., Jamieson, F., & Hollingworth, S. (2008). He was a bit of a delicate thing, *Gender and Education*, 20, 4, 399–408.

Wilson, J. (2000a). Doing justice to inclusion, *European Journal of Special Needs Education*, 15, 3, 297–304.

Wilson, J. (2000b). Reply by John Wilson, *European Journal of Special Needs Education*, 15, 3, 314–315.

Wilson, J. (2002). Defining 'special needs', *European Journal of Special Needs Education*, 17, 1, 61–66.

Winterton, R., & Parker, C. (2009). A utilitarian pursuit, *The International Journal of the History of Sport*, 26, 14, 2106–2125.

Wintour, P. (2014). Compulsory setting: Schools face being forced to separate pupils by ability, *The Guardian*, Wednesday 3 September. http://www.theguardian.com/politics/2014/sep/03/schools-separate-pupils-ability-setting, accessed 8 September 2014.

Winzer, M. (2006). Confronting difference. In L. Florian (Ed.) *The Sage handbook of special education* (pp. 21–34), London: Sage.

Wolfensberger, W. (1975). *The origin and nature of our institutional models*, New York: Human Policy Press.

Wolff, J., Gu, H., Gerig, G., Elison, J., Styner, M., Gouttard, S., et al. (2012). Differences in white matter fiber tract development present from 6 to 24 months in infants with autism, *The American Journal of Psychiatry*, 169, 6, 589–600. doi:10.1176/appi.ajp.2011.11091447

Woll, B., & Adam, R. (2012). Sign language and the politics of deafness. In M. Martin-Jones, A. Blackledge, & A. Creese (Eds) *The Routledge handbook of multilingualism*, London: Routledge.

Woolley, H., Armitage, M., Bishop, J., Curtis, M., & Ginsborg, J. (2006). Going outside together, *Children's Geographies*, 4, 3, 303–318.

World Health Organization (WHO) (2002). *Towards a common language for functioning, disability and health ICF*, Geneva: World Health Organization.

Wyse, D., & Styles, M. (2007). Synthetic phonics and the teaching of reading, *Literacy*, 41, 1, 35–42.

Zounhia, K., Hatziharistos, D., & Emmanouel, K. (2003). Greek secondary school pupils' perceived reasons for behaving appropriately and perceived teachers' strategies to maintain discipline, *Educational Review*, 55, 3, 289–303.

INDEX

Printed in Great Britain
by Amazon